IMPLEMENTING THE RIGHT TO DECIDE UNDER THE CONVENTION ON THE RIGHTS OF PERSONS WITH DISABILITIES

This book addresses one of the most controversial questions in contemporary human rights law: how can persons with severe cognitive disabilities make their own decisions?

Historically, vulnerable persons have been considered incapable, and guardians were appointed to represent their interests, which has led to serious abuses. The Convention on the Rights of Persons with Disabilities (CRPD), adopted in 2006, requires that they receive support to make their own decisions. However, governments claim it is impossible to fully implement this international requirement.

This book tackles the issue of decision-making from both a legal and theoretical perspective. It explores how supported decision-making could incorporate safeguards to protect the vital interests of vulnerable persons in order to present a viable legal alternative to guardianship. It accepts that some persons' abilities are very limited, but contends that guardianship is not the appropriate response, even in such cases. Instead, the book presents a unique Modified Support Framework, which can incorporate all persons with disabilities, fulfilling the goals of the CRPD.

Implementing the Right to Decide under the Convention on the Rights of Persons with Disabilities

Supporting the Legal Capacity of All Persons with Disabilities

János Fiala-Butora

•HART•

OXFORD • LONDON • NEW YORK • NEW DELHI • SYDNEY

HART PUBLISHING

Bloomsbury Publishing Plc

Kemp House, Chawley Park, Cumnor Hill, Oxford, OX2 9PH, UK

1385 Broadway, New York, NY 10018, USA

Bloomsbury Publishing Ireland Limited, 29 Earlsfort Terrace, Dublin 2, D02 AY28, Ireland

HART PUBLISHING, the Hart/Stag logo, BLOOMSBURY and the Diana logo are trademarks of Bloomsbury Publishing Plc

First published in Great Britain 2025

A catalogue record for this book is available from the British Library.

A catalogue record for this book is available from the Library of Congress.

ISBN: HB: 978-1-50998-032-1
ePDF: 978-1-50998-034-5
ePub: 978-1-50998-033-8

Typeset by Compuscript Ltd, Shannon

Preface

IN THE SUMMER of 2004, as a freshly graduated law student, I was asked to investigate the alleged use of 'cage beds' in social care institutions for persons with disabilities in Slovakia for a BBC documentary. I visited several of these places, found the cage beds (the documentary was a great international success), and saw other horrible forms of abuse. Yet the most striking thing about the institutions was quite an abstract matter: the legal status of their residents. The staff told me they were there voluntarily, even though they clearly did not want to be there: many of them were asking me for help to get out. I was told they could not understand their situation or make decisions, but many clearly did: they were showing me documents of their previous lives and their letters and complaints asking to get back their freedom. Many of them had worked and lived independently before being placed in the care home. They did not commit any crime, nor was there any other court order committing them to these institutions. They seemed to be in a legal limbo. Through their explanation, I slowly realised that they were all placed under guardianship, and their guardian consented to their stay in the care home on their behalf, circumventing all detention safeguards by maintaining the fiction of their voluntariness. I was shocked to see how the seemingly benign institution of incapacitation, which we spent barely five minutes studying during the five years of law school, could be abused in such a way. I was even more shocked to realise that none of my teachers and colleagues knew about this and cared that thousands of our fellow citizens were being made to disappear from society.

A few months later, I joined the Mental Disability Advocacy Centre (MDAC) as its first legal officer with the desire to help the people I had met in the institutions. Our task was to explore how international human rights law could be used to help persons with disabilities. In the following years, we took several cases to the European Court of Human Rights (some are referenced in this book), challenging guardianship and similar practices. Despite the successes, we had a feeling of growing frustration. Human rights law, as it existed at the time, highlighted the abuses connected to incapacitation but it did not help persons who were indeed unable to make decisions alone. It offered them guardianship or nothing.

The solution came through discussions with my colleague Gábor Gombos, who represented our organisation at the negotiations on drafting the Convention on the Rights of Persons with Disabilities. Gábor was a survivor of forced psychiatric treatment and was already an internationally well-known advocate when I met him. Through him, I understood how the struggle we see in Central Europe is connected to a worldwide movement and how the international negotiations could decide the fate of persons with disabilities in all countries. We talked for hours about how the law could help persons with disabilities make their decisions, how supported decision-making should be conceived as a legal institution to be able to replace guardianship, and how our experience with human rights litigation could help influence the discussions in the UN.

The adoption of the CRPD was a great success, a massive milestone for the rights of persons with disabilities, but it did not resolve all the issues we were fighting for. The advocacy continues to this day. There are still strong forces, notably governments across the world, who doubt that persons with cognitive disabilities can make their own decisions. There are still gaps in our understanding of how this could be possible for persons with high support needs. Convincing opponents to change their course and fully embrace the CRPD's vision therefore remains difficult.

This book aims to fill some of those gaps. It is based on my experience as a human rights lawyer representing victims with disabilities before international courts and my SJD studies at Harvard Law School, where I had the privilege to research this field for several years. My aim was to explore not simply how persons with cognitive disabilities could make decisions with support but how the law could ensure that all of them have access to support and that even persons with the highest support needs can be accommodated in a support framework. To fill that gap is essential for the CRPD to reach its potential and to convince governments and other stakeholders that supporting the autonomy of persons with even the most severe disabilities is not a pipe dream but a realistic alternative. I hope it will be of interest to researchers and students interested in human rights and disability rights as a window into and possible solution to some of the most intriguing academic discussions of recent years over the limits of autonomy. It can also be a valuable resource for legal practitioners, governments, and other stakeholders interested in challenging and reforming legal capacity laws.

I dedicate the book to the memory of Gábor Gombos and other friends, colleagues, and clients, victims of abusive guardianship systems and advocates for its change, who did not see guardianship abolished but were forever hopeful that that day would come. May their wish come true.

Acknowledgements

I WOULD LIKE to thank my wife, Erika, for her continuing love and support, from which I am drawing strength during difficult times. Without her, this book would never have been written. I would also like to thank our children Abigél, Tamara, Franciska, and Áron for their patience – I am just as eager for this project to finish as they are. This book is based on my SJD research at Harvard Law School, where I benefitted from the guidance and wisdom of many instructors and peers. I am particularly indebted to Professor Michael A. Stein for his never-ceasing generous mentorship over the years; to Professor Martha A. Field for the important life lessons going way beyond academia; to Professor Gerald L. Neuman for teaching me to be patient with international human rights law and understanding the subtle difference between advocacy and academia, which I have still not mastered; and to Professor William P. Alford for constantly pushing me to demand more from myself. I am also grateful for the support of my colleagues at the Centre for Disability Law and Policy at the University of Galway, in particular Professor Eilionóir Flynn. I would also like to thank for the support of my colleagues at the Mental Disability Advocacy Centre (currently Validity Foundation), who accompanied me on the journey of disability rights advocacy throughout the years, and of the many friends, clients, and allies in the disability rights movement, whose views and ideas shaped my understanding of what a just world ought to look like, and the role of legal capacity laws in getting us there. This book benefitted from comments and editing by Bob Dent and Laurie Anderson, which greatly improved it – any remaining mistakes are my fault. The funding for research into this book came from the Harvard Frederick Sheldon Travelling Fellowship, the European University Institute's Max Weber Fellowship, and the Hungarian Academy of Sciences' János Bolyai Research Scholarship (no. BO/00785/20).

Contents

Preface .... *v*
Acknowledgements .... *vii*
Table of Cases .... *xiii*
Table of Statutes .... *xv*
Table of International Law Sources .... *xvii*

1. **Introduction** 1
   1.1. The Existing Landscape of Legal Capacity Law 2
   1.2. Recent Challenges to Guardianship 4
   1.3. The Structure of this Book 7
   1.4. Note on Terminology 9

2. **Legal Capacity** 11
   2.1. What is Legal Capacity? 11
   2.2. A Historical Overview 14
   2.3. Legal Capacity as a Human Right 17
      2.3.1. Violations of Procedural Rights 20
      2.3.2. Violations of Other Substantive Rights 20
      2.3.3. Guardianship as Such 21
   2.4. Implications for the Convention on the Rights of Persons with Disabilities 23

3. **Interpreting Article 12 of the CRPD** 27
   3.1. The Conflicting Views on Interpreting Article 12 28
      3.1.1. The Absolutist Position and the Constricted Position 30
      3.1.2. Strong and Weak Points 32
         3.1.2.1. Support to Persons with Severe Disabilities 32
         3.1.2.2. The Role of Mental Capacity 34
         3.1.2.3. The CRPD's Text 35
      3.1.3. Common Ground 38
   3.2. The Text of Article 12 – And its Implications 38
      3.2.1. The Consensual Aspect 39
      3.2.2. The Suprapositive Aspect 43
      3.2.3. The Institutional Aspect 45
   3.3. Conclusion – Does Article 12 Resolve the Debate? 47

4. **The Inherent Features of Guardianship** 49
   4.1. Is the Aim of Substitute Decision-Making Ever Legitimate? 50
   4.2. The Assumptions behind Guardianship 51

4.3. Different Legal Approaches to Guardianship 53
4.3.1. The Status Approach 53
4.3.2. The Quasi-Status Approach 54
4.3.3. The Outcome Approach 55
4.3.4. The Functional Approach 57
4.3.5. The Quasi-Functional Approach 58
4.4. Evaluating the Different Approaches 59
4.4.1. Costs 61
4.4.2. Legal Certainty 61
4.4.3. Protection from Abuse 62
4.4.4. Ease of Administration and Oversight 63
4.4.5. Evaluation of the Above Approaches 65

5. The Alternative: Supported Decision-Making 67
5.1. What is Supported Decision-Making? 69
5.1.1. The Emergence of Supported Decision-Making in International Law 70
5.1.2. Supported Decision-Making in Domestic Laws 72
5.1.3. The Ideal and Existing Models of Supported Decision-Making 75
5.2. The Psychological Assumptions behind Supported Decision-Making 78
5.2.1. Interdependent Decision-Making 78
5.2.2. The Psychological Basis of Supported Decision-Making 80
5.2.2.1. Abstract Thinking and Context 81
5.2.2.2. Logical/Linguistic Intelligence 82
5.2.2.3. No Support 83
5.2.2.4. Legal and Clinical Incompetence 84
5.3. Forms of Supported Decision-Making 85
5.3.1. Supported Decision-Making as the Natural Way of Making Decisions 85
5.3.2. Supported Decision-Making as a Principle 86
5.3.3. Supported Decision-Making as an Alternative to Guardianship 87

6. Supported Decision-Making as a Legal Institution 90
6.1. Ideal v Legal Forms of Supported Decision-Making 90
6.2. The Functions of the Legal Regulation of Supported Decision-Making 92
6.2.1. The Guardian's Right to be Present and to Access Information 92
6.2.2. The Role of Supporters 94
6.2.3. Legal Certainty 96

6.2.4. Protection from Harmful Decisions 97
6.2.4.1. Abuse by Others 99
6.2.4.2. Abuse by Self 102
6.2.4.3. Abuse by the Supporter 106
6.3. Comparing Guardianship and Supported Decision-Making 108
6.3.1. Restrictiveness 109
6.3.2. Flexibility 109
6.3.3. The Pedagogic Effect 110
6.3.4. The Expressive Function 110
6.3.5. Ease of Transacting 111
6.3.6. Protection from Harmful Decisions 112
6.4. Conclusion 113

7. The Case of Persons with High Support Needs 115
7.1. Existing Solutions and their Shortcomings 115
7.1.1. The Support Only Framework – The Complete Abolition of Guardianship 116
7.1.2. The Some Guardianship Framework – The Need to Make Substituted Decisions 120
7.1.3. Common Ground and Divergence between the Two Positions 123
7.2. The Modified Support Framework – A Proposal for a Third Option 125
7.2.1. Who are 'Persons with High Support Needs' from a Legal Perspective? 126
7.2.2. The Modified Support Framework in Practice 129
7.2.3. Comparing the Three Models 132
7.3. Safeguards Ensuring that Support does not Become Substitution 135
7.4. The Equality of Persons with High Support Needs 136

8. Conclusion 139

Bibliography 145
Index 159

Table of Cases

Berková v Slovakia App no 67149/01 (ECtHR 24 March 2009) 19
Bock v Germany App no. 11118/84 (ECtHR 21 February 1989) 18
Chhedulal Tharu and others v Nepal No. 2038/2011 (Human Rights Committee, CCPR/C/114/D/2038/2011, 3 July 2015) 17
Delecolle v France Appl no 37646/13 (ECtHR 25 October 2018) 20
Egger v Austria App no 15780/89 (ECtHR admissibility decision 11 October 1993) 18
Frodl v Austria App no 20201/04 (ECtHR 8 April 2010) 46
Greens and M. T. v the United Kingdom App no 60041/08 (ECtHR 23 October 2010) 46
H.F. v Slovakia App no 54797/00 (ECtHR 8 November 2005) 19–20
H.L. v the United Kingdom App no 45508/99 (ECtHR 5 October 2004) 55
H.M. v Switzerland, App no 39187/98 (ECtHR 26 February 2002) 35
Herczegfalvy v Austria, App no. 10533/83 (ECtHR 24 September 1992) 36
Hiller v Austria, App no 1967/14 (ECtHR 22 November 2016) 33
Kiss v Hungary App no 38832/06 (ECtHR 20 May 2010) 19–21, 57, 71
Matter v Slovakia App no 31534/96 (ECtHR 5 July 1999) 18, 21
Mikhaylenko v Ukraine App no 49069/11 (ECtHR 30 May 2013) 20
Nikolyan v Armenia App no 74438/14 (ECtHR 3 October 2019) 19
Plesó v Hungary App no 41242/08 (ECtHR 2 October 2012) 55–56
Pretty v the United Kingdom App no 2346/02 (ECtHR 29 April 2002) 19
Salontaji-Drobnjak v Serbia App no 36500/05 (ECtHR 13 October 2009) 19, 57–58
Scoppola v Italy (No. 3) App no 126/05 (ECtHR 22 May 2012) 46
Shtukaturov v Russia, App no 44009/05 (ECtHR 27 March 2008) 15, 19–22, 63, 66, 71
Stanev v Bulgaria App no 36760/06 (ECtHR 17 January 2012) 20, 55, 63, 71
Sýkora v the Czech Republic App no 23419/07 (ECtHR 22 November 2012) 20–21, 23–24, 56, 63–64, 66, 87
Vaudelle v France App no 35683/97 (ECtHR 30 January 2001) 50
Winterwerp v the Netherlands App no 6301/73 (ECtHR 24 October 1979) 18
X. v Croatia App no 11223/04 (ECtHR 17 July 2008) 14, 19, 21, 57
X. and Y. v the Netherlands App no 8978/80 (ECtHR 26 March 1985) 50

Table of Statutes

Act no. IV of 1959 on the Civil Code of the Hungarian Republic (*Törvény a Magyar Köztársaság Polgári Törvénykönyvéről*) (Hungary) 10, 54, 57–58, 61–62, 74, 86, 94, 98, 107

Act no. CXX of 2009 on the Civil Code (*Törvény a Polgári Törvénykönyvről)*(Hungary).... 76, 94–97, 100–01

Act no. IV of 1952 on Family, Marriage and Custodianship (*Törvény a házasságról, a családról és a gyámságról*) (Hungary)....20

Act no. V of 2013 on the Civil Code (*Törvény a Polgári Törvénykönyvről*) (Hungary) 95

Act no. 89/2012 Col. Civil Code (*Občanský zákoník*) (Czech Republic)....76, 95, 97

Americans with Disabilities Act (ADA), 42 U.S.C. § 121103 (1990) (USA) 36

Assisted Decision-Making (Capacity) Act 2015 (Ireland)....76

German Civil Code (*Bürgerliches Gesetzbuch* (BGB)) Federal Law Gazette (*Bundesgesetzblatt*) I page 42, 2909; 2003 I page 738 (Germany)....75

Mental Capacity Act 2005 (England and Wales)....51, 57, 78, 86

Representation Agreement Act, [RSBC 1996] CHAPTER 405 (British Columbia, Canada) 73–74

The Vulnerable Persons Living with a Mental Disability Act, CCSM c V90 (Manitoba, Canada) 69, 73

Table of International Law Sources

Convention on the Elimination of All Forms of Discrimination against Women (CEDAW) (18 December 1979) 17–18
Convention on the Rights of the Child (CRC) (20 November 1989)....... 17–18, 25
Convention on the Rights of Persons with Disabilities, U.N. Doc. A/RES/61/106 (13 December 2006) 4, 27
Council of Europe Committee of Ministers, Recommendation R(99)4 on the legal protection of incapable adults (23 February 1999). 19, 71
European Convention on Human Rights (Convention for the Protection of Human Rights and Fundamental Freedoms), 213 U.N.T.S. 222 (4 November 1950).. 18–19, 35
European Union Council Directive 2000/78/EC on establishing a general framework for equal treatment in employment and occupation (27 November 2000)...36
Principles for the Protection of Persons with Mental Illness and the Improvement of Mental Health Care, UN General Assembly Resolution A/RES/46/119, 17 December 1991. 71
Standard Rules on the Equalization of Opportunities for Persons with Disabilities, UN General Assembly Resolution A/RES/48/96 (4 March 1994) 71
UN Committee on the Elimination of Discrimination against Women, General Recommendation No. 21: Equality in marriage and family relations, A/49/38 (1994) 3
UN Committee on the Rights of Persons with Disabilities, Concluding observations on Argentina, CRPD/C/ARG/CO/1 (8 October 2012) 71
UN Committee on the Rights of Persons with Disabilities, Concluding observations on Australia, CRPD/C/AUS/CO/1 (21 October 2013)...........71
UN Committee on the Rights of Persons with Disabilities, Concluding Observations on Austria, CRPD/C/AUT/CO/1 (13 September 2013) 28
UN Committee on the Rights of Persons with Disabilities, Concluding Observations on China, CRPD/C/CHN/CO/1 (15 October 2012).............28
UN Committee on the Rights of Persons with Disabilities, Concluding Observations on Hungary, CRPD/C/HUN/CO/1 (22 October 2012)... 28, 72
UN Committee on the Rights of Persons with Disabilities, Concluding Observations on Peru, CRPD/C/PER/CO/1 (9 May 2012) 28–29
UN Committee on the Rights of Persons with Disabilities, Concluding Observations on Spain, CRPD/C/ESP/CO/1 (19 October 2011) 28, 72

UN Committee on the Rights of Persons with Disabilities, General comment No. 1 (2014) – Article 12: Equal recognition before the law, CRPD/C/GC/1 (19 May 2014) 28, 53, 72, 117
UN Committee on the Rights of Persons with Disabilities, Initial reports submitted by States parties in accordance with article 35 of the Convention: Spain, CRPD/C/ESP/1 (5 October 2010) 72
UN Human Rights Committee, General Comment No. 18, Non-discrimination, U.N. Doc. HRI/GEN/1/Rev.1 (1994) 37
UN Human Rights Committee, General comment No. 35 – Article 9 (Liberty and security of person), CCPR/C/GC/35 (16 December 2014) 35
Vienna Convention on the Law of Treaties (VCLT), 1155 U.N.T.S. 331 (27 January 1980) 36, 40

1

Introduction

THIS BOOK INQUIRES into what it means to be a person before the law.[1] An assumption of our legal system is that all subjects entering legal transactions are capable of rational decision-making to pursue their interests.[2] For two millennia, persons with intellectual and psychosocial disabilities have been considered to fail to meet this criterion.[3] They have been denied the right to make their own decisions and the law has authorised other persons, their guardians, to make decisions on their behalf.[4] From subjects, they were reduced to objects of the law, unable to enter into legal transactions on their own.

This legally recognised incapacity stigmatises persons with disabilities and results in violations of their autonomy in many areas of their lives.[5] It also leads to their exclusion from conceptions of equal citizenship.[6] A long philosophical tradition from Immanuel Kant[7] through John Locke[8] and John Rawls[9] to Peter Singer[10] failed to include persons with severe disabilities in theories of justice and equal moral personhood. Considered unable to achieve the cognitive functioning required from human beings, persons with disabilities were described as having a moral status below that of some animals; their rights could be violated,

[1] G Quinn, 'Personhood and Legal Capacity – Perspectives on the Paradigm Shift of Article 12 CRPD', Harvard Law School Project on Disability Conference presentation (2010).

[2] I Bantekas, 'Mental and Intellectual Capacity and Contractual Freedom: Assistive Decision-Making Matters' (2023) 21 *Seattle Journal for Social Justice* 569, 570.

[3] I Basa, 'Gondnokság a római jogban' (2006) 43 *Állam- és Jogtudomány* 407, 443.

[4] M Rioux, J Gilmour and N Angel, 'Negotiating capacity: legally constructed entitlement and protection' in B McSherry and I Freckelton (eds), *Coercive care: rights, law and policy* (Routledge, 2013) 51.

[5] J Fiala-Butora, MA Stein, and JE Lord, 'The democratic life of the Union: towards equal voting participation for Europeans with Disabilities' (2014) 55 *Harvard International Law Journal* 71.

[6] SN Skarsaune and HM Hanisch, 'Holding and Professional Care: On Self-Determination for Persons With Profound Intellectual and Multiple Disabilities' (2023) 48(1) *Research and Practice for Persons with Severe Disabilities* 25, 25.

[7] Kant considered that men are end in themselves because they are capable of reasoning; see: I Kant, *Lectures on Ethics* (Harper Torchbooks, 1963) 239; C Kong, *Mental Capacity in Relationship* (Cambridge, Cambridge University Press, 2017) 149.

[8] J Locke, *An Essay Concerning Human Understanding* (Roger Woolhouse ed, Reprint edn, Penguin Classics 1998).

[9] M Nussbaum, 'The Capabilities of People with Cognitive Disabilities' (2009) 40 *Metaphilosophy* 331, 333; P Gooding 'Legal Capacity in the UN Convention on the Rights of Persons with Disability and its Challenges to a Rawlsian Theory of Justice', Melbourne University Postgraduate Legal Theory Conference (2010) 8.

[10] P Singer, 'Speciesism and Moral Status' (2009) 40 *Metaphilosophy* 567, 567.

and they could even be killed with impunity.[11] While the history of philosophy provides examples of personhood not based on cognition, these did not shape the mainstream understanding of the role of persons with disabilities in society.[12] Contemporary philosophers,[13] such as Martha Nussbaum,[14] Eva Kittay[15] and Anita Silvers,[16] tried to include persons with severe disabilities in social contract theories of justice, but could not overcome the obstacle[17] presented by their perceived inability to make their own decisions.[18] In these theories, persons with disabilities might deserve protection for other reasons, but they are not fully autonomous beings, their status is not equal to their fellow citizens.[19] The lack of legal capacity of persons with severe disabilities remains a central obstacle to justifying their moral personhood.[20] As noted by Gerard Quinn, a long-standing advocate for disability rights, this is not simply a question of contract or legal status, it goes to the heart of whom we recognise as equal human beings.[21]

Law is not the only cause of prejudices and stigma relating to the lack of rationality and cognitive skills of persons with disabilities, but greatly contributes to it. A legal system recognising their abilities and validating them as autonomous decision-makers would treat them as equal citizens, subjects, not objects of the law.[22] To achieve this change of status is the aim of this book.

1.1. THE EXISTING LANDSCAPE OF LEGAL CAPACITY LAW

Historically, persons with disabilities could not be accepted as autonomous subjects because they indeed make decisions differently than non-disabled

[11] J McMahan, *The Ethics of Killing: Problems at the Margins of Life* (Oxford, Oxford University Press, 2003).

[12] W Martin refers to Martin Luther, Thomas Hobbes, and Arthur Schopenhauer as examples. W Martin, 'Respect for the Will of the Person' in M Bach and N Espejo-Yaksic (eds), *Legal capacity, disability and human rights* (Larcier Intersentia, 2023) 47.

[13] J-S Beaudry, *The Disabled Contract: Severe Intellectual Disability, Justice and Morality* (Cambridge University Press, 2021).

[14] M Nussbaum, *Frontiers of justice: disability, nationality, species membership* (Harvard University Press, Belknap Press, 2006); Nussbaum, 'The Capabilities of People with Cognitive Disabilities'.

[15] EF Kittay, 'The Personal Is Philosophical: a Philosopher and Mother of a Cognitively Disabled Person Sends Notes From the Battlefield' (2009) 40 *Metaphilosophy* 606.

[16] A Silvers and LP Francis, 'Thinking About the Good: Reconfiguring Liberal Metaphysics (or not) for People with Cognitive Disabilities' (2009) 40 *Metaphilosophy* 475.

[17] A Arstein-Kerslake and E Flynn, 'The right to legal agency: domination, disability and the protections of Article 12 of the Convention on the Rights of Persons with Disabilities' (2017) 13(1) *International Journal of Law in Context* 22, 23.

[18] MS Smith and MA Stein, 'The Disabled Contract: Severe Intellectual Disability, Justice and Morality by Jonas-Sébastien Beaudry' (2022) 44(4) *Human Rights Quarterly* 839, 839.

[19] J Griffin, *On Human* Rights (Oxford University Press, 2008) 95.

[20] See the critique of Martha Nussbaum in Fiala-Butora, Stein, Lord, 'The democratic life of the Union'.

[21] G Quinn, 'Personhood and Legal Capacity – Perspectives on the Paradigm Shift of Article 12 CRPD', Harvard Law School Project on Disability Conference presentation (2010).

[22] E Flynn and A Arstein-Kerslake, 'Legislating personhood: realising the right to support in exercising legal capacity' (2014) 10 *International Journal of Law in Context* 81, 91.

individuals. Because the law could not incorporate their way of exercising their legal capacity, placing them under guardianship was accepted as a necessary intervention.[23] In order to protect their interests, guardians were appointed to make decisions on their behalf.[24] No legal alternatives were developed to replace this system of substituted decision-making until the end of the twentieth century.[25] Reforms concentrated on improving guardianship by tailoring it to individual needs and by introducing effective safeguards, but they did not question guardianship as such.[26]

Not only did guardianship undermine the position of persons with disabilities as full members of society, it also generated frequent abuses.[27] It led to the social exclusion of persons with disabilities sanctioned by law, to their 'civil death',[28] and persons subject to it as the 'legally disappeared'.[29] Currently, the Council of Europe's Commissioner for Human Rights considers it to be one of the most important and invisible human rights issues.[30] A system more respectful of disabled persons' autonomy is therefore not only crucial for philosophical theories of personhood; it also has grave practical implications for the everyday lives of millions of persons with disabilities around the world.[31]

Similar restrictions on legal capacity have existed for other groups, such as women,[32] racial and religious minorities,[33] and children.[34] Gradually, the limitations on women's and other minorities' legal capacity have been lifted, and now they are universally recognised as scientifically unfounded.[35] Persons

[23] NA Kohn, JA Blumenthal, and AT Campbell, 'Supported Decision-Making: A Viable Alternative to Guardianship?' (2013) 117 *Penn State Law Review* 1111, 1111.

[24] T Carney, 'Guardianship, Citizenship, & Theorizing Substitute-decisionmaking Law' (2012) 12/25 *Sydney Law School Research Paper* 1.

[25] K Blankman, 'Guardianship Models in the Netherlands and Western Europe' (1997) 20 *International Journal of Law and Psychiatry* 47, 47.

[26] ibid, 48.

[27] A Dhanda, 'Legal Capacity in the Disability Rights Convention: Stranglehold of the Past or Lodestar for the Future?' (2007) 34 *Syracuse Journal of International Law and Commerce* 429, 435.

[28] ML Perlin, 'Striking for the Guardians and Protectors of the Mind: The Convention on the Rights of Persons with Mental Disabilities and the Future of Guardianship Law' (2013) 117 *Penn State Law Review* 1159, 1162.

[29] G Quinn, 'An Ideas Paper', Eur. Foundation Centre, Seminar on Legal Capacity, Brussels (4 June 2009) 4.

[30] Mental Disability Advocacy Centre (MDAC), *Legal Capacity in Europe* (Budapest, MDAC, 2013) 1.

[31] G Quinn and A Arstein-Kerslake, 'Restoring the 'human' in 'human rights': personhood and doctrinal innovation in the UN disability convention' in C Gearty and C Douzinas (eds), *The Cambridge Companion to Human Rights Law* (Cambridge University Press, 2012) 41.

[32] Committee on the Elimination of Discrimination against Women, *General Recommendation No. 21: Equality in marriage and family relations*, A/49/38, 1994, para. 7.

[33] A Arstein-Kerslake, *The Right to Legal Personhood of Marginalised Groups* (Oxford University Press, 2024) 3.

[34] I Doron, 'From Lunacy to Incapacity and Beyond – Guardianship of The Elderly and Ontario's Experience in Defining "Legal Incapacity"' (1999) 19(4) *Health Law in Canada*, 95.

[35] M Rioux, J Gilmour, and N Angel, 'Negotiating capacity: legally constructed entitlement and protection' in B McSherry and I Freckelton (eds), *Coercive care: rights, law and policy* (Abingdon, Routledge, 2013).

with disabilities, together with children, are still waiting for their liberation.[36] They are still suffering from attitudes that portray them as incapable of managing their affairs, which are currently backed up by medical and psychological evidence.[37] They have still not achieved full citizenship; guardianship and exclusion from decision-making are still the norm for them, and autonomous status is the exception.

1.2. RECENT CHALLENGES TO GUARDIANSHIP

Recently, guardianship has come under challenge from international human rights law. In 2006, the United Nations adopted the Convention on the Rights of Persons with Disabilities (CRPD),[38] which, in its article 12, requires state parties to 'recognize that persons with disabilities enjoy legal capacity on an equal basis with others in all aspects of life'.[39] This is considered by many to be the most important provision[40] of the CRPD but also the most controversial one.[41] It introduces a paradigm shift in understanding legal capacity, moving from the current paradigm of substituted decision-making to a new one based on support.[42] However, it is unclear what the new paradigm ought to look like and how it can be operationalised in practice. Does it apply to everybody, including persons with the most severe disabilities? So far, there is no satisfactory answer to the question of what 'equal basis' for exercising legal capacity means in the case of persons with high support needs.[43] Without it, they cannot be incorporated into theories of full personhood. To propose such an answer is the primary aim of this book.

[36] JR Morss, 'But for the Barriers: Significant Extensions to Children's Capacity' (2004) 11 *Psychiatry, Psychology and Law* 319.

[37] Rioux, Gilmour, Angel, 'Negotiating capacity' 53; MA Stein and A Silvers, 'Essentially Empirical: The Role of Biological and Legal Classification in Effectively Prohibiting Genetic Discrimination' in R Figueroa and S Harding (eds), *Science and Other Cultures: Issues in Philosophies of Science and Technology* (Routledge, 2003) 129.

[38] Convention on the Rights of Persons with Disabilities, G.A. Res. 61/106, U.N. Doc. A/RES/61/106 (13 December 2006) [hereinafter CRPD].

[39] Article 12 (2) of the CRPD.

[40] RD Dinerstein, 'Implementing Legal Capacity Under Article 12 of the UN Convention on the Rights of Persons with Disabilities: The Difficult Road from Guardianship to Supported Decision-Making' (2012) 19 *Human Rights Brief* 4.

[41] JE Lord and MA Stein, 'Contingent participation and coercive care: feminist and communitarian theories of disability and legal capacity' in B McSherry and I Freckelton (eds), *Coercive care: rights, law and policy* (Routledge, 2013); S Wildeman, 'Protecting Rights and Building Capacities: Challenges to Global Mental Health Policy in Light of the Convention on the Rights of Persons with Disabilities' (2013) 41 *The Journal of Law, Medicine and Ethics* 48, 56.

[42] A-M Callus, 'Removing obstacles to equal recognition for persons with intellectual disability: Taking exception to the way things are' (2018) 12 *ALTER European Journal of Disability Research* 153, 159.

[43] MA Stein, F Mahomed, V Patel, and C Sunkel (eds), *Mental Health, Legal Capacity, and Human Rights* (Cambridge University Press, Cambridge, 2021) 5.

The CRPD challenges the prejudice that persons with disabilities are incapable of rational decision-making, and it requires that they be supported to make their own decisions instead of being incapacitated.[44] The UN Committee on the Rights of Persons with Disabilities (hereinafter CRPD Committee) interprets Article 12 in an absolute way by prohibiting substituted decision-making and requiring support to be provided to all persons with disabilities. However, it does not explain how persons with the most severe disabilities can benefit from this.

Several authors criticised guardianship laws' assumption of individuals as rational atomistic beings,[45] a notion that persons with disabilities cannot achieve, and proposed relational understandings of autonomy,[46] which are more reflective of how people make decisions.[47] Other scholars consider it unclear how support works in practice and suggest that more research and experiments need to be conducted before it can replace guardianship.[48] They also doubt that persons with severe disabilities can be incorporated into a support framework.[49] According to them, persons with severe disabilities cannot make decisions even with the highest degree of support and are, therefore, in need of guardianship.[50] Thus, they are outside the CRPD's mandate of equal recognition of legal capacity. Others claim that an exception read into the CRPD is not compatible with its text and undermines the Convention.[51] Therefore, persons with even the most severe disabilities must be supported to make decisions, their legal capacity cannot be restricted. They have developed an ideal vision of supported

[44] E Flynn and A Arstein-Kerslake, 'The Support Model of Legal Capacity: Fact, Fiction, or Fantasy?' (2014) 31(1) *Berkeley Journal of International Law* 124, 137.

[45] JE Lord and MA Stein, 'Contingent participation and coercive care: feminist and communitarian theories of disability and legal capacity' in B McSherry and I Freckelton (eds), *Coercive care: rights, law and policy* (Routledge, 2013) 31.

[46] C Mackenzie and S Natalie, *Relational Autonomy: Feminist Perspectives on Autonomy, Agency, and the Social Self* (Oxford University Press, 2000).

[47] A Silvers and LP Francis, 'Thinking About the Good' 487.

[48] NA Kohn, JA Blumenthal, and AT Campbell, 'Supported Decision-Making: A Viable Alternative to Guardianship?' (2013) 117(4) *Penn State Law Review* 1111, 1114.

[49] T Carney, 'Guardianship, Citizenship'; A Lawson, 'The United Nations Convention on the Rights of Persons with Disabilities: New Era or False Dawn?' (2007) 34 *Syracuse Journal of International Law and Commerce* 563; M Keys, 'Legal Capacity Law Reform in Europe: An Urgent Challenge' in G Quinn and L Waddington (eds), *European Yearbook of Disability Law* (Intersentia, 2009); P Weller, 'Supported Decision-Making and the Achievement of Non-Discrimination: The Promise and Paradox of the Disabilities Convention' (2008) 26(2) *Law in Context* 85, 102; Perlin, 'Striking for the Guardians' 1159; O Lewis, 'Advancing Legal Capacity Jurisprudence' (2011) 6 *European Human Rights Law Review* 700; Kohn, Blumenthal, and Campbell, 'Supported Decision-Making: A Viable Alternative' 1118.

[50] Carney, 'Guardianship, Citizenship' 7.

[51] T Minkowitz, 'The United Nations Convention on the Rights of Persons with Disabilities and the Right to Be Free from Nonconsensual Psychiatric Interventions' (2007) 34 *Syracuse Journal of International Law and Commerce* 405, 408–09; Dhanda, 'Legal Capacity in the Disability Rights Convention' 445.

decision-making, which should be made available to all persons with disabilities without exceptions.[52]

A handful of other books have addressed the issue of legal capacity. Anna Arstein-Kerslake's *Restoring Voice to People with Cognitive Disabilities: Realizing the Right to Equal Recognition before the Law* (Cambridge University Press, 2017) argues for universal legal capacity, which includes persons with high support needs. Two other volumes from the same author analyse legal capacity from a gender perspective (*Legal Capacity and Gender* (Springer 2021)) and its implications for different vulnerable groups (*The Right to Legal Personhood of Marginalised Groups* (Oxford University Press, 2024). Camilla Kong in *Mental Capacity in Relationship: Decision-Making, Dialogue, and Autonomy* (Cambridge University Press, 2017) argues persuasively for a relational understanding of capacity and how interventions should concentrate on the quality of relationships of persons with disabilities, intervening if these break down or become abusive. Four edited collections describe recent developments in implementing the CRPD and reforming legal capacity laws.[53] Universal legal capacity is also the subject of two commentaries on the CRPD,[54] and several books have sections dedicated to this topic.[55]

This book differs from these earlier ones in one important aspect. In my opinion, works that advocate for supported decision-making describe ideal models that go beyond the law's ability to influence behaviour. They explain how supporters should behave without fully engaging with the question of whether the law can enforce the required result.[56] They also do not explain

[52] A particularly well-known example is developed in M Bach and L Kerzner, 'A New Paradigm for Protecting Autonomy and the Right to Legal Capacity', Paper prepared for the Law Commission of Ontario (October 2010).

[53] E Flynn, A Arstein-Kerslake, C de Bhailís, and ML Serra, *Global Perspectives on Legal Capacity Reform Our Voices, Our Stories* (Abington, Routledge, 2019); M Donnelly, R Harding, and E Taşcıoğlu, *Supporting Legal Capacity in Socio-Legal Context* (Hart, 2022); C Kong, J Coggon, P Cooper, M Dunn, and AR Keene, *Capacity, Participation and Values in Comparative Legal Perspective* (Bristol, Policy Press, 2023); M Domański and B Lackoroński, *Models of Implementation of Article 12 of the Convention on the Rights of Persons with Disabilities (CRPD); Private and Criminal Law Aspects* (Routledge, 2024).

[54] VD Fina, R Cera, and G Palmisano (eds), *The United Nations Convention on the Rights of Persons with Disabilities: A Commentary* (Springer, 2017); I Bantekas, MA Stein, and D Anastasiou (eds), *The UN Convention on the Rights of Persons with Disabilities: A Commentary* (Oxford University Press, 2018).

[55] OM Arnardóttir and G Quinn (eds), *The UN Convention on the Rights of Persons with Disabilities: European and Scandinavian Perspectives* (Leiden, Martinus Nijhoff Publishers, 2009); C O'Mahoney and G Quinn (eds), *Disability Law and Policy: An Analysis of the UN Convention* (Clarus Press, 2017); G de Beco, *Disability in International Human Rights Law* (Oxford University Press, 2021); M Donnelly, *Healthcare Decision-Making and the Law: Autonomy, Capacity and the Limits of Liberalism* (Cambridge University Press 2010); Á Hynes, *Irish Capacity Law and Assisted Decision-Making* (Bloomsbury Publishing, 2018); AS Kanter, *The Development of Disability Rights under International Law: From Charity to Human Rights* (Routledge 2014); B McSherry and P Weller, *Rethinking Rights Based Mental Health Laws* (Bloomsbury Publishing, 2010); P Gooding, *A New Era for Mental Health Law and Policy* (Cambridge University Press, 2017); A Nilsson, Compulsory Mental Health Interventions and the CRPD: Minding Equality (Hart, 2021).

[56] V Perju, 'Constitutional Transplants, Borrowing, and Migrations' (2011) *Boston College Law School Faculty Papers* 360, 36.

why guardianship continues to be used around the world despite its serious shortcomings when a superior alternative is available. This book will therefore concentrate on the legal rules constituting guardianship and supported decision-making. It will analyse the functions of guardianship laws and how these functions could be fulfilled by laws based on support. To incorporate persons with high support needs in a support framework, I will argue that one assumption of the paradigm shift endorsed by the CRPD is flawed: the rational atomistic man whose decisions are never overturned is not the standard of current guardianship laws, which persons with disabilities would be required to achieve. Approaches that utilise relational autonomy quite rightly challenge the way the imagined rational man makes decisions, but they still presume that the decisions reached are final and legally binding. Instead, I argue that the law already allows certain decisions of even fully legally capable individuals to be set aside in their interest. Equality, therefore, does not require rules that would never overturn a decision made by a disabled person; instead, I propose a framework in which this is done on an equal basis, regardless of capacity status and disability.

The book will not analyse guardianship and supported decision-making as currently applied in a specific jurisdiction to avoid the trap of conflating problems of practical implementation with inherent problems of these legal institutions. Instead, it breaks them down into its components and reconstructs them as stylised notions from their intrinsic features, and then compares the rules of the two institutions in the abstract. The generalisation involved in this exercise naturally leaves some issues unaddressed and leads to some simplification. All claims can have factual assumptions that might not be true under some specific circumstances. I hope the conclusions drawn from this analysis will justify the method and will lead to a more realistic understanding of how law can enable rather than hinder the exercise of legal capacity. The goal, then, is to propose legal rules that achieve the objectives of the ideal version of supported decision-making rather than ones that simply adopt the ideal version as a blueprint.

1.3. THE STRUCTURE OF THIS BOOK

Chapter two of this book will explain what legal capacity means and how legal capacity laws developed historically. It will also describe why guardianship is currently considered one of the most important human rights violations in the world.[57] A number of abuses related to guardianship have been documented by academic research, reports of human rights organisations, and the work of international human rights tribunals that underlie the need for reform.[58] To understand how guardianship has failed to protect persons with disabilities, it

[57] G Quinn, 'Personhood and Legal Capacity – Perspectives on the Paradigm Shift of Article 12 CRPD', Harvard Law School Project on Disability Conference presentation (2010) 3.

[58] Mental Disability Advocacy Centre (MDAC), *Legal Capacity in Europe*.

is necessary to separate abuses that are a result of the system's malfunctioning from shortcomings that are inherent in guardianship.

Chapter three will introduce the Convention on the Rights of Persons with Disabilities (CRPD) and will delve into the debate on the interpretation of its Article 12. There are broadly two conflicting positions in the literature concerning the meaning of Article 12 and the obligations following from it, both of which have weaknesses. I will show that these attempts cannot fully resolve the issue at hand and, therefore, this chapter will offer a different analysis, applying a structure based on the various aspects of international human rights norms, to establish what limits the CRPD sets for legal capacity laws, within which several possible interpretations of Article 12 can be imagined.

Chapter four analyses how guardianship laws operate. Contrary to other approaches, which are usually interested in their negative features, I am taking a holistic approach, describing the often overlooked positive aspects of guardianship as well. Only by understanding these can we explain why countries are not abandoning their guardianship systems, and what features supported decision-making laws have to possess in order to constitute an adequate alternative to guardianship.

Chapter five will analyse the theoretical writings on supported decision-making to establish its essential features and to compare it with the existing legislation recognising supported decision-making in Canada, Sweden, and Germany. Supported decision-making was proposed by the drafters of the CRPD as an alternative that could replace guardianship and supposedly fulfil the goal of fully respecting the autonomy of persons with disabilities. However, it is unclear what supported decision-making exactly means, and how it operates in practice.[59] It has been so far mainly described by disability advocates as a theoretical proposal, possibly overstating its potential. Nevertheless, it has certain inherent features that make it a very promising alternative to guardianship.

Chapter six will compare supported decision-making to the ideal version of guardianship in order to establish their advantages and disadvantages. The aim will be to describe the trade-offs present in replacing guardianship with supported decision-making and exploring ways to mitigate them. The main question is whether it is possible to design safeguards that could ensure that supported decision-making can take on the functions of guardianship, including maintaining legal certainty and protection from abuse.

Chapter seven will analyse how persons with high support needs can be incorporated into a support framework. Any model is as good as its ability to deal with its exceptions.[60] Persons with the most profound disabilities, who might completely lack decision-making abilities in some or all areas, therefore

[59] R Dinerstein, EG Grewa, and J Martinis, 'Emerging International Trends and Practices in Guardianship Law for People with Disabilities' (2016) 22 *ILSA Journal of International and Comparative Law* 435, 442.

[60] G Quinn, 'Personhood and Legal Capacity – Perspectives on the Paradigm Shift of Article 12 CRPD', Harvard Law School Project on Disability Conference presentation (2010).

represent a challenge for the concept of supported decision-making. They might not be able to make decisions even with full support, therefore, supposedly, they will always be dependent on some form of substitute decision-making. I will propose a solution, the Modified Support Framework, to incorporate the decisions taken on behalf of persons with the highest support needs into the supported decision-making framework. If this proposal is successful, even persons with the most severe disabilities could achieve full legal personhood in the framework suggested by this book, an attribute which they have been denied so far.

Chapter eight will conclude by situating legal capacity laws and the proposal of this book in a wider context of factors contributing to and undermining the autonomy of persons with disabilities, and how these relate to the interpretation of the CRPD.

1.4. NOTE ON TERMINOLOGY

This book is concerned with persons who have decision-making difficulties. This primarily involves persons with intellectual disabilities (mental retardation, cognitive disabilities, developmental disabilities), autism, brain injury, psycho-social disabilities (mental illness), and some of their important sub-categories, such as persons suffering from dementia and substance abuse problems and other addictions, and persons in persistent vegetative states (coma). Although an umbrella term, 'mental disability' was suggested and used by some to refer to all these groups,[61] this is both outdated and misleading, as in other contexts, it is used to refer to persons with psychosocial disability or persons with intellectual disability, which are just a subset of the overall category. Therefore, instead of coining a new umbrella term, I will use 'persons with disabilities' throughout this book to refer to all the above categories of persons with decision-making difficulties. In practice, persons with sensory impairments,[62] communication difficulties,[63] cerebral palsy and other types of mobility impairments[64] may be all placed under guardianship despite the absence of a rational connection

[61] This is reflected in the names of two important international organisations working in the area of disability rights: Mental Disability Advocacy Centre (MDAC), and Mental Disability Rights International (MDRI).

[62] Dhanda, 'Legal Capacity in the Disability Rights Convention' 431.

[63] See, for example, descriptions of Civil Codes in Mexican States that provide for the incapacitation of deaf persons and persons with physical disabilities in: Rehabilitation International, 'Legal Capacity and Guardianship of Persons with Disabilities in Mexico', Seminar on Legal Capacity and Access to Justice (Mexico 2010) 11 and 25; also, see I Hoffman and G Konczei, 'Legal Regulations Relating to the Passive and Active Legal Capacity of Persons with Intellectual and Psychosocial Disabilities in Light of the Convention on the Rights' (2010) 33 *Loyola of Los Angeles International and Comparative Law Review* 150, also Mental Disability Advocacy Centre (MDAC), *Legal Capacity in Europe*, 79.

[64] G Quinn, 'An Ideas Paper', Eur. Foundation Centre, Seminar on Legal Capacity, Brussels (4 June 2009) 7.

between its legal basis and their condition.[65] They are, nevertheless, typically not the primary objects of guardianship legislation.

The above groups are diverse in many of their characteristics, but from the perspective of guardianship they are treated surprisingly similarly: in many countries, the same legal regime is applicable to them.[66] I will note important differences where they matter. For the most part, the examples provided come from the realm of persons with intellectual disability.

[65] Hoffman and Konczei, 'Legal Regulations Relating to the Passive and Active Legal Capacity'.

[66] Typically, the same guardianship legislation applies to persons with psychosocial disabilities as well as persons with intellectual disabilities; see, for example, Act no. IV of 1959 on the Civil Code of the Hungarian Republic, § 14(4) and 15(4).

2

Legal Capacity

THE OPERATION OF legal capacity laws undermines the status of persons with disabilities as autonomous members of society.[1] I use the term legal capacity laws to include all legislation regulating decision-making on behalf of persons with disabilities, laws that permit or prohibit persons to make legally valid decisions based on their actual or perceived (in)ability to make these decisions.[2] Those recognised as capable can make decisions on their own; for those found to be incapable, the law has various alternative mechanisms to allow substitute decision-makers to make decisions on their behalf.[3]

The idea that some persons with disabilities are incapable of managing their affairs and that, therefore, it is society's duty to protect them by intervening in their decision-making goes back to at least ancient Roman times.[4] It has been accepted and practised as a natural reaction to the situation of persons with some types of disabilities since then as an indispensable element of life and law.[5] This chapter describes how the flawed foundations of substituted decision-making led to violations of human rights and how these were captured in international human rights law.

2.1. WHAT IS LEGAL CAPACITY?

To analyse the human rights implications of 'legal capacity' and 'guardianship', I need to clarify these terms. Both concepts can be found in all legal systems of the world in various forms, but they lack a universal definition.[6]

[1] A Arstein-Kerslake, *Restoring Voice to People with Cognitive Disabilities* (Cambridge University Press, 2017).

[2] JE Lord and MA Stein, 'Contingent participation and coercive care: feminist and communitarian theories of disability and legal capacity' in B McSherry and I Freckelton (eds), *Coercive care: rights, law and policy* (Routledge, 2013) 31.

[3] P Gooding, 'Supported Decision-Making: A Rights-Based Disability Concept and its Implications for Mental Health Law' (2013) 20(3) *Psychiatry, Psychology and Law* 431, 434.

[4] AF Johns, 'Guardianship Folly: The Misgovernment of Parens Patriae and the Forecast of its Crumbling Linkage to Unprotected Older Americans in the Twenty-first Century – A March of Folly? Or just a Mask of Virtual Reality?' (1997) 27 *Stetson Law Review* 28, 38.

[5] NA Kohn, JA Blumenthal, and AT Campbell, 'Supported Decision-Making: A Viable Alternative to Guardianship?' (2013) 117(4) *Penn State Law Review* 1111.

[6] J Dawson and G Szmukler, 'The "Fusion Law" Proposals and the CRPD' in MA Stein, F Mahomed, V Patel, and C Sunkel (eds), *Mental Health, Legal Capacity, and Human Rights* (Cambridge University Press, 2021) 100.

For the purposes of this book, *legal capacity* is defined as the right of individuals to be recognised as subjects of rights and obligations before the law and the ability to acquire rights and obligations by their own actions. These two components of legal capacity are sometimes referred to as the *capacity to have rights* and the *capacity to act*,[7] or *legal standing* and *legal agency*.[8] In some jurisdictions, typically in common law countries,[9] they are expressed in one legal institution; in others, they are constituted separately,[10] causing a great deal of confusion in translations.[11] All persons are born with the *capacity to have rights*, which is recognised and cannot be taken away under modern law.[12] The *capacity to act*, on the other hand, is subject to limitations in all countries around the world.[13] This book is concerned with this second component only, and it will use *legal capacity* in this sense.

Historically, legal capacity restrictions applied to a wide circle of persons,[14] including women[15] and members of racial minorities.[16] Medieval law contained various restrictions on the legal capacity of women, which depended on their personal status. Married women, for example, could not own or dispose of property; only their husbands could do it on their behalf.[17] Similar legal limitations existed for racial minorities.[18] Anna Arstein-Kerslake makes a compelling case for how denial of legal personhood continues to affect various marginalised

[7] T Minkowitz, 'The United Nations Convention on the Rights of Persons with Disabilities and the Right to Be Free from Nonconsensual Psychiatric Interventions' (2007) 34 *Syracuse Journal of International Law and Commerce* 405, 411.

[8] Gooding, 'Supported Decision-Making' 437.

[9] M Keys, 'Article 12' in VD Fina, R Cera, and G Palmisano (eds), *The United Nations Convention on the Rights of Persons with Disabilities. A Commentary* (Springer, 2017).

[10] G de Beco, *Disability in International Human Rights Law* (Oxford University Press, 2021) 95.

[11] The translation of 'legal capacity' to Arabic, Chinese and Russian led to controversies already during the CRPD's drafting process, because it could have changed its meaning; see A Lawson, 'The United Nations Convention on the Rights of Persons with Disabilities: New Era or False Dawn?' (2007) 34 *Syracuse Journal of International Law and Commerce* 563; Hungarian law, for example, differentiates between capacity to have rights, capacity to act, procedural capacity (capacity to participate in legal proceedings), and delictual capacity (capacity to bear the consequences of breaking the law by one's actions).

[12] The CRPD Committee has so far not found a situation involving the deprivation of capacity to have rights.

[13] J Dawson, 'A realistic approach to assessing mental health laws' compliance with the UNCRPD.' (2015) 40 *International Journal of Law and Psychiatry* 70, 72.

[14] Z Benincasa and M Nowak, 'Outline of the legal situation of persons with mental disabilities (furiosi) in Roman law' in M Domański and B Lackoroński (eds), *Models of Implementation of Article 12 of the Convention on the Rights of Persons with Disabilities (CRPD); Private and Criminal Law Aspects* (Routledge, 2024) 49.

[15] A Arstein-Kerslake, *Legal Capacity and Gender* (Springer, 2021).

[16] C Dayan, *The Law Is a White Dog: How Legal Rituals Make and Unmake Persons* (Princeton University Press, 2013); G Pavlich, 'Criminal Justice and Cape Law's Persons' (2014) 23 *Social and Legal Studies* 55.

[17] MM Sheehan, 'The Influence of Canon Law on the Property Rights of Married Women in England' (1963) 25(1) *Medieval Studies* 109, 119–21.

[18] See E Foner and J Brown, *Forever Free: A Story of Emancipation and Reconstruction* (Knopf, 2005); HT Catterall, *Judicial Cases Concerning Slavery and the Negro* (Carnegie Institution of Washington, 1926) 247.

groups.[19] Nevertheless, legal capacity in modern law is most often limited by reasons of age, in the case of minors, and the person's inability to make decisions alone on account of some impairment, the focus of this book.[20] These limitations can take many forms and many names, such as guardianship, conservatorship,[21] tutelage,[22] custodianship,[23] representation,[24] trusteeship,[25] administratorship,[26] and others.[27] But the central feature is always the transfer of the adult's ability to acquire rights and obligations by her own actions to another person, the *guardian*. The incapacitated adult's actions thus lose their legal relevance; they are not binding because only the guardian is entitled to act on her behalf.[28]

This book will use the umbrella term *guardianship* to refer to these types of interventions, which are the primary example of substitute decision-making. Their common feature is that once they are imposed on the disabled person, she loses her ability to make legally valid decisions, and this decision-making power is transferred to another person.[29] The scope of the measure can be general, affecting all decisions, which is often called *plenary guardianship*.[30] On the other hand, *partial guardianship* can be limited to only certain decisions or certain types of decisions, such as management of immovable property, family matters, medical choices, and others.[31]

[19] A Arstein-Kerslake, *The Right to Legal Personhood of Marginalised Groups* (Oxford University Press, 2024).

[20] T Carney, 'Guardianship, Citizenship, & Theorizing Substitute-decisionmaking Law' (2012) 12/25 *Sydney Law School Research Paper* 1.

[21] M Bushko, 'Toxic: A Feminist Legal Theory Approach to Guardianship' (2022) 81 *Maryland Law Review Online* 141, 143.

[22] N Henckes, 'Between tutelage and assistance: The debate over the reform of the 1838 French law on insane people from the 1870s to the 1910s' (2017) 35(2) *Sciences sociales et santé* 81.

[23] T Grisso, *Evaluating Competencies: Forensic Assessments and Instruments,* Perspectives in Law and Psychology 16 (Kluwer Academic Plenum Publishers, 2nd Edition, 2003) 12.

[24] Á Hynes, *Irish Capacity Law and Assisted Decision-Making* (Bloomsbury Publishing, 2018).

[25] I Bantekas, 'Mental and Intellectual Capacity and Contractual Freedom: Assistive Decision-Making Matters' (2023) 21(2) *Seattle Journal for Social Justice* 569, 584.

[26] SS Herr, 'Self Determination, Autonomy, and Alternatives for Guardianship' in SS Herr, LO Gostin, and HH Koh (eds), *The Human Rights of Persons with Intellectual Disabilities* (Oxford University Press, 2003) 435.

[27] S Castillo-Wyszogrodzka, 'Implementation of Article 12 of the UN Convention on the Rights of Persons with Disabilities in France' in M Domański and B Lackoroński (eds), *Models of Implementation of Article 12 of the Convention on the Rights of Persons with Disabilities (CRPD); Private and Criminal Law Aspects* (Routledge, 2024) 203.

[28] A-M Callus, 'Removing obstacles to equal recognition for persons with intellectual disability: Taking exception to the way things are' (2018) 12 *ALTER European Journal of Disability Research* 153, 163.

[29] R Dinerstein, EG Grewal, and J Martinis, 'Emerging International Trends and Practices in Guardianship Law for People with Disabilities' (2016) 22 *ILSA Journal of International and Comparative Law* 435, 452.

[30] M Hamilton, 'Supported Decision-making as an Alternative to Guardianship' (2023) *Trends in State Courts* 87, 88.

[31] O Lewis, 'Advancing Legal Capacity Jurisprudence' (2010) 6 *European Human Rights Law Review* 700, 701.

Besides guardianship, other mechanisms limiting the decision-making ability of persons with disabilities in specific areas also exist. Mental health laws contain provisions on overriding the objections of persons who are refusing treatment;[32] laws on adoption can have specific provisions for not taking into account the disabled person's opinions in the process;[33] electoral laws can decide whether disability can be a basis for disenfranchisement;[34] banking regulations can forbid persons with various impairments to operate a bank account without an assistant;[35] etc. Whether decision-making in a particular area is governed by general guardianship laws or specific sectorial provisions varies among jurisdictions, but all these regulations can have an impact on a person's legal capacity. This book is mainly concerned with general guardianship laws, but I will also comment on how its findings can be applied to laws regulating specific areas.

2.2. A HISTORICAL OVERVIEW

The notion that some persons are unable to protect their interests, and therefore others have to make decisions on their behalf, is as old as the law itself.[36] In ancient Rome, the Law of Twelve Tables prescribed the appointment of guardians (curators) to 'fools' (persons with mental illness)[37] to manage their property and thus protect the financial interests of their family and heirs.[38] In the middle ages, the reception of Roman law in the European continent resulted in the adoption of guardianship as a general framework for managing all decisions of the disabled person.[39] In England, the King's Parens Patriae powers justified appointing guardians to noblemen with mental illness or intellectual disability to manage their estate and arrange for the care of the person[40] since

[32] The academic literature is particularly rich in discussions whether mental health treatment should be governed by specific mental health laws or general incapacity laws. See, for example, N Rees, 'The Fusion Proposal: A Next Step?' in B McSherry and P Weller (eds), *Rethinking Rights Based Mental Health Laws* (Hart, 2010) 73; J Dawson and G Szmukler, 'Fusion of Mental Health and Incapacity Legislation' (2006) 188 *British Journal of Psychiatry* 504; G Richardson, 'Mental Disabilities and the Law: From Substitute to Supported Decision-Making?' (2012) 65 *Current Legal Problems* 333.

[33] *X. v Croatia* App no 11223/04 (ECtHR 17 July 2008).

[34] J Fiala-Butora, MA Stein, and JE Lord, 'The democratic life of the Union: towards equal voting participation for Europeans with Disabilities' (2014) 55 *Harvard International Law Journal* 71.

[35] A Dhanda, 'Legal Capacity in the Disability Rights Convention: Stranglehold of the Past or Lodestar for the Future?' (2007) 34 *Syracuse Journal of International Law and Commerce* 429, 431.

[36] Benincasa and Nowak, 'Outline of the legal situation'.

[37] I Basa, 'Gondnokság a római jogban' (2006) 43 *Állam- és Jogtudomány* 407.

[38] Johns, 'Guardianship Folly' 10.

[39] K Blankman, 'Guardianship Models in the Netherlands and Western Europe' (1997) 20 *International Journal of Law and Psychiatry* 47, 48.

[40] L Salzman, 'Guardianship for persons with mental illness – a legal and appropriate alternative?' (2011) 4 *Saint Louis University Journal of Health Law & Policy* 279, 286.

the thirteenth century.[41] The sovereign's power over persons with disability was absolute, relating to their body and property.[42]

Guardianship has survived to the twenty-first century, but not without changes. As Blankman describes, in Western Europe, inflexible plenary guardianship systems have been phased out since the 1960s and have been replaced with more limited forms of guardianship tailored to the disabled person's needs.[43] Also, the intervention's purpose shifted from protecting the adult's property for the sake of her heirs to safeguarding the adult's interests themselves, including not only financial but also healthcare and social care matters.[44] Alternatives to guardianship have also been developed, such as enduring powers of attorney, allowing patients to decide on their medical treatment in the event of their incapacity.[45] However, these alternatives have not eliminated guardianship: it remains the prevalent model of intervention even in the most progressive jurisdictions.[46] The adoption of the CRPD initiated a new wave of reforms[47] of legal capacity laws across the globe,[48] some of which seem very promising.[49] Nevertheless, no country has managed to eliminate guardianship from its laws yet,[50] which remains the main form of intervention in the decision-making of adults with cognitive disabilities.[51]

The situation is even worse in the countries of post-communist Central and Eastern Europe, which were behind the Iron Curtain and thus did not participate in the reform movement of the 1960s. They rely heavily on outdated plenary guardianship,[52] which in some states is the only form of legal response to the needs of persons with disabilities who have difficulties making their own decisions.[53]

[41] Carney, 'Guardianship, Citizenship' 1.

[42] Rees, 'The Fusion Proposal' 73.

[43] Blankman, 'Guardianship Models in the Netherlands and Western Europe' 47.

[44] ibid.

[45] Carney, 'Guardianship, Citizenship' 2.

[46] See M Rioux, J Gilmour, and N Angel, 'Negotiating capacity: legally constructed entitlement and protection' in B McSherry and I Freckelton (eds), *Coercive care: rights, law and policy* (Routledge, 2013) 51, 71, describing the situation in Canada, considered to be one of the most progressive countries in the area of legal capacity regulation.

[47] C Kong, J Coggon, P Cooper, M Dunn, and A R Keene, *Capacity, Participation and Values in Comparative Legal Perspective* (Bristol University Press, 2023).

[48] M Domański and B Lackoroński, *Models of Implementation of Article 12 of the Convention on the Rights of Persons with Disabilities (CRPD); Private and Criminal Law Aspects* (Routledge, 2024) 203.

[49] P Marshall, P Vasquez, V Purin, and L Godoy, 'Are We Closing the Gap? Reforms to Legal Capacity in Latin America in Light of the Convention on the Rights of Persons with Disabilities' (2023) 56(1) *Vanderbilt Journal of Transnational Law* 119.

[50] RAC Caycho, 'The flag of imagination: Peru's new reform on legal capacity for persons with intellectual and psychosocial disabilities and the need for new understandings in private law' (2020) 14 *Age of Human Rights Journal* 155, 169.

[51] E Flynn, A Arstein-Kerslake, C de Bhailís, and ML Serra, *Global Perspectives on Legal Capacity Reform Our Voices, Our Stories* (Routledge, 2019).

[52] Mental Disability Advocacy Centre (MDAC), *Legal Capacity in Europe* (MDAC, 2013) 20.

[53] See, for example, *Shtukaturov v Russia* App no 44009/05 (ECtHR 27 March 2008).

Persons with disabilities were not the only ones suffering from restrictions of their legal capacity. However, the limitations on women's legal capacity have been gradually lifted[54] and are now universally recognised as scientifically unfounded.[55] The same development took place with regard to racial and religious minorities.[56] Legal capacity laws no longer formally restrict somebody's decision-making ability just because she is a woman or a member of a disfavoured minority, at least as far as the Western world is concerned.[57] These vulnerable groups might still be subject to denials of their legal personhood, but not through the application of guardianship laws.[58]

Persons with disabilities, together with children,[59] are still waiting for their liberation to take place. They have still not achieved full citizenship.[60] They are still suffering from age-old attitudes portraying them as incapable of managing their affairs.[61] These are currently accepted and justified by medical and psychological evidence that show that they lack the ability to make fully autonomous decisions.[62] Contrary to other historically oppressed groups, for persons with disabilities guardianship and exclusion from decision-making is still the norm, and autonomous status the exception.[63] Their objectively existing decision-making difficulties are often still addressed by the law by relying on the same principle as was used in medieval times.[64]

[54] See Rioux, Gilmour, Angel, 'Negotiating capacity' for a description of how women's legal capacity in Colombia was denied until the legal reforms of 1932 and 1974.

[55] MA Stein and A Silvers, 'Essentially Empirical: The Role of Biological and Legal Classification in Effectively Prohibiting Genetic Discrimination' in R Figueroa and S Harding (eds), *Science and Other Cultures: Issues in Philosophies of Science and Technology* (Routledge, 2003).

[56] The situation of some racial minorities, such as the Roma, might constitute an exception. In some European states, the unwillingness of authorities to register births and issue identity documents to Roma results in denial of personhood and the loss of civil rights. For the description of this problem in Italy, see A Nolan, '"Aggravated Violations", Roma Housing Rights and Forced Expulsions in Italy: Recent Development under the European Social Charter Collective Complaints System' (2011) 11 *Human Rights Law Review* 343, 355.

[57] The situation might be different in some countries, where the rights of women are considerably curtailed in many areas of life. See HM Fattah, 'Kuwait Grants Political Rights to Its Women', *New York Times*, 17 May 2005, 9, about the recent granting of the right to vote to women in Kuwait.

[58] Arstein-Kerslake, *The Right to Legal Personhood.*

[59] See JR Morss, 'But for the Barriers: Significant Extensions to Children's Capacity' (2004) 11 *Psychiatry, Psychology and Law* 319, for a description of a recent Australian court decision expanding the scope of children's legal capacity.

[60] Arstein-Kerslake, *Restoring Voice.*

[61] T Carney, 'Australian Guardianship Tribunals: An adequate response to CRPD disability rights recognition and protection of the vulnerable over the lifecourse?' (2017) 10 *Journal of Ethics in Mental Health* 1, 2.

[62] Grisso, *Evaluating Competencies.*

[63] Flynn, Arstein-Kerslake, de Bhailís, Serra, *Global Perspectives on Legal Capacity.*

[64] J Fiala-Butora and MA Stein, 'The Law as a Source of Stigma or Empowerment: Legal Capacity and Persons with Intellectual Disabilities' in K Scior and S Werner (eds), *Intellectual Disability & Stigma: Stepping out from the Margins* (Palgrave Macmillan, 2016).

2.3. LEGAL CAPACITY AS A HUMAN RIGHT

Regardless of its variations across jurisdictions, the core of guardianship is always the same and is always problematic: it transfers the adult's decision-making power over her affairs to the guardian.[65] The person is thus reduced from a subject to an object of law; her will and actions become legally irrelevant. Depending on the scope and type of the guardianship order, the guardian enjoys control over all or some of her affairs and may be authorised to decide where the adult lives, with whom she associates, what medical procedures she undergoes, what happens to her property and so on.[66] Not surprisingly, guardianship, especially in its plenary form, is referred to as 'civil death',[67] and persons subject to it as the 'legally disappeared'.[68]

Guardianship is no doubt a problematic institution because it constitutes a serious intrusion into personal autonomy.[69] The concern for the rights of the person placed under guardianship was already recognised in ancient Roman law, and it gradually replaced the protection of the person's family's property interests as the only consideration motivating incapacitation.[70] It is, therefore, surprising that guardianship has only recently been recognised as a human rights issue.

At the United Nations level, the International Covenant on Civil and Political Rights (ICCPR), adopted in 1966, guarantees the right to recognition as a person before the law, but this protects only the capacity to have rights, not the capacity to act.[71] Guardianship has, therefore, remained permissible under the ICCPR.[72] Newer instruments, such as the Convention on the Elimination of Discrimination Against Women (CEDAW) signed in 1973, and the Convention on the Rights of the Child (CRC) signed in 1990, contain provisions guaranteeing the capacity to

[65] Gooding, 'Supported Decision-Making' 434.

[66] Lewis, 'Advancing Legal Capacity Jurisprudence' 701.

[67] W Blackstone, *Commentaries on the Laws of England: A Facsimile of First Edition of 1765–1769 with an Introduction by Stanley N. Katz* (Blackwells, 1979).

[68] G Quinn, 'An Ideas Paper', Eur. Foundation Centre, Seminar on Legal Capacity, Brussels (4 June 2009) 4.

[69] Dinerstein, Grewal, and Martinis, 'Emerging International Trends' 452.

[70] Basa, 'Gondnokság a római jogban' 411.

[71] Article 16 of the International Covenant on Civil and Political Rights (16 December 1966).

[72] As explained by the commentary to the ICPRR by Manfred Nowak, 'limitations on the capacity to act … do not represent a violation of Art. 16', see M Nowak, *U.N. Covenant on Civil and Political Rights: CCPR Commentary* (N.P. Engel, 1993) 283. The Human Rights Committee have recently expanded the scope of Article 16 in enforced disappearance cases, holding that 'intentional removal of a person from the protection of the law constitutes a denial of the right to recognition everywhere as a person before the law' – see *Chhedulal Tharu and others v Nepal* No. 2038/2011 (Human Rights Committee, CCPR/C/114/D/2038/2011, 3 July 2015). These developments have not resulted in changes in the Committee's views regarding guardianship.

act.[73] Nevertheless, there is very little jurisprudence or discussion of guardianship issues under these instruments relevant to the topic of this book.[74]

Guardianship became an important human rights issue recently through the activities of the Council of Europe, and its flagship body, the European Court of Human Rights. Although the European Convention on Human Rights, adopted in 1950, contains no reference to a right to legal capacity, it has been gradually recognised by the case law of the European Court. The first case to deal with the subject was *Winterwerp v the Netherlands* in 1979,[75] where the Court had to consider whether the European Convention's fair trial guarantees were relevant for the restriction of legal capacity. The Netherlands government argued that legal capacity is a matter of status, not rights and obligations.[76] The European Court rejected this line of reasoning and held that procedural guarantees apply to placement under guardianship. It did not, however, question the fact of incapacitation as such. The legitimacy of placing disabled persons under guardianship was also accepted in other cases following *Winterwerp*, such as *Egger v Austria*[77] and *Bock v Germany*.[78] Despite its widespread nature in Western Europe, the restriction of legal capacity as a substantive issue had not been addressed by the European Court.

This state of affairs changed only after the post-communist countries of Central and Eastern Europe ratified the European Convention on Human Rights. Although guardianship in those countries was formally often similar to that in the west, it has been applied in a very abusive way with significant procedural flaws which lead to a number of applications challenging it.[79]

Matter v Slovakia was the first case that considered that the restriction of legal capacity as such could be a problem under the European Convention.[80] The European Court held that incapacitation is a serious interference with the right to respect for private life under Article 8 of the European Convention, although

[73] Article 15(2) of the Convention on the Elimination of All Forms of Discrimination against Women (CEDAW) (18 December 1979); Articles 5, 12 and 14(2) of the Convention on the Rights of the Child (CRC) (20 November 1989).

[74] A detailed discussion is provided in Arstein-Kerslake, *Restoring Voice*. On the relevance of CEDAW during the CRPD negotiation process see Dhanda, 'Legal Capacity in the Disability Rights Convention' 442. On the relevance of ICCPR, see European Union Agency for Fundamental Rights, *Legal capacity of persons with intellectual disabilities and persons with mental health problems* (February 2013) 16.

[75] *Winterwerp v the Netherlands* App no 6301/73 (ECtHR 24 October 1979).

[76] ibid, §73.

[77] *Egger v Austria* App no 15780/89 (ECtHR admissibility decision 11 October 1993).

[78] *Bock v Germany* App no. 11118/84 (ECtHR 21 February 1989).

[79] For the flaws of guardianship systems in Central Easter Europe, see the reports of the Mental Disability Advocacy Centre (MDAC) on several countries of the region: *Guardianship and Human Rights in Serbia* (MDAC, 2006), *Guardianship and Human Rights in Bulgaria* (MDAC, 2007), *Guardianship and Human Rights in the Czech Republic* (MDAC, 2007), *Guardianship and Human Rights in Georgia* (MDAC, 2007), *Guardianship and Human Rights in Hungary* (MDAC, 2007), *Guardianship and Human Rights in Kyrgyzstan* (MDAC, 2007), *Guardianship and Human Rights in Russia* (MDAC, 2007).

[80] *Matter v Slovakia* App no 31534/96 (ECtHR 5 July 1999).

it did not find a violation in that specific case.[81] That came in *Shtukaturov v Russia*, where the European Court decided that placing the applicant under plenary guardianship violated his right to private life.[82] That reasoning was later confirmed in *Nikolyan v Armenia*.[83] Guardianship also led to violations in cases such as *X. v Croatia*,[84] *Salontaji-Drobnjak v Serbia*[85] and *Alajos Kiss v Hungary*.[86] Procedural aspects of guardianship were criticised in *H.F. v Slovakia*[87] and *Berková v Slovakia*.[88]

Another significant development was the adoption of the Council of Europe's Committee of Ministers' Recommendation R(99)4 *on the legal protection of incapable adults*, which proscribed detailed rules and principles for guardianship.[89] Although not a binding instrument, the European Court took its standards into account when interpreting the European Convention, providing it an almost-binding status.[90]

The European Court has not recognised the central importance of legal capacity for the autonomy of persons with disabilities. In fact, it has not yet recognised a right to personal autonomy as such. The closest it came to this was in *Pretty v the United Kingdom*.[91] The Court will, however, have plenty of opportunities to do so in the near future, as the number of cases concerning disability rights before the Court is growing.[92]

Cases concerning legal capacity decided by the European Court can be divided to three groups based on what types of violations they are concerned with. The first relates to violations of procedural rights.[93] The second involves situations where guardianship results in violations of fundamental rights.[94] The third group is concerned with limitations of the person's decision-making powers itself.

[81] ibid, § 68.

[82] *Shtukaturov v Russia.*

[83] *Nikolyan v Armenia* App no 74438/14 (ECtHR 3 October 2019).

[84] *X. v Croatia* App no 11223/04 (ECtHR 17 July 2008).

[85] *Salontaji-Drobnjak v Serbia* App no 36500/05 (ECtHR 13 October 2009).

[86] *Kiss v Hungary* App no 38832/06 (ECtHR 20 May 2010).

[87] *H.F. v Slovakia* App no 54797/00 (ECtHR 8 November 2005).

[88] *Berková v Slovakia* App no 67149/01 (ECtHR 24 March 2009).

[89] Council of Europe Committee of Ministers, Recommendation R(99)4 on the legal protection of incapable adults (23 February 1999).

[90] See, for example, in *Shtukaturov v Russia*, § 95.

[91] *Pretty v the United Kingdom* App no 2346/02 (ECtHR 29 April 2002).

[92] J Fiala-Butora, 'The influence of the convention on the rights of persons with disabilities on the European court of human rights in the area of mental health law: Divergence and unexplored potential' (2024) 94 *International Journal of Law and Psychiatry* 101965.

[93] In the legal literature, these have been addressed, for example, in M Keys, 'Legal Capacity Law Reform in Europe: An Urgent Challenge' in G Quinn and L Waddington (eds), *European Yearbook of Disability Law* (Intersentia, 2009); O Lewis, 'Mental Disability Law in Central and Eastern Europe: Paper, Practice, Promise' (2014) *International Journal of Mental Health and Capacity Law* 293, 297; O Lewis, 'Protecting the Rights of People with Mental Disabilities: The European Convention on Human Rights' (2002) 9 *European Journal of Health Law* 293, 307.

[94] Dinerstein, Grewal, Martinis, 'Emerging International' 452.

2.3.1. Violations of Procedural Rights

In many countries, the incapacitation procedure is not accompanied by the necessary safeguards.[95] As a result, persons whose capacity is in question are often not heard by the courts and have no opportunity to submit evidence or appoint a representative.[96] In some states, it is even possible to place persons under guardianship without them being aware of it, since the law allows courts not to notify them about the proceedings, not to hear them during it, and not to deliver the decision to them.[97] In others, persons under guardianship have no right to request the review of their incapacitation.[98] The type and quality of evidence used in incapacitation proceedings were also criticised by the European Court. If medical assessments are too general or outdated,[99] or they are prepared without the psychiatrist in fact examining the person,[100] the guardianship order based on them loses its validity. These and other problems can lead to a violation of their right to a fair trial under Article 6 of the European Convention, as has already occurred in many cases.[101]

2.3.2. Violations of Other Substantive Rights

The second group involves situations in which the victim cannot exercise a fundamental right because of the limitation of her legal capacity. In other words, in this category, the European Court does not contest placement under guardianship itself; it only questions some effects guardianship has on the enjoyment of a wide range of human rights. For example, if a person under guardianship cannot marry, either because her guardian does not consent to it or because it is prohibited by law,[102] this can constitute a violation of the right to marry under Article 12 of the European Convention – although in the case of *Delecolle v France*, in which the European Court considered this issue, it did not find a violation.[103] If she cannot join an association, this can breach her rights under Article 11 of the European Convention. If she cannot vote, it can lead to the violation of the right to vote, as found by the European Court in *Alajos Kiss*

[95] Lewis, 'Advancing Legal Capacity'.
[96] *Sýkora v the Czech Republic* App no 23419/07 (ECtHR 22 November 2012); *Stanev v Bulgaria* App no 36760/06 (ECtHR 17 January 2012); *Shtukaturov v Russia*.
[97] See *Sýkora v the Czech Republic*, for a particularly blatant example of disregard for procedural fairness.
[98] *Mikhaylenko v Ukraine* App no 49069/11 (ECtHR 30 May 2013); *Stanev v Bulgaria*.
[99] *H.F. v Slovakia*; *Sýkora v the Czech Republic*, § 111.
[100] *Sýkora v the Czech Republic*.
[101] *Sýkora v the Czech Republi*; *H.F. v Slovakia*; *Shtukaturov v Russia*.
[102] See, for example, Article 9(1) of the Hungarian Act no. IV of 1952 on the Family, Marriage and Custodianship.
[103] *Delecolle v France* Appl no 37646/13 (ECtHR 25 October 2018).

v Hungary.[104] If she is hospitalised against her will but with the consent of her guardian, as happened to the applicants in *Shtukaturov v Russia*[105] and in *Sýkora v the Czech Republic*,[106] it can lead to the violation of the right to liberty. If incapacitation precludes the person from being involved in the proceedings concerning the adoption of her own child, it can lead to the violation of her right to family life, as happened in *X. v Croatia*.[107]

It is not difficult to develop hypothetical scenarios that would likely engage every single article of the European Convention and where guardianship would be the central reason for the violation. Even freedom from torture is not immune to its power: some guardians have a right to consent to procedures such as surgical castration,[108] electroconvulsive therapy (ECT),[109] psychosurgery (lobotomy), and the use of 'cage beds' and other restraints.[110] If the person objects to these procedures, but her guardian consents to them, she is considered to be a voluntary patient under domestic guardianship laws since consent is obtained from the legally authorised person.[111] Therefore, a court review of the medical procedure or other legal safeguards are not available for the person under guardianship.[112] From the perspective of the European Court, this domestic legal fiction of consent matters little: these interventions constitute an arbitrary application of severely intrusive measures on a patient who clearly objects.[113]

2.3.3. Guardianship as Such

The third type of violations concerns the essence of guardianship: a limitation of the person's ability to make decisions. The European Court held in 2006 that this constitutes a serious interference with the person's right to private life under Article 8 of the European Convention.[114] In 2008, in *Shtukaturov v Russia*, it found a violation of that right because of the deprivation of the applicant's legal capacity.[115] The mere placement under guardianship, if unjustified, can constitute a human rights violation even if the scope of the guardianship order does not affect other protected rights.

[104] *Kiss v Hungary*.

[105] *Shtukaturov v Russia*.

[106] *Sýkora v the Czech Republic*.

[107] *X. v Croatia*.

[108] Comm. on Soc. Affairs, Health and Sustainable Dev., *Putting an End to Coerced Sterilisations and Castrations*, Doc. 13215 (28 May 2013) (by Liliane Maury Pasquier) 5.

[109] See Egészségügyi Minisztérium, *Az Egészségügyi Minisztérium szakmai protokollja: Az ECT kezelés* (Budapest, Egészségügyi Közlöny, 2005) §§ II(5.2)–II(5.3).

[110] See, for example, Mental Disability Advocacy Centre (MDAC), *Cage Beds: Inhuman and Degrading Treatment in Four EU Accession Countries* (MDAC, 2003) 18–19.

[111] *Sýkora v the Czech Republic*, § 80 and 84.

[112] *Sýkora v the Czech Republic*.

[113] See the unambiguous wording in *Shtukaturov v Russia*, §108.

[114] *Matter v Slovakia*, § 68.

[115] *Shtukaturov v Russia*.

Shtukaturov v Russia is currently the leading case in the area of plenary guardianship.[116] The decision is often praised for its firm stance against incapacitation.[117] The European Court declared that the applicant's total deprivation of legal capacity was not compatible with his right to private life even though the domestic courts had no other, less restrictive options under domestic law.[118] Article 8 of the European Convention, therefore, requires an answer proportionate to the individual circumstances of each person, and where less restrictive alternatives do not exist, they must be created through legislative reform.

A fourth category of potential problems should be mentioned, which has not been directly considered by the European Court and does not fit neatly in any of the above categories. Many guardianship systems do not provide safeguards for the person under guardianship to challenge their guardian's decisions.[119] This can lead to abuse and arbitrary decisions by guardians,[120] in particular if the law provides only very vague indications on what the guardian should base its decisions.[121] There is no reason why the person herself should be unable to initiate a court proceeding to contest her guardian's decisions. Since the matter will be resolved by a court, the person should be allowed to participate in the proceeding and, by extension, to initiate the proceeding.[122]

The above description shows that legal capacity is of central importance for persons with disabilities. It is key to their self-determination and independence, and it is also a precondition for the effective enjoyment of all other human rights. Vice versa, its restriction is a breeding ground for violations of the complete list of rights protected by the European Convention. Its prevalence makes it one of the most critical and most invisible human rights violations today in the opinion of the Council of Europe's Commissioner for Human Rights.[123] The reform of guardianship is, therefore, one of the main goals of the international disability rights movement as it symbolises the paternalistic approach to disabled peoples' autonomy and curtailment of their independence.[124]

[116] Lewis, 'Advancing Legal Capacity' 713.

[117] O Lewis, 'Council of Europe' in L Waddington and A Lawson, *The UN Convention on the Rights of Persons with Disabilities in Practice: A Comparative Analysis of the Role of Courts* (Oxford University Press, 2018), 112; O Lewis, 'Disabling Legal Barriers' (2017) 1 *European Human Rights Law Review* 49, 49.

[118] *Shtukaturov v Russia*, § 95.

[119] Salzman, 'Guardianship for persons with mental illness' 287.

[120] KB Glen, 'Introducing a New Human Right: Learning from Others, Bringing Legal Capacity Home' (2018) 49 *Columbia Human Rights Law Review* 1.

[121] NA Kohn, 'Legislating Supported Decision-Making' (2021) 58 *Harvard Journal on Legislation* 313, 338.

[122] Callus, 'Removing obstacles to equal recognition for persons with intellectual disability'.

[123] Mental Disability Advocacy Centre (MDAC), *Legal Capacity in Europe*, 1.

[124] Inclusion Europe, 'Key Elements of a System of Supported Decision-Making: Position Paper of Inclusion Europe' (Inclusion Europe, 2008); International Disability Alliance (IDA) CRPD Forum, 'Principles for Implementation of CRPD Article 12, Submitted for the Day of General Discussion on "Article 12 of the CRPD – The right to equal recognition before the law" at the UN'

2.4. IMPLICATIONS FOR THE CONVENTION ON THE RIGHTS OF PERSONS WITH DISABILITIES

The CRPD has been frequently declared not to create new human rights but only adapt and specify existing general human rights norms to the situation of persons with disabilities.[125] When interpreting the obligations it creates, existing human rights law serves as a helpful starting point.[126] To analyse the right to equal recognition as a person before the law in Article 12 of the CRPD, the existing international case-law on guardianship therefore has to be taken into account.

The description of the European Court's jurisprudence shows that limitations of legal capacity can lead to many types of serious violations of human rights. However, not all of these are an inherent feature of guardianship, they do not make guardianship problematic as such.

From the perspective of this book's topic, the procedural problems are incidental to the substantive issues. They can be solved relatively easily – at least, it does not require too much theorising to recognise that rules excluding persons with disabilities from their own legal capacity proceedings should have no place in modern guardianship laws. They seem to be a remnant of old prejudices that serve no purpose apart from the appearance of efficiency.

The concerned person should always be notified about the proceedings and should always be heard by the judge directly, even if she cannot attend the trial for medical reasons. The fact that decisions about incapacitation are not delivered to the person and she, therefore, cannot make use of her right to appeal[127] can be dealt with similarly: such limitations of procedural rights should not be allowed because there is nothing to be gained by them. If a person is unable to understand the decision, she will not read it but suffer no harm from receiving it. That is not a legitimate concern for authorising non-delivery.

The lack of effective representation by court-appointed attorneys is a more complicated issue, but neither specific to this area nor unsolvable. For a start, attorneys should be appointed in a reasonable time before the court hearing, and should be required to meet with their client before the hearing to learn about her position. A training of attorneys in disability-related issues would also be beneficial. Legal representation should be of a certain quality, which means that representatives should be sufficiently trained in matters of legal capacity, sufficiently remunerated and have enough time between their appointment and the

(21 October 2009); Quinn, G, 'Personhood and Legal Capacity – Perspectives on the Paradigm Shift of Article 12 CRPD', Harvard Law School Project on Disability Conference presentation (2010) 3.

[125] R Kayess and P French consider the notion that the CRPD does not create new rights an 'official fiction'; see R Kayess and P French, 'Out of Darkness into Light? Introducing the Convention on the Rights of Persons with Disabilities' (2008) 8 *Human Rights Law Review* 32.

[126] See P Weller, 'Supported Decision-Making and the Achievement of Non-Discrimination: The Promise and Paradox of the Disabilities Convention' (2008) 26(2) *Law in Context* 87, 85.

[127] *Sýkora v the Czech Republic.*

hearing to consult their clients and prepare their defence.[128] All these problems can and should be remedied, but that does not change guardianship's inherent features. The substantive issues – when and how it is applied and for what purpose – remain the same.

Similarly, many restrictions automatically connected to guardianship can be easily removed by legal reform. A person under guardianship should not have to automatically lose her right to vote, her right to marry, her right to join associations, her right to work, and other fundamental rights. If any restrictions should apply in these areas, they should not be automatic but related to the person's ability to make decisions in the specific area and proportional to the potential harm society is trying to prevent, if there is any at all.[129]

If the matter of restriction of a specific right of the person under guardianship is decided in a court procedure, the person should not be excluded just because she is under guardianship. Excluding her from proceedings concerning divorce, adoption, abortion, other medical procedures and similar issues is not warranted because nothing is to be gained by it. If the person is unable to participate meaningfully in the proceedings, no harm is done by attempting to include her. On the other hand, if she is excluded on the basis of her guardianship status, the court is risking the exclusion of individuals who would be able to make their wishes known. Even if their involvement is minor, it can only be of benefit to the proceeding. Relying exclusively on their guardians has no advantages: if the person herself is also involved in making her opinion known, it does not prevent the guardian from taking steps on her behalf.

An analysis of the right to vote, for example, suggests that disenfranchisement should never take place because of the lack of voting capacity, not even in a separate court procedure concerned specifically with this matter.[130] A similar closer look at any of these areas would be beneficial and would uncover what exactly is pursued by prohibiting persons under guardianship from marrying, being eligible for civil servant positions, joining associations, and under what conditions, if at all, these can be justified.

It is possible to modify guardianship in a way that would lead to fewer automatic limitations of fundamental rights and, at the same time, retain guardianship's core features. For example, procedural rules could be changed to permit also persons under guardianship to apply for a court review of involuntary hospitalisation.[131] Such a system would still be guardianship if it restricts the person's ability to make legally valid decisions and appoints a substitute

[128] ML Perlin, *International human rights and mental disability law: when the silenced are heard* (Oxford University Press, 2012).

[129] L Turner-Stokes, K Benaichouche-Motam, W Goodison, A Altaie, A Howard, P McKnight, and J Alfonso, 'Improving the systematic screening and documentation of mental capacity for patients with severe brain injury: The Mental Capacity Screening assessment tool (MCScreen)' (2024) 24(5) *Clinical Medicine, Journal of the Royal College of Physicians of London*, 1.

[130] Fiala-Butora, Stein, and Lord, 'The democratic life of the Union'.

[131] As suggested by the European Court in *Sýkora v the Czech Republic*.

decision-maker to make these decisions, as this is the *sine qua non* feature of guardianship.

This is not to suggest that the above problems are unworthy of attention. Quite the contrary, they highlight real and serious problems that cause human suffering and make guardianship an intolerable abuse of the most vulnerable.[132] These issues should be emphasised in the political debate or advocacy campaigns because they build momentum for change. Nevertheless, they can be remedied relatively easily because the cure is known. They do not touch on the substantive issues, the inherent problematic features of guardianship. This book is, therefore, not concerned with procedural matters and violations of other fundamental rights, which all deserve a specific analysis but are tangential to the issue of legal capacity limitations discussed here. The further analysis will concentrate on the inherent features of guardianship, which cannot be overcome by legal reform without discarding the whole system.

Two conclusions can be drawn from the above discussion for the purposes of analysing the meaning of Article 12 of the CRPD: first, despite its importance, both in terms of the number of persons affected and the severity of the violations, legal capacity of persons with disabilities has been recognised a serious human rights issue only relatively recently. This is entirely consistent with other human rights violations specific to persons with disabilities: as Michael Stein notes, under general human rights instruments, the issues of persons with disabilities were ignored, they did not enjoy actual human rights protection.[133] The CRPD aims to overcome this invisibility of disability in human rights treaties.[134] Specifically, Article 12 of the CRPD should be seen as a reaction to the ignorance of mainstream human rights standards about legal capacity issues.

The second issue is what exactly the CRPD is reacting to. The above description of human rights violations constitutes a particular narrative of what guardianship as a human rights violation entails. The typical victim is a relatively capable person who is unjustly restricted by a court order and is legally prohibited from making certain decisions when, in fact, she would functionally be able to make them. The other type of scenario, involving a person clearly unable to make decisions on her own, who is denied the support to make them, is invisible in the international jurisprudence for obvious reasons: these persons would find it particularly hard to seek legal assistance and turn to international bodies. There is no substantive discussion by human rights tribunals of their

[132] Lewis, 'Disabling Legal Barriers' 49.

[133] MA Stein, 'Disability Human Rights' (2007) 95 *California Law Review* 75, 82, noting that persons with disabilities do not receive specific protection under human rights treaties apart from an article of the Convention on the Rights of the Child, which does not consider children with disabilities equal to non-disabled children.

[134] P Bartlett, 'Implementing a paradigm shift: Implementing the convention on the rights of persons with disabilities in the context of mental disability law' in *Torture in healthcare settings: Reflections on the special rapporteur on Torture's 2013 thematic report* (American University Washington College of Law: Center for Human Rights & Humanitarian Law, 2014) 170.

experience and the human rights implications and solutions to the problems these are raising.

International bodies are not the only ones shaping narratives; stories of victimisation can reach the public through other means as well.[135] However, the lack of attention on these fora to one side of the problem affects the understanding of the issue by other human rights bodies, and the richness of the various solutions and alternatives developed. The importance of this experience also affects the interpretation of the CRPD.

[135] Flynn, Arstein-Kerslake, de Bhailís, Serra, *Global Perspectives on Legal Capacity*.

3

Interpreting Article 12 of the CRPD

THE CRPD ENTERED into force on 3 May 2008.[1] It was welcomed as the dawn of a new era, as a significant step towards recognising the rights of persons with disabilities worldwide.[2] From its many innovative provisions, Article 12 has been appraised as one of the most progressive as well as one of the most controversial.[3] It requires that persons with disabilities enjoy legal capacity on an equal basis with others in all aspects of their lives.[4] Many commentators consider it a paradigm shift in approaching legal capacity, which requires the introduction of measures supporting the exercise of legal capacity.[5] Some go further, arguing that Article 12 requires the abolition of all guardianship schemes based on the limitation of legal capacity.[6]

[1] Convention on the Rights of Persons with Disabilities, G.A. Res. 61/106, U.N. Doc. A/RES/61/106 (13 December 2006).

[2] Secretary-General hails adoption of landmark Convention on the Rights of Persons with Disabilities, U.N. Secretary-General, SG/SM/10797, HR/4911, L/T/4400 (13 December 2006).

[3] A Arstein-Kerslake, *Restoring Voice to People with Cognitive Disabilities* (Cambridge University Press, 2017) 15.

[4] Article 12(2) of the CRPD.

[5] T Carney, 'Prioritising Supported Decision-Making: Running on Empty or a Basis for Glacial-To-Steady Progress?' (2017) 6(4) *Laws* 18; B McSherry, 'Legal Capacity under the Convention on the Rights of Persons with Disabilities' (2012) 20 *Journal of Law and Medicine* 22; P Weller, 'Supported Decision-Making and the Achievement of Non-Discrimination: The Promise and Paradox of the Disabilities Convention' (2008) 26(2) *Law in Context* 87; A Lawson, 'The United Nations Convention on the Rights of Persons with Disabilities: New Era or False Dawn?' (2007) 34 *Syracuse Journal of International Law and Commerce* 563; M Keys, 'Legal Capacity Law Reform in Europe: An Urgent Challenge' in G Quinn and L Waddington (eds), *European Yearbook of Disability Law* (Intersentia, 2009); G Quinn and A Arstein-Kerslake, 'Restoring the "human" in "human rights": personhood and doctrinal innovation in the UN disability convention' in C Gearty and C Douzinas (eds), *The Cambridge Companion to Human Rights Law* (Cambridge University Press, 2012) 47; L Salzman, 'Guardianship for persons with mental illness – a legal and appropriate alternative?' (2011) 4 *Saint Louis University Journal of Health Law & Policy* 279.

[6] E Flynn and A Arstein-Kerslake, 'Legislating personhood: realising the right to support in exercising legal capacity' (2014) 10(1) *International Journal of Law in Context* 81; T Minkowitz, 'The United Nations Convention on the Rights of Persons with Disabilities and the Right to Be Free from Nonconsensual Psychiatric Interventions' (2007) 34 *Syracuse Journal of International Law and Commerce* 405; N Devi, J Bickenbach, and G Stucki, 'Moving towards substituted or supported decision-making? Article 12 of the Convention on the Rights of Persons with Disabilities' (2011) 5 *ALTER European Journal of Disability Research* 261; S Pathare and LS Shields, 'Supported decision-making for persons with mental illness: a review' (2012) 34(2) *Public Health Review* 1; P Gooding, 'Supported Decision-Making: A Rights-Based Disability Concept and its Implications for Mental Health Law' (2013) 20(3) *Psychiatry, Psychology and Law* 431; A Dhanda, 'Constructing a new Human Rights Lexicon: Convention on the Rights of persons with Disabilities' (2008) 8 *SUR*

While there is agreement on the importance of Article 12, it is unclear what exactly it requires from states implementing it. The brief text leaves a broad scope for different interpretations. This is not surprising, given that international treaties such as the CRPD tend to be the result of compromises between various stakeholders.[7] Rather than providing a blueprint for legislators and a detailed list of obligations state parties must comply with, Article 12 is more a statement of basic principles legal reforms will have to follow. Nor has its content been sufficiently clarified by the CRPD Committee's published concluding observations[8] or a General Comment on Article 12.[9] While the Committee stressed the importance of introducing supported decision-making and denounced guardianship, it did not explain how supported decision-making should completely replace guardianship and what should happen to persons who are unable to make decisions with support.

This chapter argues that traditional methods of interpretation cannot resolve the dispute over the meaning of Article 12. Even the most convincing positions based on the traditional methods either create unreasonable expectations or frustrate the CRPD's goals. The disagreement over interpretation hinders clarity in understanding the implications and realising the full potential of the CRPD. The most contentious issue, the decision-making of persons with high support needs, cannot currently be resolved simply by deducing a solution from the text of the CRPD. The current interpretation of Article 12 therefore has to leave this question open, and solutions to accommodate persons with high support needs in a support framework have to be derived from other sources. That will be the goal of subsequent chapters of this book.

3.1. THE CONFLICTING VIEWS ON INTERPRETING ARTICLE 12

As explained above, Article 12 of the CRPD aims to overcome the inability of existing human rights instruments to protect persons with disabilities from the violation of their right to legal capacity. Its paragraph 1 guarantees the 'right to recognition everywhere as persons before the law', or the capacity to have

International Journal on Human Rights 43; C de Bhailís and E Flynn, 'Recognising legal capacity: commentary and analysis of Article 12 CRPD' (2017) 13(1) *International Journal of Law in Context* 6.

[7] A Aust, *Modern Treaty Law and Practice* (Cambridge University Press, 2012) 205; A Chayes and AH Chayes, *The new sovereignty: compliance with international regulatory agreements* (Harvard University Press, 1995) 4; A Dhanda, 'Legal Capacity in the Disability Rights Convention: Stranglehold of the Past or Lodestar for the Future?' (2007) 34 *Syracuse Journal of International Law and Commerce* 429.

[8] See the CRPD Committee's Concluding Observations on Austria (CRPD/C/AUT/CO/1, 13 September 2013) § 28; Hungary (CRPD/C/HUN/CO/1, 22 October 2012) § 26; Peru (CRPD/C/PER/CO/1, 9 May 2012) § 25; Spain (CRPD/C/ESP/CO/1, 19 October 2011) § 34; China (CRPD/C/CHN/CO/1, 15 October 2012) § 22.

[9] UN Committee on the Rights of Persons with Disabilities, General comment No. 1 (2014) – Article 12: Equal recognition before the law, Committee on the Rights of Persons with Disabilities, CRPD/C/GC/1 (19 May 2014).

rights, the passive aspect of legal capacity.[10] This causes little controversy: the denial of legal personhood on the basis of disability would be hard to justify in the current world.[11] The views of the CRPD Committee have so far dealt with Article 12.1 only once, with regard to the lack of identity cards in Peru.[12]

Article 12(2), however, is much more ambiguous. It requires States Parties to 'recognize that persons with disabilities enjoy legal capacity on an equal basis with others in all aspects of life'.[13] Its plain reading forbids discrimination on the basis of disability in the exercise of legal capacity, which is a common practice around the world.[14] It is, however, unclear whether this prohibits all differential treatments, including those based on objective and reasonable criteria,[15] a question addressed below.[16] Guardianship, a measure limiting legal capacity, has been developed precisely to apply only to persons with disabilities.[17] It is thus hardly compatible with the notion of enjoying legal capacity 'on an equal basis with others' if the prohibition of discrimination excludes all disability-specific differential treatment.

Article 12(3) posits what guardianship and other measures limiting legal capacity have to be replaced with. It obliges states 'to provide access by persons with disabilities to the support they may require in exercising their legal capacity'.[18] Article 12(2) and (3) together mark a paradigm shift in understanding legal capacity: measures of substituted decision-making that limit legal capacity are forbidden and have to be replaced by solutions based on supported decision-making.[19]

This shift is no doubt a major breakthrough in international law for persons with disabilities. Many of the practices described previously now constitute impermissible human rights violations under the CRPD, going beyond the issues so far considered by the European Court of Human Rights. However, it is not at all clear how far exactly the wording of Article 12 extends. Essentially, two conflicting views have emerged in the literature about its limits, which differ mainly on the question of how Article 12 applies to persons with the most severe disabilities.

[10] Article 12.1 of the CRPD.

[11] Arstein-Kerslake, *Restoring Voice*, 38.

[12] Concluding observations prepared by the Committee on the Rights of Persons with Disabilities with regard to Peru, CRPD/C/PER/CO/1, 20 April 2012, §§ 22–23.

[13] Article 12.1 of the CRPD.

[14] 'Legal capacity', Background conference document prepared by the Office of the United Nations High Commissioner for Human Rights for the Sixth Session of the Ad Hoc Committee (August 2005), available at www.un.org/esa/socdev/enable/rights/documents/ahc6ohchrlegalcap.doc.

[15] GL Neuman, 'Divergent Human Rights Approaches to Capacity and Consent' in MA Stein, F Mahomed, V Patel, and C Sunkel (eds), *Mental Health, Legal Capacity, and Human Rights* (Cambridge University Press, 2021) 59.

[16] See chapter 3.1.2.3 below.

[17] K Blankman, 'Guardianship Models in the Netherlands and Western Europe' (1997) 20 *International Journal of Law and Psychiatry* 47.

[18] Article 12.3 of the CRPD.

[19] E Flynn and A Arstein-Kerslake, 'The Support Model of Legal Capacity: Fact, Fiction, or Fantasy?' (2014) 31(1) *Berkeley Journal of International Law* 124, 129.

3.1.1. The Absolutist Position and the Constricted Position

The first position, named Absolutist in this chapter, rests on a literal reading of Article 12, which prohibits any differential treatment on the basis of disability. Its proponents argue that the CRPD achieved the goal of outlawing all legal capacity limitations.[20] Guardianship and other forms of substitute decision-making must be replaced by a support model of legal capacity.[21] According to this view, since the wording of Article 12(2) does not provide for exceptions, it applies to all persons with disabilities, not a specific subset of them, such as persons judged sufficiently capable to make their own decisions. There certainly are individuals who cannot exercise their legal capacity in the traditional sense; they have to be accommodated under Article 12(3).[22] The state, under this reading, is obliged to support the decision-making of persons with even the highest support needs and is not allowed to resort to measures of substituted decision-making in their case.[23]

The main protagonists of the Absolutist Position are disability rights advocates who participated in the drafting of the CRPD.[24] This was adopted by the Office of the High Commissioner for Human Rights of the United Nations (OHCHR) as early as 2009[25] and confirmed in 2017.[26] It was endorsed by the Council of Europe's Commissioner for Human Rights.[27] Importantly, the CRPD Committee supports the Absolutist Position by rejecting all forms of substituted decision-making in its concluding observations[28] and its General Comment No. 1

[20] Minkowitz, 'The United Nations Convention on the Rights of Persons with Disabilities' 408–411.

[21] Flynn and Arstein-Kerslake, 'Legislating personhood'.

[22] A Arstein-Kerslake and E Flynn, 'The General Comment on Article 12 of the Convention on the Rights of Persons with Disabilities: a roadmap for equality before the law' (2016) 20(4) *The International Journal of Human Rights* 471.

[23] Minkowitz, 'The United Nations Convention on the Rights of Persons with Disabilities' 408–411.

[24] For example, the International Disability Alliance and Inclusion Europe; see International Disability Alliance (IDA) CRPD Forum, 'Principles for Implementation of CRPD Article 12, Submitted for the Day of General Discussion on "Article 12 of the CRPD – The right to equal recognition before the law" at the UN' (21 October 2009); Inclusion Europe, 'Key Elements of a System of Supported Decision-Making: Position Paper of Inclusion Europe' (Brussels, Inclusion Europe, 2008); S Trömel, 'A Personal Perspective on the Drafting History of the United Nations Convention on the Rights of Persons with Disabilities' in OM Arnadóttir and G Quinn (eds), *The United Nations Convention on the Rights of Persons with Disabilities: European and Scandinavian Perspectives* (Martinus Nijhoff, 2009) 128.

[25] Office of the United Nations High Commissioner for Human Rights, Thematic Study on enhancing awareness and understanding of the Convention on the Rights of Persons with Disabilities, A/HRC/10/48 (26 January 2009) §§ 43–45.

[26] Mental health and human rights, Report of the United Nations High Commissioner for Human Rights, UN Human Rights Council, Thirty-fourth session, A/HRC/34/32 (27 February–24 March 2017) § 26.

[27] Council of Europe Commissioner for Human Rights, 'Who gets to decide? Right to legal capacity for persons with intellectual and psychosocial disabilities', CommDH/IssuePaper (20 February 2012) 14.

[28] See the list of observations in (n 8).

on Legal Capacity.[29] The Absolutist Position is also widely supported in legal scholarship.[30]

The other view, named Constricted Position for the purposes of this analysis, relies on a narrower reading of the CRPD. It recognises that Article 12 requires the replacement of substituted decision-making by supported decision-making. However, it denies that this would apply to all decisions of all persons with disabilities.[31] The proponents of the Constricted Position argue for using substituted decision-making for exceptional situations, at least for some persons and at least for some decisions.[32] The remaining guardianship laws should be improved, even renamed, but nevertheless retained.[33] The protagonists of this view are mainly legal[34] and medical[35] academics and professionals.

[29] General comment No. 1.

[30] S Cifuentes and 30 other legal scholars, 'Legal Opinion on Article 12 of the CRPD' (21 June 2008) 4–5; Flynn and Arstein-Kerslake, 'Legislating personhood'; Minkowitz, 'The United Nations Convention on the Rights of Persons with Disabilities'; Devi, Bickenbach, Stucki, 'Moving towards substituted or supported decision-making?'; Pathare and Shields, 'Supported decision-making for persons with mental illness'; Gooding, 'Supported Decision-Making: A Rights-Based Disability Concept'; Dhanda, 'Constructing a new Human Rights Lexicon'; A-M Callus, 'Removing obstacles to equal recognition for persons with intellectual disability: Taking exception to the way things are' (2018) 12 *ALTER European Journal of Disability Research* 153.

[31] T Carney, 'Guardianship, Citizenship, & Theorizing Substitute-decisionmaking Law', *Sydney Law School Research Paper* No. 12/25 (7 April 2012) 7.

[32] MC Freeman, K Kolappa JMC de Almeida, A Kleinman, N Makhashvili, S Phakathi, B Saraceno, G Thornicroft, 'Reversing Hard Won Victories in the Name of Human Rights: A Critique of the General Comment on Article 12 of the UN Convention on the Rights of Persons with Disabilities' (2015) 2(9) *Lancet Psychiatry* 844.

[33] See the discussion of 'facilitated decision-making' in Mental Disability Advocacy Centre (MDAC), *Legal Capacity in Europe* (MDAC, 2013) 28.

[34] T Carney, 'Prioritising Supported Decision-Making: Running on Empty or a Basis for Glacial-To-Steady Progress?' (2017) 6(4) *Laws* 18; B McSherry, 'Legal Capacity under the Convention on the Rights of Persons with Disabilities' (2012) 20 *Journal of Law and Medicine* 22; P Weller, 'Supported Decision-Making and the Achievement of Non-Discrimination: The Promise and Paradox of the Disabilities Convention' (2008) 26(2) *Law in Context* 87; Lawson, 'The United Nations Convention on the Rights of Persons with Disabilities'; Keys, 'Legal Capacity Law Reform in Europe', PS Appelbaum, 'There Are All Kinds of Rights' (2016) 46(2) *Hastings Center Report* inside back cover; ML Perlin, '"Striking for the Guardians and Protectors of the Mind": The Convention on the Rights of Persons with Mental Disabilities and the Future of Guardianship Law' (2013) 117 *Pennsylvania State Law Review* 1159; O Lewis,' Advancing Legal Capacity Jurisprudence' (2010) 6 *European Human Rights Law Review* 700; NA Kohn, JA Blumenthal, and AT Campbell, 'Supported Decision-Making: A Viable Alternative to Guardianship?' (2013) 117(4) *Penn State Law Review* 1111; Carney, 'Guardianship, Citizenship, & Theorizing Substitute-decisionmaking Law'; M Scholten and J Gather, 'Adverse consequences of article 12 of the UN Convention on the Rights of Persons with Disabilities for persons with mental disabilities and an alternative way forward' (2018) 44 *Journal of Medical Ethics* 226; M Burch, 'Autonomy, respect, and the rights of persons with disabilities in crisis' (2017) 34(3) *Journal of Applied Philosophy* 389; G Szmukler, 'The UN Convention on the Rights of Persons with Disabilities: "Rights, will and preferences" in relation to mental health disabilities' (2017) 54 *International Journal of Law and Psychiatry* 90; RA Keene, NB Kane, SYH Kim, and GS Owen, 'Mental capacity – Why look for a paradigm shift?' (2023) 31(3) *Medical Law Review* 340.

[35] Freeman et al, 'Reversing Hard Won Victories' 844; P Gosney and P Bartlett, 'The UK Government Should Withdraw from the Convention on the Rights of Persons with Disabilities' (2020) 216(6) *British Journal of Psychiatry* 296; J Dawson and G Szmukler 'Fusion of Mental Health and Incapacity Legislation' (2006) 188(6) *British Journal of Psychiatry* 504; G Szmukler and

3.1.2. Strong and Weak Points

In order to find a common ground between the two positions presented above, we have to understand their strengths and weaknesses. There are strong arguments on both sides of the debate, used by persons taking the rights of persons with disabilities seriously.[36] They can be divided to three categories.

3.1.2.1. Support to Persons with Severe Disabilities

The Absolutist Position's weak point is the Constricted Position's strong one: it is hard to imagine how persons with very high support needs can lead their lives without some form of substituted decision-making.[37] It is true that the CRPD requires that all persons with disabilities have access to the support they need to make decisions, but what does this mean in the case of a person with severe intellectual disability whose parents just died and now has to decide whether she wants to live in her home or move to a group home?[38] How does it apply to a person who has to make a decision about a non-life-saving psychiatric treatment? There is no doubt that persons in these situations have been abused in the past due to faulty guardianship laws. That, however, does not exclude that others can genuinely find themselves in a situation in which they cannot communicate a decision, even with the highest possible level of support available.[39]

Proponents of the Absolutist Position have so far not developed a comprehensive theory of how legislation based only on supported decision-making would solve these difficult situations.[40] An elaborate proposal by Bach and Kerzner introduces a new category, facilitated decision-making, for persons unable to make decisions themselves.[41] However, since facilitated decisions are taken by others on behalf of the persons with disability,[42] they are in substance

BD Kelly, 'We should replace conventional mental health law with capacity-based law' (2016) 209(6) *British Journal of Psychiatry* 449; JMC de Almeida, 'The UN Committee's interpretation of "will and preferences" can violate human rights' (2019) 18(1) *World Psychiatry* 45.

[36] Keene, Kane, Kim, Owen, 'Mental capacity – Why look for a paradigm shift?' 348.

[37] D Bilchitz, 'Dignity, fundamental rights and legal capacity: Moving beyond the paradigm set by the general comment on article 12 of the convention on the rights of persons with disabilities' (2016) 32(3) *South African Journal on Human Rights* 410, 410.

[38] MA Stein, F Mahomed, V Patel, and C Sunkel (eds.), *Mental Health, Legal Capacity, and Human Rights* (Cambridge University Press, 2021) 5.

[39] A Ward, 'Abolition of Guardianship? "Best Interests" versus "Best Interpretation"' (2015) 32 *Scots Law Times* 150, 150.

[40] L Barclay, 'Paternalism, Supported Decision-Making and Expressive Respect' (2024) 27(1) *Journal of Ethics and Social Philosophy* 121, 139.

[41] M Bach and L Kerzner, 'A New Paradigm for Protecting Autonomy and the Right to Legal Capacity', Paper prepared for the Law Commission of Ontario (2010) 182.

[42] L Series and A Nilsson, 'Article 12 CRPD Equal Recognition before the Law' in I Bantekas, MA Stein, and D Anastasiou (eds), *The UN Convention on the Rights of Persons with Disabilities: A Commentary* (Oxford University Press, 2018) 365.

not different from improved substitute decision-making.[43] Another proposal by Eilionóir Flynn and Anna Arstein-Kerslake allows for the appointment of substitute decision-makers in case of emergency situations, such as refusal of life-saving treatment.[44] Their framework does not address non-emergency situations in which a person with a disability is unable to make a decision. Another proposal rests in formally reclassifying certain substitute decisions as supported decisions if the person's will and preferences clash.[45]

What proponents of the Absolutist Position share is a preference for full formal legal capacity, the prohibition of any formal incapacitation as an obligation derived from Article 12.[46] Relying on the CRPD and claiming it requires supporting everybody is insufficient to explain how to make decisions on behalf of persons with severe disabilities.[47] Unless a credible and workable suggestion is developed, governments are unlikely to leave all substituted decision-making behind because they would not have a solution to meet the needs of persons with severe disabilities who are unable to make decisions with support.[48]

The Absolutist Position seems to be concerned mainly with the restrictions on legal capacity, with legal limitations on decision-making ability. However, some persons' impairment is so severe they are unable to make decisions if they are left to their own devices, regardless of any legal limitations.[49] Their incapacity is not simply a societal restriction imposed upon them, unlike in the situations dealt with by the European Court considered in chapter two above. It is a result of the interaction between their impairment and the societal framework.[50] Failing to make important decisions about their care and management of their property can be a violation of their fundamental rights.[51] The proponents of the Absolutist Position, however, have so far not explained how these decisions would be made. They argue that all persons can make decisions in a support framework – which, however, is a very tenuous proposition.[52]

[43] T Carney, 'Searching for workable alternatives to guardianship for vulnerable populations?' (2015) 1 *Ethics, Medicine and Public Health* 115; Burch, 'Autonomy, Respect' 7.

[44] A Arstein-Kerslake and E Flynn, 'The General Comment on Article 12'.

[45] Szmukler, 'The UN Convention on the Rights of Persons with Disabilities'.

[46] Flynn and Arstein-Kerslake, 'Legislating personhood'.

[47] T Carney, 'Globalisation and Guardianship – Harmonisation or Postmodern Diversity?' (2001) 24 *International Journal of Law and Psychiatry* 95, 104.

[48] Neuman, 'Divergent Human Rights Approaches to Capacity and Consent' 64.

[49] AE Buchanan and DW Brock, *Deciding For Others: The Ethics of Surrogate Decision Making* (Cambridge University Press, 1989) 19.

[50] M Donnelly, 'Judging Values in a Time of Transition: An Irish Perspective' in: C Kong, J Coggon, P Cooper, M Dunn, and AR Keene, *Capacity, Participation and Values in Comparative Legal Perspective* (Bristol University Press, 2023) 66.

[51] For an example, see the case of *Hiller v Austria* App no 1967/14 (ECtHR 22 November 2016), where the applicant, who was hospitalised with mental illness, was left unsupervised and committed suicide. While the European Court did not find a violation of the right to life, both Judge Sajó's concurring opinion and Judge Motoc's dissenting opinion highlight the difficult trade-off between promoting personal autonomy and security from self-harm.

[52] M Parker, 'Getting the Balance Right: Conceptual Considerations Concerning Legal Capacity and Supported Decision-Making' (2016) 13 *Bioethical Inquiry* 389.

3.1.2.2. The Role of Mental Capacity

The disagreement over the interpretation of Article 12 centres around the question of the CRPD Committee's rejection of the mental capacity approach, that is, using mental capacity to determine who could be incapacitated.[53] The Committee requires that all persons should receive support to exercise their legal capacity.[54] It separates mental capacity from legal capacity and states in the General Comment that the former should not be the basis for limiting the latter because mental capacity does not have an objective basis and it discriminates against persons with disabilities.[55] Critics take issue with this argument.[56] They argue that mental capacity can be assessed objectively,[57] and more importantly, it is not discriminatory against persons with disabilities because it can be applied in a disability-neutral way.[58] The latter argument seems to be undermined by the fact that capacity assessments disproportionately affect persons with disabilities[59] because their mental capacity is disproportionately compromised.[60] The argument then ultimately turns on the question of whether this disproportionate effect should be considered discrimination and, therefore, prohibited under the CRPD or not.[61] Critics of the CRPD Committee's position argue that it is not discriminatory because it does not lead to the disadvantage of persons with disabilities.[62] In fact, the mental capacity approach is the only way to safeguard the interest of persons who cannot make decisions even with support,[63] and by pretending that such persons do not exist, the Committee seriously endangers their lives and well-being.[64]

These arguments miss their mark. The Committee does not deny that some person's mental capacity can be very low.[65] It does not even expressly claim that all persons are able to make decisions with support, even though it could be argued that this is what the General Comment implies. Instead, the CRPD Committee rejects the idea that mental capacity is a suitable basis for selecting which individuals should be in need of help and intervention. The Committee

[53] Keene, Kane, Kim, Owen, 'Mental capacity – Why look for a paradigm shift?' 344.
[54] General comment No. 1, §16.
[55] General comment No. 1, §15.
[56] Bilchitz, 'Dignity, fundamental rights and legal capacity' 417.
[57] de Almeida, 'The UN Committee's interpretation' 46.
[58] Scholten and Gather, 'Adverse consequences of article 12' 228.
[59] Flynn and Arstein-Kerslake, 'Legislating personhood' 87.
[60] LA Schaefer and TJ Farrer, *A Casebook of Mental Capacity in US Legislation. Assessment and Legal Commentary* (Routledge, 2022) 5.
[61] Series and Nilsson, 'Article 12 CRPD Equal Recognition before the Law' 356.
[62] G Szmukler, '"Capacity", "best interests", "will and preferences" and the UN Convention on the Rights of Persons with Disabilities' (2019) 18(1) *World Psychiatry* 34, 37.
[63] M Scholten, J Gather, and J Vollmann, 'Equality in the Informed Consent Process: Competence to Consent, Substitute Decision-Making, and Discrimination of Persons with Mental Disorders' (2021) 46(1) *Journal of Medicine and Philosophy* 108, 110.
[64] Burch,' Autonomy, respect' 391.
[65] Series and Nilsson, 'Article 12 CRPD Equal Recognition before the Law' 353.

clearly considers the limitation of legal capacity a serious disadvantage,[66] and in light of its overuse[67] and the connected abuses,[68] there can be no doubt that the Committee is, in general, correct. The remaining open question is whether the Committee is mistaken with regard to persons with high support needs. If the critics are correct, these persons can be identified and their interests secured only through the mental capacity approach. According to the Committee's position, these persons suffer disadvantage by incapacitation because they can be helped by another approach, which is more favourable to them. The disagreement and the interpretation of Article 12, therefore, turns on the question of whether this approach indeed exists and what obligations exactly follow from it for States Parties to the CRPD.

3.1.2.3. The CRPD's Text

The Absolutist Position's is more in line with the CRPD's text. Indeed, Article 12 does not provide for explicit exceptions to the prohibition of substituted decision-making, which seems to be a significant weakness of the Constricted Position.[69] However, this issue is not decisive for the whole debate.

In the history of international law, several seemingly all-inclusive provisions were interpreted to exclude persons with disabilities from the enjoyment of certain rights. The right to vote is a good example.[70] While the text of human rights treaties contained no specific exclusion on the grounds of disability,[71] some form of lack of capacity to vote has become an accepted ground for disenfranchisement through interpretation.[72] The right to liberty, which had no disability-specific exception in the International Covenant on Civil and Political Rights, was later similarly interpreted to permit the detention of persons perceived to be in need of psychiatric treatment against their will.[73] While the European Convention on Human Rights expressly allowed the detention of 'persons of unsound mind',[74] this was later expanded to cover not only persons in need of psychiatric treatment but also persons dependent on social care.[75] Even torture has not been

[66] General comment No 1.

[67] M Hamilton, 'Supported Decision-making as an Alternative to Guardianship' (2023) *Trends in State Courts* 87, 88.

[68] RM Powell and MA Stein, 'People with Disabilities and Sexual and Reproductive Rights: an International Comparative Analysis' (2016) 11 *Frontiers of Law in China* 53, 77.

[69] de Bhailís and Flynn, 'Recognising legal capacity' 13.

[70] J Fiala-Butora, MA Stein, and JE Lord, 'The democratic life of the Union: towards equal voting participation for Europeans with Disabilities' (2014) 55 *Harvard International Law Journal* 71 (2014).

[71] ibid, 75.

[72] ibid, 76.

[73] See UN Human Rights Committee, General comment No. 35 (2014) – Article 9 (Liberty and security of person), CCPR/C/GC/35 (16 December 2014) § 19.

[74] Article 5(1)e) of the European Convention on Human Rights (Convention for the Protection of Human Rights and Fundamental Freedoms), 213 U.N.T.S. 222 (4 November 1950).

[75] *H.M. v Switzerland* App no 39187/98 (ECtHR 26 February 2002).

immune to an exception on the grounds of disability.[76] In its famous judgment of *Herczegfalvy v Austria*, the European Court of Human Rights held that a measure, which would otherwise violate Article 3 of the European Convention, can be justified if a 'medical necessity' exists; that is, if a psychiatrist decides a person should be strapped to a bed for weeks, it is acceptable.[77]

This book does not argue that Article 12 should be construed to allow limitations of legal capacity for some persons with disabilities or for some decisions. Rather, the point is that this is possible as a matter of international law. The text is not explicit enough to prevent this reading of Article 12. If the CRPD Committee, the main body interpreting the CRPD, wished to depart from an absolute prohibition of differential treatment under Article 12 by formulating exceptions based on reasonable and objective criteria, it can do so. The Committee's General Comment on Legal Capacity shows that its position is still ambiguous: it rejects all forms of substituted decision-making and endorses support, but it does not state what follows from this for persons who are unable to make decisions with support.[78]

In fact, it is inevitable to read some exceptions into the CRPD. Its text seemingly prohibits all discrimination based on disability.[79] If this were understood to preclude all differential treatment based on disability, it would lead to unreasonable results. For example, it would be difficult to argue that a person with total loss of vision should be given a driver's licence under the CRPD and allowed to work as a taxi driver. The CRPD's text does not contain the exception of genuine occupational requirements, known from other texts on disability.[80] Nevertheless, an interpretation insisting on blind taxi drivers would be hard to sustain because it would be impossible to implement and, therefore, considered unreasonable by the States Parties to the CRPD.[81]

If differential treatment on the basis of disability in some instances can be justified, and the CRPD does not specify what could be accepted as a justification, exceptions will have to be construed through interpretation. A starting point can be using analogies from other human rights treaties.[82] In the UN system, according to the Human Rights Committee's General Comment No. 18 on Non-discrimination, the prohibition on discrimination establishes a

[76] J Fiala-Butora, 'Disabling Torture: The Obligation to Investigate Ill-treatment of Persons with Disabilities' (2013) 45 *Columbia Human Rights Law Review* 214.

[77] *Herczegfalvy v Austria*, App no. 10533/83 (ECtHR 24 September 1992) § 82.

[78] General comment No. 1, § 17.

[79] Article 5 of the CRPD.

[80] See Article 4.1 of the European Union's Council Directive 2000/78/EC on establishing a general framework for equal treatment in employment and occupation (27 November 2000); Sec. 12113 of the Americans with Disabilities Act (ADA), 42 U.S.C. § 121103 (1990).

[81] Article 32 b) of the Vienna Convention on the Law of Treaties (VCLT), 1155 U.N.T.S. 331 (27 January 1980).

[82] GL Neuman, 'Submission to the Committee on the Rights of Persons with Disabilities Regarding Draft General Comment on Article 5, Equality and Non-Discrimination', UN OHCHR (18 June 2017).

presumption of equal treatment, which can be overruled by measures based on objective and reasonable criteria following a legitimate aim.[83] A reading applying these criteria to the CRPD is implausible for one reason: it would justify violations of the rights of persons with disabilities that the CRPD was adopted to overcome, not conserve.[84] Differential treatment of persons with disabilities has been subject to scrutiny under existing human rights treaties using objective and reasonable criteria, and these have not been able to overcome the frequent and severe violations of disabled people's rights.[85] According to the official fiction, the CRPD did not create new rights for persons with disabilities, it only specified existing rights for them because these have been inadequately protected under existing instruments.[86] It follows that the criteria of the existing treaties cannot be used to justify differential treatment on the basis of disability under the CRPD, at least not in the same way, not to produce the same outcomes. Some heightened form of justification is required, but also not an absolute form of equality, as explained above. What exactly is meant by 'on an equal basis with others' is therefore not clear from the text.[87]

There are no doubt good reasons for not specifying exceptions to equal treatment in the CRPD. Highlighting them might have invited States Parties to rely on them increasingly, subjecting all disability discrimination to individual justifications. Future practice will show whether this approach is the most effective in preventing abuse. Nevertheless, this does not mean that there are no exceptions to the prohibition of differential treatment. Once the CRPD Committee faces them, it will have to specify their criteria to curtail them as much as possible.

The Committee has so far had a very consistent position rejecting all substitute decision-making measures.[88] It ordered governments to replace, not modify, their guardianship systems.[89] Its General Comment on Legal Capacity formally rejects all forms of substituted decision-making.[90] This, however, can change as the composition of the Committee changes and as it is faced with the more difficult issues of countries that do their best to comply with Article 12 but cannot. As one member of the Committee noted, the Committee has so far not decided on the question of whether there ever is an exception from the prohibition of

[83] Human Rights Committee, General Comment 18, Non-discrimination, U.N. Doc. HRI/GEN/1/Rev.1 (1994), § 13.

[84] P Bartlett, 'The UN Convention on the Rights of Persons with Disabilities: great opportunities and dangerous interpretations' (2019) 18(1) *World Psychiatry* 47, 48.

[85] MA Stein, 'Disability Human Rights' (2007) 95 *California Law Review* 82, 82.

[86] R Kayess and P French, 'Out of Darkness into Light? Introducing the Convention on the Rights of Persons with Disabilities' (2008) 8(1) *Human Rights Law Review* 32.

[87] Series and Nilsson, 'Article 12 CRPD Equal Recognition before the Law' 362.

[88] See the CRPD Committee's Concluding Observations on Russia (CRPD/C/RUS/CO/1, 9 April 2018) § 27; Slovenia (CRPD/C/SVN/CO/1, 16 April 2018) § 19; Haiti (CRPD/C/HTI/CO/1, 13 April 2018) § 23; Austria (n 8) § 28; Hungary (n 8) § 26; Peru (n 8) § 25; Spain (n 8) § 34; China (n 8) § 22.

[89] ibid.

[90] General comment No. 1, § 17.

substituted decision-making.[91] The question is thus not settled, not by the text of the CRPD.

3.1.3. Common Ground

Proponents of the above two positions agree that the skills of persons with disabilities are undervalued, and many could benefit from support instead of guardianship.[92] What the two positions also share is both the necessity and the inability to explicitly address the exceptional cases, the situation of persons with high support needs. The Absolutist position requires that persons with severe disability utilise a support framework, but its proponents have so far been unable to explain how this can be operationalised or what obligations follow from it.[93] Full legal capacity is strategically treated as a useful legal fiction, which can nevertheless potentially harm persons with high support needs: if substitute decisions are prohibited, some of their decisions will not be made because these persons will not be accommodated in a support framework.[94]

The Constricted position has a solution for them: retaining guardianship. However, this cannot ensure that substituted decisions are utilised only in their case, that they are applied only in exceptional situations of genuine inability to reach a supported decision. This has the potential to harm a large number of persons with disabilities who are able to utilise support and who will be denied support because they will be subject to substitute decision-making.[95]

These problems are insurmountable by interpretation. It will be the goal of subsequent chapters to find a solution to the situation of persons with high support needs that can best fulfil the goal of the CRPD. The remaining part of this chapter analyses how the CRPD constrains interpretative choices.

3.2. THE TEXT OF ARTICLE 12 – AND ITS IMPLICATIONS

The two positions described above are both concerned with the interpretation of the CRPD; they deduce normative conclusions about legal capacity reform from the text of Article 12. They rely on the traditional canons of interpretation found in the Vienna Convention on the Law of Treaties from 1969 (hereinafter VCLT). This section will undertake a more detailed analysis of the text to ascertain which of these conclusions are justified.

[91] T Degener, 'Challenges and Compliance of the UN CRPD' (2013) Working Paper of the Academy of European Law 4.

[92] See, for example, Callus, 'Removing obstacles to equal recognition'.

[93] Stein, Mahomed, Patel, Sunkel, *Mental Health, Legal Capacity, and Human Rights*, 5.

[94] Appelbaum, 'There Are All Kinds of Rights'.

[95] A Dhanda, 'Advocacy Note on Legal Capacity', World Network of Users and Survivors of Psychiatry (undated), available from www.un.org/esa/socdev/enable/rights/art9legal.htm.

The CRPD is an international treaty subject to the rules of interpretation of treaties listed in Section 3 of the VCLT.[96] However, these rules do not entirely determine the outcome. They have to be respected, but within the limits set by them, the interpreter can choose various methods of interpretation, which can lead to different results.[97] The aim of this section is, therefore, not to provide the correct or preferred interpretation of Article 12 because more results contradicting each other are possible that are fully compliant with the VCLT's requirements.[98] Rather, it will assess to what extent the text limits our understanding of legal capacity reform and whether any alternatives can be excluded.

In its method, this part of the chapter will go above the VCLT and will rely on the specific nature of the CRPD as a human rights treaty developed by Gerald Neuman.[99] Neuman identifies three aspects specific to human rights treaties that create a useful framework for understanding and interpreting them: the consensual, the suprapositive, and the institutional aspects. These will structure the following analysis.

3.2.1. The Consensual Aspect

The consensual aspect reflects the fact that human rights norms are adopted by the mutual agreement of all parties, and can be interpreted through their subsequent mutual agreements and practice.[100]

Concerning the text that the parties agreed to, the general rule of treaty interpretation according to Article 31(1) of the VCLT is to give the treaty's terms their ordinary meaning in their context and in light of the treaty's object and purpose. This does not settle the difficult questions identified above. There is no ordinary meaning to how the enjoyment of legal capacity 'on an equal basis with others' applies to persons with high support needs under Article 12(2) CRPD. The different positions agree that they exercise their capacity differently than others, either with high levels of support or with substitution. Currently,

[96] B Schlütter, 'Aspect of Human Rights Treaty Interpretation by the UN Treaty Bodies' in H Keller and G Ulfstein (eds), *UN Human Rights Treaty Bodies: Law and Legitimacy* (Cambridge University Press, 2012) 261; J Christoffersen, 'Impact on General Principles of Treaty Interpretation', in MT Kamminga and M Scheinin (eds), *The Impact of Human Rights Law on General International Law* (Oxford University Press, 2009) 37; K Mechlem, 'Treaty Bodies and the Interpretation of Human Rights' (2009) 42 *Vanderbilt Journal of Transnational Law* 905; M Fitzmaurice, 'Dynamic (Evolutive) Interpretation of Treaties, Part I', *Hague Yearbook of International Law XXI* (Martinus Nijhoff, 2008) 101.

[97] M Villiger, *Commentary on the 1969 Vienna Convention on the Law of Treaties* (Martinus Nijhoff, 2009) 421.

[98] M Fitzmaurice, 'Interpretation of Human Rights Treaties' in D Shelton (ed), *The Oxford Handbook of International Human Rights Law* (Oxford University Press, 2013) 739.

[99] GL Neuman, 'Human Rights and Constitutional Rights: Harmony and Dissonance' (2003) 55 *Stanford Law Review* 1863, 1866.

[100] ibid, 1867.

all domestic guardianship systems permit substituted decision-making.[101] The CRPD aims to overcome outdated guardianship regimes, but it is not at all certain what it wants to replace them with. Regardless of how the content of 'equal basis for exercising legal capacity' will be defined, it will not be deduced from the ordinary meaning of the term, as that is too ambiguous.

The VCLT recognises the instruments of ratification by the parties as sources of the context for the purpose of the interpretation of the treaty.[102] A number of States Parties addressed Article 12 in reservations or interpretative declarations when ratifying the CRPD, with the aim of retaining their domestic laws based on substituted decision-making.[103] A country making a reservation wishes not to be bound by a specific provision.[104] This seems to suggest that the States Party making the reservation considers Article 12 to forbid substituted decision-making. On the contrary, the interpretative declarations express that the States Parties consider Article 12 not to prohibit substituted decision-making.[105] The States Parties' understanding of the provision is thus varied; we cannot deduce from it a common understanding about the legal capacity of persons with high support needs.

Article 32 of the VCLT lists the preparatory works of the treaty among the supplementary means of interpretation to be used in the case of ambiguous or obscure meaning. Article 12 has been one of the most controversial issues of the CRPD's drafting process, referenced a number of times in the travaux.[106] However, the sources do not make it clear what the parties agreed on. Quite the contrary, it seems that leaving the terms of Article 12 ambiguous was a necessary part of the compromise.[107]

The text produced by the working group for the third session of the Ad Hoc Committee included a reference to full legal capacity that shall not be limited on the basis of impairment.[108] During the third session of the Ad Hoc Committee, Canada noted the lack of consensus about the meaning of legal capacity and proposed wording that expressly allowed for limitations on legal capacity.[109] Until the fifth session of the Ad Hoc Committee, the delegations debated both

[101] J Dawson, 'A realistic approach to assessing mental health laws' compliance with the UNCRPD' (2015) 40 *International Journal of Law and Psychiatry* 70, 72.

[102] Article 31 (2) b) of the Vienna Convention on the Law of Treaties (VCLT).

[103] Canada, Ireland, the Netherlands, Venezuela, Poland, Syria, Singapore, Australia, Egypt, Estonia, Kuwait, Georgia, and Norway.

[104] See the reservation of Canada and Singapore to Article 12.

[105] See the declarations of Australia, Poland, Syria, the Netherlands, Egypt, Estonia, Kuwait, Norway to Article 12 of the CRPD, and France's declaration to Article 29 of the CRPD.

[106] JE Lord and MA Stein, 'Contingent participation and coercive care: feminist and communitarian theories of disability and legal capacity' in B McSherry and I Freckelton (eds), *Coercive care: rights, law and policy* (Routledge, 2013) 45.

[107] Dhanda, 'Legal Capacity in the Disability Rights Convention' 435.

[108] Chair's Draft Elements of a Comprehensive and Integral International Convention on Protection and Promotion of the Rights and Dignity of Persons with Disabilities (December 2003), available at www.un.org/esa/socdev/enable/rights/wgcontrib-chair1.htm.

[109] UN CRPD, Third session of the Ad Hoc Committee, Daily Summary, Volume 4, #3 (26 May 2004), available at www.un.org/esa/socdev/enable/rights/ahc3sum26may.htm.

proposals simultaneously.[110] A number of delegations proposed that the CRPD expressly permits guardianship,[111] while others wished to prohibit it expressly.[112]

For the sixth session, the OHCHR prepared a background document concluding that restrictions of active legal capacity are permissible in all legal systems, including international law.[113] The discussion continued in the seventh session.[114] The working text contained explicit references to restrictions of legal capacity as a last resort.[115] So did, although implicitly, a proposal by the EU elaborated together with Canada, Australia, Norway, Costa Rica, the USA, and Liechtenstein.[116] The International Disability Caucus submitted an alternative proposal that explicitly endorsed the exercise of full legal capacity to act and prohibited restrictions.[117] In the ensuing discussion, several delegations expressed that, while they preferred supported decision-making, limitations of legal capacity were sometimes necessary.[118] New Zealand proposed a compromise by deleting an explicit reference to limitations of legal capacity, whereby the text 'should neither promote nor prohibit substitutive decision making'. During the eighth session, delegates reformulated the text along the lines of the compromise proposed by New Zealand earlier. A new sub-paragraph 4 about safeguards was included without an explicit reference to restrictions of legal capacity.[119]

[110] See the Coordinator's remarks in: UN Ad Hoc Committee; see UN CRPD, Fifth session of the Ad Hoc Committee, Daily Summary, Volume 6, #2 (25 January 2005), available at www.un.org/esa/socdev/enable/rights/ahc5sum25jan.htm.

[111] See, for example, the position of Kenya, Syria, Iran and Yemen during the fifth session of the UN Ad Hoc Committee; see UN CRPD, Fifth session of the Ad Hoc Committee, Daily Summary, Volume 6, #2 (25 January 2005), available at www.un.org/esa/socdev/enable/rights/ahc5sum25jan.htm.

[112] The first states to suggest so were Mexico and Lebanon during the fourth session of the UN Ad Hoc Committee drafting the CRPD's text; see UN CRPD, Fourth session of the Ad Hoc Committee, Daily Summary, Volume 5, #4 (August 26, 2004).

[113] 'Legal capacity', Background conference document prepared by the Office of the United Nations High Commissioner for Human Rights, available at www.un.org/esa/socdev/enable/rights/documents/ahc6ohchrlegalcap.doc.

[114] UN CRPD, Seventh session of the Ad Hoc Committee, Daily Summary, Volume 8, #2 (January 17, 2006), available at www.un.org/esa/socdev/enable/rights/ahc7sum17jan.htm.

[115] See Article 12(2)b) at: Working text, International Convention on the Rights of Persons with Disabilities, available at www.un.org/esa/socdev/enable/rights/ahc7ann2rep.htm; Annex II to Report of the Ad Hoc Committee on a Comprehensive and Integral International Convention on the Protection and Promotion of the Rights and Dignity of Persons with Disabilities on its seventh session, A/AC.265/2006/2 (13 February 2006), available at https://www.un.org/esa/socdev/enable/rights/ahc7report-e.htm.

[116] See Article 12(4) in: Contribution by Governments, European Union (30 January 2006), available at www.un.org/esa/socdev/enable/rights/ahc7eu.htm.

[117] Chairman's Text as amended by the International Disability Caucus (undated), available at www.un.org/esa/socdev/enable/rights/ahc7docs/ahc7idcchairamend1.doc.

[118] For example China, Russia, Canada, Yemen, Japan, Kenya on behalf of the African Group, Australia, UN CRPD, Seventh session of the Ad Hoc Committee, Daily Summary, Volume 8, #3 (18 January 2006), available at www.un.org/esa/socdev/enable/rights/ahc7sum18jan.htm.

[119] Interim report of the Ad Hoc Committee on a Comprehensive and Integral International Convention on the Protection and Promotion of the Rights and Dignity of Persons with Disabilities

However, to appease some states with contrary views, a footnote was included that restricted the scope of Paragraph Article 12(2) only to the 'legal capacity for rights' rather than the 'legal capacity to act' in the Arabic, Chinese, and Russian translation of the Convention.[120] This would have explicitly permitted limitations of legal capacity in these language versions. Twenty-one countries of the Arab group addressed a letter to the Chairman on 5 December 2006, maintaining their position that Article 12(2) does not cover the capacity to act.[121] The EU and 18 other delegations expressed their understanding that the Arabic translation is only a technical issue and that the concept of legal capacity has the same meaning in all language versions.[122] The last meeting of the Ad Hoc Committee eventually deleted the footnote in the text presented to the UN General Assembly, ensuring that the term legal capacity covers the capacity to act in all language versions.[123] The intense debate shows the States Parties were aware that the CRPD would have an impact on their guardianship systems, but they could not agree on whether to permit or prohibit substituted decision-making. The compromise was found in a text that does neither.

There is thus no clear consensus concerning the exact meaning of the provision. However, there is some common denominator between the two Positions and the States Parties' understandings. All share the view that the CRPD protects all persons with disabilities from violations of their right to legal capacity. The aim is to maximise their autonomy and minimise arbitrary interferences with their decision-making. An approach bringing the CRPD the closest to this aim through interpretation should satisfy all involved.

There is so far no subsequent agreement between the States Parties about the implementation of Article 12. There is, however, a manifest tension between the practice of domestic states and the principles expressed in the CRPD as interpreted by the CRPD Committee.[124] While the latter requires maximising

on its eighth session, UN Doc A/AC.265/2006/4 (1 September 2006), available at www.un.org/esa/socdev/enable/rights/ahc8intreporte.htm#btta.

[120] AHC8 Drafting Committee – First revised text (13 September 2006), available at www.un.org/esa/socdev/enable/documents/ahc8docs/firstrevtxt13sep.doc.

[121] Letter dated 5 December 2006 from the Permanent Representative of Iraq to the United Nations addressed to the Chairman, UN Doc A/AC.265/2006/5 (7 December 2006), available at www.un.org/esa/socdev/enable/rights/ahclet5deciraq.doc.

[122] Letter dated 5 December 2006 from the Permanent Representative of Finland to the United Nations addressed to the Chairman, UN Doc A/AC.265/2006/6 (7 December 2006), available at www.un.org/esa/socdev/enable/rights/ahc8docs/ahc8l5decfin.doc.

[123] Final report of the Ad Hoc Committee on a Comprehensive and Integral International Convention on the Protection and Promotion of the Rights and Dignity of Persons with Disabilities, UN Doc A/61/611, 6 December 2006, available at www.un.org/esa/socdev/enable/rights/ahcfinalrepe.htm.

[124] See, for example, the German and the Danish governments' position on the Committee's draft general comment on article 12: German Statement on the Draft General Comment on Article 12 CRPD, Federal Republic of Germany (20 February 2014); Response from the Government of Denmark with regards to Draft General Comment on Article 12 of the Convention – Equal Recognition before the Law, Ministry of Children, Gender Equality, Integration and Social Affairs (20 February 2014).

autonomy, current guardianship regimes blatantly violate it. No States Party to the CRPD currently complies with Article 12.[125] Many are very far from it.

This is not surprising, given that the purpose of human rights treaties generally, and specifically that of the CRPD, is to reform restrictive domestic legislation.[126] However, if the influence between human rights and domestic norms is mutual, this blatant and widespread non-compliance must have some relevance for constructing the meaning of the CRPD. The situation would be different if the majority, or at least some States Parties, have already managed to create a legal capacity regime based solely on supported decision-making.[127]

Since that is not the case, the implementation process has to adapt to this reality. An interpretation that all states of the world would find impossible to implement would no doubt be rejected by them and would have little impact in changing domestic practices.[128] It could lead to an explicit subsequent understanding that rejects the complete abolition of guardianship.

3.2.2. The Suprapositive Aspect

The Suprapositive aspect relates to the fact that human rights norms derive legitimacy not only from their text but also from non-legal principles superior to their embodiment in positive law.[129] These principles can have various sources, and the fact that States Parties agreed to a certain text does not necessarily mean they also accepted the suprapositive principle on which it rests.[130] Indeed, State Parties to the CRPD represent various cultures with different religious and moral systems with potentially very different understandings of disability. It can therefore be very contentious to establish a unified understanding of the CRPD's superior principles.[131]

The text, however, serves as a useful starting point. The preamble stresses the importance of individual ability and independence of persons with disabilities, including the freedom to make their own choices.[132] The same is repeated in Article 3(a), among the General Principles, together with full and effective

[125] Peru might be the first country to comply with the CRPD, see A Martinez-Pujalte, 'Legal Capacity and Supported Decision-Making: Lessons from Some Recent Legal Reforms' (2019) 8(1) *Laws* 15; however, other authors refute this claim, see RAC Caycho, 'The flag of imagination: Peru's new reform on legal capacity for persons with intellectual and psychosocial disabilities and the need for new understandings in private law' (2020) 14 *Age of Human Rights Journal* 155, 169.

[126] Neuman,' Human Rights and Constitutional Rights' 1866.

[127] Keene, Kane, Kim, Owen, 'Mental capacity – Why look for a paradigm shift?' 344.

[128] R Uerpmann-Wittzack, 'The Law-Making Function of the UN Committee on the Rights of Persons with Disabilities' (2018) 8(2) *Wroclaw Review of Law, Administration & Economics* 36, 43.

[129] Neuman,' Human Rights and Constitutional Rights' 1868.

[130] ibid, at 1873.

[131] Carney, 'Guardianship, Citizenship, & Theorizing Substitute-decisionmaking Law'.

[132] Preamble, Article n) of the CRPD.

participation and inclusion in society.[133] Article 1 states that the CRPD's purpose is the full and equal enjoyment of all human rights by all persons with disabilities.

These provisions signify that the question of decision-making and legal capacity is an important part of the treaty and that the drafters wanted to overcome the current exclusionary practices. However, this does not make it clear how they wanted to overcome them. It cannot be taken as an automatic endorsement of the Absolutist position. The Constricted position's main line of reasoning is not that persons with high support needs should be excluded from society or that they should be incapacitated. Rather, the argument is that preventing them from accessing substituted decision-making harms them because they are unable to make all their necessary decisions with support.[134] To prove this claim wrong one would have to show that its factual basis is incorrect, which has not yet taken place. Seen in this light, the Constricted position fulfils the purpose of the treaty, while the Absolutist position frustrates it because it allows persons with high support needs to enjoy some of their rights only in a supported way, which they are unable to make use of.

The contradictory claims on which the two positions are based cannot be resolved by reliance on the CRPD's purpose because they are factual in nature. Arguing for one position based on the purpose leads to circular argumentation.[135] It inherently entails claims about how the purpose should be achieved, which leads to specifying the purpose itself beyond that expressed in the text.[136] Ascertaining the object of a treaty is not a mechanical task, it is itself an interpretative question and an exercise in value judgment.[137] Proponents of the two positions fall into this trap of implying their preferred means into the interpretation of the treaty's aim.[138]

There is no doubt that as the CRPD's interpretation develops and its provisions become more specific, the understanding of its object and purpose will also evolve. However, the direction of this evolution in the case of Article 12 is not determined by the current understanding of the treaty's purpose.

Nevertheless, the suprapositive principles are a valuable source of inspiration for proponents of the abolition of all substituted decision-making. The dignity of persons with disability, their equality and full participation in society, including the right to make their own decisions, could be recognised as the maxims on which Article 12 rests and which States Parties accepted by ratification. Although they do not prescribe how Article 12 should be implemented, they underline that any particular substituted decision-making regime violates the autonomy of at least some persons with disabilities. Reliance on the CRPD's norms, therefore,

[133] Article 3(c) of the CRPD.

[134] Freeman et al, 'Reversing Hard Won Victories'.

[135] Aust, 'Modern Treaty Law and Practice' 209.

[136] Keene, Kane, Kim, Owen, 'Mental capacity – Why look for a paradigm shift?' 348.

[137] G Letsas, 'Strasbourg's Interpretive Ethic: Lessons for the International Lawyer' (2010) 21(3) *The European Journal of International Law* 510, 533; see also R Gardiner, 'The Vienna Convention on Treaty Interpretation' in DB Hollis (ed), *The Oxford Guide to Treaties* (Oxford University Press, 2012) 496.

[138] Series and Nilsson, 'Article 12 CRPD Equal Recognition before the Law' 343.

allows the CRPD Committee, if it wishes to do so, to push for further reforms until guardianship is completely eliminated.

3.2.3. The Institutional Aspect

The institutional aspect refers to the effectiveness of oversight of compliance with human rights norms by human rights bodies.[139] In the case of the CRPD, the Committee on the Rights of Persons with Disabilities is the body entrusted with interpreting and enforcing the CRPD. Its powers, resources, authority, and the methods of ensuring compliance it chooses, will all have an impact on its success in resolving the tensions between the international and domestic norms through the treaty's implementation.

The VCLT does not address the authority of treaty bodies when interpreting human rights treaties.[140] Opinions vary on the legal power of their pronouncements, but few would doubt they have some relevance for interpretation.[141] The CRPD itself does not grant binding power to the CRPD Committee's views.[142] Its powers can, therefore, be likened to other specialized UN treaty bodies, whose pronouncements have legal force to the degree of their persuasiveness.[143]

The Committee can approach the difference in the understanding of Article 12 between itself and the States Parties in two basic ways. It either accepts the states' claims about the impossibility of providing supported decision-making for all[144] and interprets Article 12 to allow for the retention of substitution in exceptional situations, or the Committee can convince the states that the specific requirements it formulates under Article 12 are reasonable and possible to implement, and indeed should be implemented.[145] In any case, the Committee cannot simply unilaterally decide how the CRPD should be understood; its opinion is not formally binding on States Parties.[146] The states' opinion on what

[139] Neuman,' Human Rights and Constitutional Rights' 1869.

[140] M Scheinin, 'The Art and Science of Interpretation in Human Rights Law' in BA Andreassen, HO Sano, and S McInerney-Lankford (eds), *Research Methods in Human Rights: A Handbook* (Edward Elgar, 2017) 22.

[141] S Besson, 'Sources of International Human Rights Law: How General is General International Law' in S Besson and J d'Aspremont (eds), *The Oxford Handbook on the Sources of International Law* (Oxford University Press, 2017) 859.

[142] See Article 34–39 of the CRPD, dealing with the composition, powers and duties of the CRPD Committee.

[143] N Rodley, 'The Role and Impact of Treaty Bodies' in D Shelton (ed), *The Oxford Handbook of International Human Rights Law* (Oxford University Press, 2013) 641.

[144] See, for example, the German and the Danish governments' position on the Committee's draft general comment on article 12: 'German Statement on the Draft General Comment on Article 12 CRPD', Federal Republic of Germany (20 February 2014); 'Response from the Government of Denmark with regards to Draft General Comment on Article 12 of the Convention – Equal Recognition before the Law', Ministry of Children, Gender Equality, Integration and Social Affairs of Denmark (20 February 2014).

[145] Uerpmann-Wittzack, 'The Law-Making Function' 45.

[146] Fourth report on subsequent agreements and subsequent practice in relation to the interpretation of treaties, Georg Nolte, Special Rapporteur, International Law Commission, UN Doc A/CN.4/694 (7 March 2016); see a similar argument with regard to the UN Human Rights Committee:

can be implemented and how, matters. Implementation itself is a dialogue, and the Committee needs to be strategic to achieve the result it considers optimal. Periodic reviews, individual communications and general comments are tools in the Committee's hand to convince the States Parties to follow its opinion.

If the Committee's views are unconvincing, the states have several options at their disposal to challenge them. They can, over time, influence the Committee's composition to change it to one more receptive to their views. They can pressure the Committee by reaching mutual agreements in the yearly Conference of States Parties about substantive issues relating to the CRPD, that depart from the Committee's views.[147] Moreover, they can resort to wilful non-compliance. It is not unheard of for even better-established bodies, such as the European Court of Human Rights, to change their opinion on substantive matters after a credible threat of non-implementation, even from a single member state.[148] In the face of general non-compliance with certain of its views, the CRPD Committee would probably consider it wise to revise them.

The interpretation of Article 12, therefore, turns on the question of whether the CRPD Committee can convince States Parties about the correctness of its position in requiring the full abolition of guardianship. If States Parties accept the Committee's position, it will become an authoritative interpretation of the CRPD, either formally as a subsequent practice under Article 31(3)b) of the VCLT or informally through the States' Parties agreement under Article 31(2)a).[149] If States Parties reject the Committee's position, it will arguably have no formal authority and, in any case, will be ignored in practice. Acceptance of the Committee's opinion, in turn, depends on whether it is able to accommodate the situation of persons with high support needs. If it cannot, it will be rejected as a manifestly absurd or unreasonable interpretation of Article 12 because it would require states to do the impossible. If the Committee's position can accommodate persons with high support needs, it should be followed, because any alternative maintaining guardianship would frustrate the purpose of the CRPD, which is to overcome limitations on legal capacity.

The CRPD Committee has so far not addressed explicitly the question of whether there are any exceptional circumstances that permit substituted decision-making under Article 12. Its published concluding observations[150] and General

W Martin and S Michalowski, 'The Legal Status of General Comments', Essex Autonomy Project, Essex University (23 May 2014).

[147] Article 40 of the CRPD; International Law Commission, 'Subsequent practice and subsequent agreements in relation to the interpretation of treaties: Text of the draft conclusions', UN Doc A/CN.4/L.907 (11 May 2018), Conclusion 2.

[148] See, for example, the European Court of Human Rights' decision in *Scoppola v Italy (No. 3)* App no 126/05 (ECtHR 22 May 2012), which partly overruled the decision of *Frodl v Austria* App no 20201/04 (ECtHR 8 April 2010), to accommodate the United Kingdom's resistance expressed in *Greens and M. T. v the United Kingdom* App no 60041/08 (ECtHR 23 October 2010).

[149] International Law Commission, 'Subsequent practice and subsequent agreements', Conclusion 2.

[150] See the CRPD Committee's Concluding Observations on Russia (n 88) § 27; Slovenia (n 88) § 19; Haiti (n 88) § 23; Austria (n 8) § 28; Hungary (n 8) § 26; Peru (n 8) § 25; Spain (n 8) § 34; China (n 8) § 22.

Comment on Legal Capacity[151] consistently require the abolition of guardianship and the introduction of supported decision-making without specifying how persons with high support needs would make decisions in a support framework. One possible way for the Committee to accommodate exceptions in the future lies in its definition of substitute decisions in the General Comment: according to para. 27, substitute decision-making regimes are based on a best interest standard.[152] Presumably, this means decisions taken on behalf of a person using a different standard, such as a substituted judgment standard based on the represented person's will and preferences,[153] could be formally accepted by the CRPD Committee as complying with Article 12. Accepting facilitated decisions as complying with the CRPD would provide states with an opportunity to experiment with formally reclassifying substitute decisions as something else.[154] The Committee has not relied on this exception so far, but the situation will get more complicated once the dialogue enters the difficult areas when states already undertaking progressive guardianship reform, such as Peru,[155] will get reviewed or the Committee receives individual applications from individuals testing the edges of Article 12.

The institutional aspect highlights that the Committee needs to choose its position carefully to convince states about the best possible way to implement the CRPD. It needs to formulate rules that are possible for States Parties to implement,[156] and are capable of convincing States Parties that they should implement them.[157]

3.3. CONCLUSION – DOES ARTICLE 12 RESOLVE THE DEBATE?

This chapter showed that current approaches are failing to provide a convincing interpretation of Article 12. Neither the Absolutist position, which excludes all substituted decision-making, nor the Constricted position, which permits some substituted decisions for exceptional circumstances, can rely authoritatively on the text of Article 12. They both provide a possible interpretation of it, but they cannot exclude the alternative. Deciding among them would require settling the difficult question of how persons with high support needs could be incorporated into a support framework under Article 12. The solution cannot be deduced from the text of the CRPD.

[151] General comment No. 1, § 8.

[152] General comment No. 1, § 27.

[153] P Skowron, 'Giving substance to 'the best interpretation of will and preferences' (2019) 62 *International Journal of Law and Psychiatry* 125, 128.

[154] T Minkowitz, 'CRPD and transformative equality' (2017) 13(1) *International Journal of Law in Context* 77, 82.

[155] RAC Caycho, 'The flag of imagination'.

[156] Neuman,' Human Rights and Constitutional Rights' 1871.

[157] Uerpmann-Wittzack, 'The Law-Making Function' 41.

This difficulty is partly caused by the development of legal capacity as a human right. In its relatively short history, international jurisprudence concerning this issue has concentrated on questions of relatively capable individuals who were unjustly restricted by guardianship laws. The issue of persons with severe disabilities in need of support has not been at the forefront of international litigation. Little attention has therefore been given to their concerns.

The CRPD as a human rights treaty has some specific features that help interpret it. Analysing its consensual, suprapositive and institutional aspects showed that maximising the decision-making autonomy of all persons with disabilities is the main objective of Article 12. The existing positions share this goal, but in proposing how to reach it, they read specific value judgments into the CRPD that are not supported by its text. Both the Absolutist position and the Constricted position, if adopted, would unavoidably create situations that would harm some persons with disabilities, contrary to the goal of the CRPD. Harming a small group of persons might be inevitable and indeed could turn out to be the best possible result, depending on the gravity and nature of the harm. However, the CRPD's text does not specify who should be harmed and how; that will have to be decided in the future. Views based on authoritatively resolving this question relying on the CRPD's aim are based on circular argumentation.

The CRPD Committee's position expressed in its General Comment on legal capacity endorses the Absolutist position. Nevertheless, the Committee's position is not binding on states.[158] Its success depends on whether States Parties accept the CRPD Committee's position as authoritative.[159] If the Committee's opinion prevails, States Parties will follow it as binding; if it does not, it will be ignored, and State Parties will maintain guardianship.[160] To convince them, the Committee must interpret Article 12 in a way that does not create unreasonable obligations. By ignoring the need for a gradual change in the social context, the Committee has so far failed to specify obligations that are possible to implement, and therefore, it can not convince States Parties that its interpretation is a reasonable one.

This chapter thus argues that the question of how persons with high support needs should be accommodated in a support framework, cannot currently be answered by interpreting Article 12. The rest of the book will develop a proposal that is in line with Article 12, it does not lead to absurd results and therefore cannot be rejected on that basis, and arguably provides the maximum level of autonomy for all persons with disabilities.

[158] ibid.
[159] Keene, Kane, Kim, Owen, 'Mental capacity – Why look for a paradigm shift?' 344.
[160] Scheinin, 'The Art and Science of Interpretation' 22.

4

The Inherent Features of Guardianship

If Article 12 does not determine how specifically persons with disabilities can be incorporated into a support framework, a solution to this problem must be found elsewhere. A framework that maximises the autonomy of persons with disabilities and provides better results than its alternatives has the potential to be accepted by all stakeholders as the preferred interpretation of Article 12.[1] To develop such a framework, we have to understand which features of guardianship are problematic from a human rights perspective – and whether it perhaps has overlooked advantages. After all, if guardianship was as unacceptable as the literature often portrays it,[2] it would not withstand the challenge of legal reform. Its stubborn perseverance in all legal systems suggests that it has certain qualities that any proposed alternative must take into account to be successful.

As chapter two described, guardianship has several problematic features from a human rights perspective. Nevertheless, some of these are relatively easy to overcome. Putting aside these abuses connected to guardianship, the inherent feature of all legal capacity limitations is the transfer of a person's decision-making powers to her guardian.[3] This is a serious interference with the person's autonomy: she loses the right to make decisions about her own life.[4] In order to understand why guardianship is still used, we need to analyse the aims and assumptions behind this intervention. This allows us to assess by what other means the same goals could be achieved, and under what conditions and from what perspective are these preferable to guardianship. The following is an abstract assessment of the assumptions behind the use of various forms of guardianship, with the aim of distilling their advantages and disadvantages. It should not be taken as an endorsement of these interventions; for the sake of

[1] R Uerpmann-Wittzack, 'The Law-Making Function of the UN Committee on the Rights of Persons with Disabilities' (2018) 8(2) *Wroclaw Review of Law, Administration & Economics* 36, 41.

[2] O Lewis, 'Disabling Legal Barriers' (2017) 1 *European Human Rights Law Review* 49, 49.

[3] P Gooding, 'Supported Decision-Making: A Rights-Based Disability Concept and its Implications for Mental Health Law' (2013) 20(3) *Psychiatry, Psychology and Law* 431, 434.

[4] E Flynn and A Arstein-Kerslake, 'Legislating personhood: realising the right to support in exercising legal capacity' (2014) 10(1) *International Journal of Law in Context* 81, 91.

analysis, I need to put aside their compliance with the CRPD and present them in the best light possible.

4.1. IS THE AIM OF SUBSTITUTE DECISION-MAKING EVER LEGITIMATE?

Why would the law ever allow the limitation of somebody's legal capacity? One might accept that there are certain individuals in a society, whether labelled as disabled or not, who can find themselves in a situation in which they are unable to make competent decisions. Since they cannot take care of their interests, society is concerned about their safety and well-being, life and health. It therefore assists them in various ways.[5] Legal capacity laws are part of this framework of care.[6] They protect vulnerable persons from two types of evils: from their own decisions that are potentially harmful to them, and from the failure to make crucial decisions necessary for their well-being.[7] Protection from abuse is an example of the first situation: a person can be tricked into a transaction that is harmful to her, such as selling her property below its value.[8] Arranging for care and treatment and managing property (investing funds, applying for social benefits, maintaining an apartment, paying bills) are examples of the latter; they are transactions necessary to secure well-being, which some persons are unable to make.[9]

All these are valid concerns and should not be taken lightly. The welfare state was created to take care of vulnerable individuals, and most people would feel uncomfortable if society abandoned those most in need of care.[10] Indeed, in terms of human rights law, protecting the rights of persons with decreased capacity is a state's positive duty, failure of which can result in violation of fundamental rights. In *Vaudelle v France*[11] and *X. and Y. v the Netherlands*,[12] the European Court of Human Rights criticised the respondent governments for not adequately protecting the legal interests of disabled persons. Caring about the well-being of vulnerable persons is a legitimate state concern and, sometimes,

[5] A Szerletics, 'Paternalism', Essex Autonomy Project, Essex University (2011).

[6] MC Freeman, K Kolappa JMC de Almeida, A Kleinman, N Makhashvili, S Phakathi, B Saraceno, G Thornicroft, 'Reversing Hard Won Victories in the Name of Human Rights: A Critique of the General Comment on Article 12 of the UN Convention on the Rights of Persons with Disabilities' (2015) 2(9) *Lancet Psychiatry* 844.

[7] Flynn and Arstein-Kerslake, 'Legislating personhood' 98.

[8] T Carney and D Tait, 'Adult Guardianship: Narrative Readings in the "Shadow" of the Law?' (1998) 21/2 *International Journal of Law and Psychiatry* 147, 149.

[9] CP Guzelian, MA Stein, and HS Akiskal, 'Credit Scores, Lending and Psychosocial Disability' (2015) 95 *Boston University Law Review* 1807.

[10] K Mackay and P McCusker, 'Adult safeguarding legislation: Navigating the borderlands between mental capacity, mental health and social care law and practice' (2024) 94 *International Journal of Law and Psychiatry* 6.

[11] *Vaudelle v France* App no 35683/97 (ECtHR 30 January 2001).

[12] *X. and Y. v the Netherlands* App no 8978/80 (ECtHR 26 March 1985).

indeed, a duty.[13] This, however, does not justify all interventions taken for this purpose – it remains to be seen whether appropriate means are used to achieve it.

4.2. THE ASSUMPTIONS BEHIND GUARDIANSHIP

Notwithstanding the intervention's legitimate goal, the state uses guardianship to protect the interests only of persons with disabilities. Only their legal capacity gets questioned, which raises the obvious concern of discrimination.[14] Singling out persons with disabilities for the intervention can only be justified if it can be shown that they are the only ones having diminished capacity.[15] This brings us to a key assumption underlying guardianship: that the person to whom it is applied is unable to make competent decisions.[16] If this assumption turns out to be incorrect in a particular case, guardianship is unjustified. If an individual is able to make competent decisions, these should be followed, rather than her autonomy violated and her decisions overruled.[17]

This leads us to the conclusion that the legitimacy[18] of guardianship depends on the quality of the fit between the affected persons' actual decision-making ability and the legal intervention.[19] The more over-inclusive guardianship is, the more persons it restricts unjustly, and conversely, the more underinclusive it is, the more vulnerable persons it fails to protect.[20] This is the first criterion I shall examine and later use to evaluate alternative approaches.

A typical application of guardianship looks like the following: a person is identified by others as lacking the capacity to protect her interests. An authorised person, who can be a family member or a public official, initiates a court procedure for placement under guardianship. The person's legal capacity is assessed during the proceedings by medical experts, and the court decides to

[13] J Herring, *Caring and the Law* (Hart, 2013).

[14] T Minkowitz, 'Legal Capacity: Alternatives to Functional Capacity' in O'Mahoney, C and G Quinn (eds), *Disability Law and Policy: An Analysis of the UN Convention* (Clarus Press, 2017).

[15] E Flynn and A Arstein-Kerslake, 'State intervention in the lives of people with disabilities: the case for a disability-neutral framework' (2017) 13(1) *International Journal of Law in Context* 39, 40; G Szmukler, R Daw, and F Callard, 'Mental health law and the UN convention on the rights of persons with disabilities' (2014) 37(3) *International Journal Law Psychiatry* 245; W Martin, S Michalowsky, T Jütten, and M Burch, 'Achieving CRPD Compliance, Is the Mental Capacity Act of England and Wales Compatible with the UN CRPD? If not, what next?', Essex Autonomy Project, Essex University (2014).

[16] PS Appelbaum, 'Assessment of Patients' Competence to consent to treatment' (2007) 357 *New England Journal of Medicine* 1834, 1836.

[17] AE Buchanan and DW Brock, *Deciding for Others: The Ethics of Surrogate Decision Making* (Cambridge University Press, 1989) 37.

[18] Which is not the same as permissibility. A measure may be impermissible even if it is legitimate.

[19] LA Schaefer and TJ Farrer, *A Casebook of Mental Capacity in US Legislation. Assessment and Legal Commentary* (Abington, Routledge, 2002) 3.

[20] NA Kohn, JA Blumenthal, and AT Campbell, 'Supported Decision-Making: A Viable Alternative to Guardianship?' (2013) 117(4) *Penn State Law Review* 1111, 1117.

limit her legal capacity in areas where she is found to lack capacity. A guardian is then appointed to make decisions on her behalf in these areas.

The described system of legal capacity restrictions is not the only way to protect incompetent individuals. Instead, each decision of the incapable person could be reviewed on an ad hoc basis: every time she makes a decision, and her carer thinks the decision harms the person's interests, the carer could ask a court for the decision to be set aside and replaced with a different one if the person is shown to have been incapable of making that specific decision. Similarly, if the person fails to make a decision, the carer could ask the court for a specific decision to be made if it is necessary for the disabled person, and if she failed to make it because she lacked capacity.

There are at least two good reasons why in most situations the law does not rely on such an ad hoc review of decisions: first, it is very time-consuming to turn to the courts with every single decision; and second, it undermines legal certainty if all transactions of a person with a disability are open to doubt until a court approves them.[21] This could hinder potential partners from engaging in legal transactions with persons with disabilities, contrary to all parties' interests.

Guardianship facilitates legal certainty. By limiting a person's legal capacity, a court certifies to other parties that the person's legal transactions will be null and void,[22] and by appointing a guardian it certifies them to make legally valid decisions on behalf of the person without the need for individual court approvals.[23] Guardianship thus provides a convenient and effective solution to making decisions for individuals considered incompetent. Provided, of course, that it is used properly.

Guardianship requires the court to predict which decisions the person will be unable to make in the future. This is difficult for two reasons: capacity can fluctuate, therefore a person can be unable to make a decision at some point and able to make it at another time;[24] and capacity assessments are at their most reliable if they are not general but are specific to a particular decision.[25] It is easier to assess whether the person is unable to comprehend a specific financial transaction than to make a general statement about the person's ability to make financial transactions.[26] The person can find some problems easier and others more difficult within the general category, depending on the particular circumstances of decision-making.

[21] M Domański and B Lackoroński, 'Comparative analysis of the transposition of Article 12 of the UN Convention on the Rights of Persons with Disabilities' in M Domański and B Lackoroński (eds), *Models of Implementation of Article 12 of the Convention on the Rights of Persons with Disabilities (CRPD); Private and Criminal Law Aspects* (Routledge, 2024) 600.

[22] I Bantekas, 'Mental and Intellectual Capacity and Contractual Freedom: Assistive Decision-Making Matters' (2023) 21(2) *Seattle Journal for Social Justice* 569, 570.

[23] AR Keene, NB Kane, SYH Kim, and GS Owen, 'Mental capacity – Why look for a paradigm shift?' (2023) 31(3) *Medical Law Review* 340, 346.

[24] Buchanan and Brock, *Deciding for Others*, 18.

[25] LA Schaefer and TJ Farrer, *A Casebook of Mental Capacity in US Legislation. Assessment and Legal Commentary* (Routledge, 2022).

[26] M Scholten, E Braun, J Gather, and J Vollmann, 'Combining Supported Decision-Making with Competence Assessment: A Way to Protect Persons with Impaired Decision-Making Capacity against Undue Influence' (2021) 21(11) *American Journal of Bioethics* 45, 46.

No prediction is perfect except the one concerning persons[27] in a coma,[28] but perhaps absolute accuracy is not necessary. If the prediction expressed in the guardianship order is reasonably close to the person's real circumstances, there is less cause for concern – guardianship is reasonably related to the person's ability and needs.[29]

The correlation between presumption and reality is crucial for the legitimacy of guardianship.[30] There could be small or large divergences between persons' actual ability to make decisions and their legal capacity determined by the courts. Guardianship does not involve an ad hoc consideration of the person's ability to make a particular decision at a particular time. It is a restriction imposed in advance, which applies to decisions made in the future. In essence, it is a prediction that the person will lack the capacity to decide certain matters in the future.

4.3. DIFFERENT LEGAL APPROACHES TO GUARDIANSHIP

The fit between the guardianship order and the person's actual capacity is crucial for evaluating the legitimacy of guardianship. This fit depends on the approach used to limit capacity. Amita Dhanda lists three limitation methods: the status, outcome and functional approaches.[31] The following analysis uses her typology as a starting point but adds two additional approaches, the quasi-status approach and the quasi-functional approach.

4.3.1. The Status Approach

The status approach is the oldest, and considered the most outdated.[32] It involves depriving a person's legal capacity purely on the basis of her disability.[33] Examples would include a prohibition on opening a bank account for blind persons or

[27] Buchanan and Brock, *Deciding for Others*, 19.

[28] That is, with regard to their capacity to make decisions: they are incapable of making any kind of decision. That, however, does not automatically mean that all decisions need to be made to protect their interests.

[29] P Appelbaum, 'Assessment of Patients' Competence to consent to treatment' (2007) 357 *New England Journal of Medicine* 1834, 1836.

[30] T Grisso, *Evaluating Competencies: Forensic Assessments and Instruments,* Perspectives in Law and Psychology 16 (Kluwer Academic Plenum Publishers, 2nd Edition, 2003) 12.

[31] A Dhanda, 'Legal Capacity in the Disability Rights Convention: Stranglehold of the Past or Lodestar for the Future?' (2007) 34 *Syracuse Journal of International Law and Commerce* 429, 431; the same typology was adopted by the Committee on the Rights of Persons with Disabilities in General comment No. 1 (2014) – Article 12: Equal recognition before the law, UN Committee on the Rights of Persons with Disabilities, General comment No. 1 (2014) – Article 12: Equal recognition before the law, Committee on the Rights of Persons with Disabilities, CRPD/C/GC/1 (19 May 2014) §15.

[32] Dhanda, 'Legal Capacity in the Disability Rights Convention' 431.

[33] M Scholten, J Gather, and J Vollmann, 'Equality in the Informed Consent Process: Competence to Consent, Substitute Decision-Making, and Discrimination of Persons with Mental Disorders' (2021) 46(1) *Journal of Medicine and Philosophy* 108, 118.

placement under guardianship purely on the basis of intellectual disability.[34] The latter example is probably historic and would nowadays be considered prejudiced. It is now widely accepted that the abilities of persons with intellectual disabilities vary, and it is hard to imagine a law that would base legal capacity limitations merely on the existence of disability.[35]

4.3.2. The Quasi-Status Approach

Plenary guardianship is not, at least formally, based purely on disability.[36] It is usually conditioned on other criteria, such as the inability to make decisions because of one's disability,[37] which brings these restrictions into the realm of the functional approach, at least formally.

In practice, however, it seems that in many jurisdictions, the application of the additional functional criteria is a mere formality, and the most critical or the sole factor determining placement under guardianship is the person's disability.[38] In Hungary, for example, one in-depth study of nearly 300 guardianship decisions found that courts and guardianship authorities find the existence of a disability very often sufficient in itself for placement under guardianship.[39] Statistics and human rights reports show that the situation in other countries is similar and,[40] to some degree, can be true for any jurisdiction[41] where guardianship proceedings are characterised by the prevalence of formal procedures and superficial inquiries.[42] It seems appropriate to create a separate category in this book for these cases of 'diagnostic testimony': the quasi-status approach is formally based on functional criteria but in practice, determined purely by the existence of a disability.[43]

[34] Dhanda, 'Legal Capacity in the Disability Rights Convention' 431.

[35] Buchanan and Brock, *Deciding for Others*, 18.

[36] That is, in the jurisdictions I am aware of; nor does Amita Dhanda or other authors mention them.

[37] An example for many: Act no. IV of 1959 on the Civil Code of the Hungarian Republic, § 15(4).

[38] NA Kohn, 'Legislating Supported Decision-Making' (2021) 58 *Harvard Journal on Legislation* 313, 325.

[39] K Szegediné Sebestyén, 'A gondnokság alá helyezés iránti perekről' (1982) 7 *Magyar Jog* 606, 607.

[40] Mental Disability Advocacy Centre (MDAC), *Legal Capacity in Europe* (MDAC, 2013) 24.

[41] JM Jameson, T Riesen, S Polychronis, B Trader, S Mizner, J Martinis, and D Hoyle, 'Guardianship and the Potential of Supported Decision Making With Individuals with Disabilities' (2015) 40 *Research and Practice For Persons With Severe Disabilities* 36.

[42] If the application of guardianship provisions was deficient, any system could be considered a 'quasi-status' approach. Even the most carefully designed functional approach would be useless if in practice it reflected nothing but a bias of its operators against persons with disabilities. The guardianship systems of post-communist countries, where the existence of a disability is an accurate prediction of incapacitation in the proceedings, are good examples. I am grateful to my colleague Maroš Matiaško for raising this point.

[43] Grisso, *Evaluating Competencies*, 12.

4.3.3. The Outcome Approach

The outcome approach is not based merely on disability but on the result of the decisions the person with disability makes.[44] If her carers or other decision-makers, such as the court deciding on her legal capacity, consider that her decisions are harmful to herself or otherwise not in her interest, her legal capacity is denied.[45] If her decisions are in conformity with others' views on what is the 'right' decision, her legal capacity remains intact. An example would include a person offered psychiatric treatment. If she accepted it, her consent would be considered valid, but if she refused, it would be viewed as a sign of incapacity, and she would be given the treatment involuntarily.[46] Similarly, if a person agreed to be placed in a care home, she would be moved there with her consent; however, if she refused to give her consent, she would be incapacitated and moved with the consent of her guardian.[47]

While the outcome approach seems outdated, there is no shortage of specific examples of its use.[48] For example, the legal incapacitation proceedings against one of the richest persons in France, Liliane Betancourt, were motivated by the outcome approach. The proceedings were initiated by her heirs because of her habit of indulging her assistant with lavish gifts, which was also the stated justification for her incompetence.[49] An interesting widespread use of the outcome approach in England was revealed by the European Court of Human Rights' decision in *H.L. v the United Kingdom*.[50] The applicant, a man with intellectual disability, was 'informally placed' in a psychiatric hospital – because he did not try to leave, no involuntary placement procedure was initiated, but the government made clear that had he tried to leave, the hospital would have applied for a court order to commit him.[51] Mr. H. L. and patients in similar situations are thus considered capable when agreeing with their doctors and considered incapable if they express disagreement with the offered course of treatment.[52]

[44] N Pickering, G Newton-Howes, and G Young, 'Harmful Choices, the Case of C, and Decision-Making Competence' (2022) 22(10) *American Journal of Bioethics* 38, 38.

[45] BD Earp, J Demaree-Cotton, and J Savulescu, 'Against Externalism in Capacity Assessment – Why Apparently Harmful Treatment Refusals Should Not Be Decisive for Finding Patients Incompetent' (2022) 22(10) *American Journal of Bioethics* 65, 65.

[46] *Plesó v Hungary* App no 41242/08 (ECtHR 2 October 2012).

[47] *Stanev v Bulgaria*.

[48] P Appelbaum, 'Assessment of Patients' Competence to consent to treatment' (2007) 357 *New England Journal of Medicine* 1834, 1836.

[49] Kim Willsher, 'Liliane Bettencourt is not fit to manage fortune, judge rules' *The Guardian* (17 October 2011) www.theguardian.com/world/2011/oct/17/liliane-bettencourt-manage-fortune-judge; 'French court places L'Oreal heiress under guardianship' *France24* (17 October 2011) www.france24.com/en/20111017-french-court-place-loreal-heiress-under-guardianship-bettencourt-paris/.

[50] *H.L. v the United Kingdom* App no 45508/99 (ECtHR 5 October 2004).

[51] ibid, § 83.

[52] Scholten, Gather, Vollmann, 'Equality in the Informed Consent Process' 120.

Amita Dhanda rejects the legitimacy of the outcome approach on the basis that it merely ensures conformity with social expectations, regardless of their actual benefit to the person or his actual capacity.[53] The European Court is also critical of it.[54] Paul Appelbaum, on the other hand, defends the outcome approach on effectiveness grounds: it would be inefficient to inquire in detail about the capacity of a person who, in any case, agrees to the socially accepted course of action.[55] Even if she were found incompetent and placed under guardianship, the resulting decision of the guardian would be the same as the person herself agreed to at the beginning; therefore, time and cost can be saved by simply accepting her decision. An incapacity procedure should be initiated only in cases where there is an actual disagreement between the person and her caretaker, the eventual guardian or a doctor suggesting a particular course of treatment.

In my view, both opinions are correct, but they address different issues. Applebaum's argument relates to the initiation of incapacity proceedings. It does seem to be more economical to accept the person's opinion as valid if she agrees with the prospective substituted decision. In certain contexts, such as medical treatment, the outcome approach can be a useful tool to speed up decision-making. Dhanda's argument, on the other hand, is concerned with the substantive standard of capacity. If incapacity proceedings are commenced, and the person's disagreement with the eventual guardian is the basis for finding her incompetent, the result is very problematic. There can be good reasons why the person disagrees with the socially acceptable outcome, for instance why she rejects a course of treatment or a particular handling of her property.[56] Reasonable people can disagree about what her best interests are in a difficult situation. This in itself does not equal incompetence, and if it results in incapacitation, it should be rejected.

The above leads to the conclusion that the outcome approach can be helpful in deciding when to initiate the incapacitation proceedings but not in determining its result. However, in practice, this differentiation is problematic. The fact that incapacity proceedings were commenced against somebody can prejudge the final result. The actors of the procedure, judges and medical experts, are already assessing the person's condition with the notion in mind that another actor already considered her incompetent.[57] This spill-over of the outcome approach from initiation to a substantive decision should not be accepted. Because it is difficult to notice, it is also hard to police, it therefore delegitimises even the narrowest use of the outcome approach as suggested by Paul Applebaum.

[53] Dhanda, 'Legal Capacity in the Disability Rights Convention' 433.
[54] *Plesó v Hungary* 67.
[55] Appelbaum, 'Assessment of Patients' Competence to consent' 1836.
[56] *Plesó v Hungary* 67.
[57] For a good example, see the government's argumentation in *Sýkora v the Czech Republic* 59.

4.3.4. The Functional Approach

The functional approach is based on mental capacity, that is, on the psychological ability of the person to make the specific decision in question.[58] It is based on a psychological assessment of the person's capacity to perform the given task.[59] It can be legally expressed by a single term, such as the ability to make competent decisions,[60] or it can be broken down into its elements, such as in the United Kingdom's Mental Capacity Act, in which inability to make a decision is defined as inability:

(a) to understand the information relevant to the decision,
(b) to retain that information,
(c) to use or weigh that information as part of the process of making the decision, or
(d) to communicate the decision (whether by talking, using sign language or any other means).[61]

The functional approach is used every time incapacitation to a specific decision requires the evaluation of a person's ability to make that specific decision.[62] In *Kiss v Hungary*, for example, the European Court held that disenfranchisement of all persons under guardianship is a disproportionate measure because this group is made up of persons of varying capacities with regard to voting.[63] The obvious reading suggests that disenfranchisement can be based on an individual assessment of a person's capacity to vote, which is an example of the functional approach.[64] Similarly, in *X. v Croatia*, the European Court criticised the applicant's exclusion from her child's adoption proceedings on the basis of her general incapacitation.[65] For such a serious measure, an assessment of X.'s capacity to participate in the adoption proceedings would have been necessary. In *Salontaji-Drobnjak v Serbia*, the Court found a violation because the applicant was not allowed to initiate court proceedings due to his general incapacitation,

[58] S O'Keeffe, 'Functional Capacity Assessments by Healthcare Professionals: Problems and Mitigating Strategies' in M Donnelly, R Harding, and E Taşcıoğlu (eds), *Supporting Legal Capacity in Socio-Legal Context* (Hart, 2022) 79.

[59] E Flynn and A Arstein-Kerslake, 'Legislating personhood: realising the right to support in exercising legal capacity' (2014) 10(1) *International Journal of Law in Context* 81, 87.

[60] An example for many: *belátási képesség* in the Hungarian Civil Code, Act no. IV of 1959 on the Civil Code of the Hungarian Republic, § 15(4).

[61] Sec. 3(1) of the UK Mental Capacity Act 2005 (c 9).

[62] M Scholten and J Gather, 'Adverse consequences of article 12 of the UN Convention on the Rights of Persons with Disabilities for persons with mental disabilities and an alternative way forward' (2018) 44 *Journal of Medical Ethics* 226, 231.

[63] *Kiss v Hungary* 44.

[64] Another possible reading suggests that disenfranchisement should never be permitted, not even in the case of proven incapacity to vote. See J Fiala-Butora, MA Stein, and JE Lord, 'The democratic life of the Union: towards equal voting participation for Europeans with Disabilities' (2014) 55 *Harvard International Law Journal* 71.

[65] *X. v Croatia* 51–53.

without an assessment of his actual capacity to participate in proceedings.[66] All these are examples where the functional approach was suggested by the European Court as a measure more tailored to the individual's circumstances, one which makes any interference with their legal capacity more proportionate.

4.3.5. The Quasi-Functional Approach

The functional approach could be equated with partial guardianship, but the matter is more complicated.[67] As explained above, partial guardianship is not based on a person's ability to make a specific decision, but on a prediction of the person's ability to make that particular decision in the future. The relationship between partial guardianship and the functional approach is a matter of degree. The closer in time that placement under partial guardianship is to any decision the person is not allowed to make due to her incapacitation, the closer the fit between the restriction and the functional approach. Similarly, the more specific the incapacitation order is about the types of decisions the person cannot make, the closer partial guardianship is to the functional approach.

To make this clear with an example, imagine a person having difficulty with managing her house during her treatment for manic depression. She is unable to let it out or sell it, she is not paying the utility bills, and a psychological assessment finds her incapable of performing these tasks. A court then places her under partial guardianship. If the guardianship order relates to managing her house, it is closely related to her functional inabilities. On the other hand, if the order covers 'management of property',[68] it is too broad. It also incapacitates her in the area of buying clothes, notwithstanding that her inability to manage her house is not the best predictor of whether she can buy clothes.[69] The assessment serving as the basis of incapacitation was not focused on her ability to buy clothes.

Similarly, if she is prevented from buying clothes only two weeks after the court order, it is easier to argue that the results of the assessment are likely still valid.[70] On the other hand, if she still cannot buy clothes or pay her utility bills ten years after the evaluation, there is much less certainty about the relationship between her legal capacity and her functional ability.[71] Her condition might have changed significantly in the meantime.

[66] *Salontaji-Drobnjak v Serbia.*

[67] Dhanda, 'Legal Capacity in the Disability Rights Convention' 432.

[68] This was one of the listed grounds of placement under partial guardianship in Hungary, which was therefore utilised heavily by the courts. See Act no. IV of 1959 on the Civil Code of the Hungarian Republic, § 14 (6) 2.

[69] Buchanan and Brock, *Deciding for Others*, 18.

[70] A Peterson, J Karlawish, and E Largent, 'Supported Decision Making With People at the Margins of Autonomy' (2021) 21(11) *American Journal of Bioethics* 4, 6.

[71] M Scholten, E Braun, J Gather, and J Vollmann, 'Combining Supported Decision-Making with Competence Assessment: A Way to Protect Persons with Impaired Decision-Making Capacity against Undue Influence' (2021) 21(11) *American Journal of Bioethics* 45, 46.

Also, if she was unable to give consent to a specific medical procedure, that should not be used as a predictor of whether she will be able to give consent to a different medical procedure two weeks later when her health situation might have stabilised.[72] If she is placed under guardianship with regard to healthcare decisions on the first occasion, she might be unjustly deprived of the right to decide on her treatment later.

Based on the above, the functional approach should refer only to incapacitation based on an ad hoc assessment of the person's ability to make the actual specific decision the incapacitation is related to.[73] Partial guardianship does not belong to this category. It is based on a prediction of this ability in the future, which can never be perfect. Because functional capacity is defined with regard to a specific action at a given time, there is always a possibility of a divergence between the person's actual capacity and her legal capacity as determined by the guardianship order sometime earlier and with some level of generality. This is not caused by faulty application – even the most carefully applied guardianship system suffers from this principal problem.[74] I will therefore consider partial guardianship to be based on a quasi-functional approach in this book.

The difference between the functional and quasi-functional approach is a matter of degree. The closer the guardianship order is to its future effects, and the more specific it is to decisions based on the person's functional abilities, the closer it is to a functional approach. A guardianship order of short duration or reviewed in short intervals, and covering only a specific decision, is very close to the functional approach.

4.4. EVALUATING THE DIFFERENT APPROACHES

The above analysis allows ranking the different approaches to guardianship based on their relationship to the person's actual functional ability to make decisions. On one end of this scale is the status-based approach, followed by the quasi-status approach (plenary guardianship), the quasi-functional approach (partial guardianship), with the functional approach on the other end. I omitted the outcome approach, because it should not be used as a substantive test for assessing capacity, only to signalise a need for capacity assessments.

The more closely related an approach is to the person's functional ability, the less restrictive it is. The functional approach is restricting a person only

[72] LA Schaefer and TJ Farrer, *A Casebook of Mental Capacity in US Legislation. Assessment and Legal Commentary* (Abington, Routledge, 2002) 3.

[73] L Turner-Stokes, K Benaichouche-Motam, W Goodison, A Altaie, A Howard, P McKnight, and J Alfonso, 'Improving the systematic screening and documentation of mental capacity for patients with severe brain injury: The Mental Capacity Screening assessment tool (MCScreen)' (2024) 24(5) *Clinical Medicine, Journal of the Royal College of Physicians of London* 1.

[74] B Hurme and PS Appelbaum, 'Defining and Assessing Capacity to Vote: The Effect of Mental Impairment on the Rights of Voters' (2007) 38 *McGeorge Law Review* 931, 962.

with regard to decisions she is unable to perform. The status approach might be based on no actual relationship between the person's abilities and her legal capacity. Plenary and partial guardianships are in between and do not represent discrete points on this scale but are spread over it. Depending on the duration of the order or the frequency of review in the case of both types, as well as on the narrowness and specificity of the order in the case of partial guardianship, they can predict more or less accurately the person's functional ability in a given area.

It might be tempting to conclude that the less restrictive an approach is, the better it is. Indeed, the history of guardianship shows a clear tendency to move towards more individually tailored approaches.[75] This is reflected in domestic law and also in international law, including the Council of Europe's Recommendation R(99), and the European Court's jurisprudence described earlier. However, such a conclusion would be premature. It would suggest that all countries should be using only the functional approach, which is not the case. In fact, some countries use solely the quasi-status approach,[76] and all the rest use the quasi-functional approach besides the functional approach. Prejudice and reliance on outdated concepts might partly explain this phenomenon, but the picture is more complicated.

Restrictiveness is not the only value determining the appropriateness of a given approach or the usefulness of a particular type of guardianship.[77] More restrictive approaches have some advantages as well. They should not be overlooked when searching for alternatives to guardianship. Newer forms of more individually tailored guardianships are often referred to as less restrictive alternatives,[78] which expresses a value judgment about them being preferable to plenary guardianship. While this might be generally correct and definitely true on the specific axis of restrictiveness, it clouds the issue that other properties of incapacitation have to be considered and that only a complex evaluation could show which methods are performing better overall or with regard to specific values. These other values, followed by different incapacitation approaches, have to be uncovered in order to outline alternative solutions. These are costs, legal certainty, protection from abuse, and ease of administration and oversight.

[75] K Blankman, 'Guardianship Models in the Netherlands and Western Europe' (2007) 20 *International Journal of Law and Psychiatry* 47, 48.

[76] That is, countries where only plenary guardianship and partial guardianship with general limitation is available, such as in Russia, Bulgaria, and Lithuania. See Mental Disability Advocacy Centre (MDAC), *Guardianship and Human Rights in Bulgaria* (MDAC, 2007); Mental Disability Advocacy Centre (MDAC), *Guardianship and Human Rights in Russia* (MDAC, 2007); Mental Disability Advocacy Centre (MDAC), *Guardianship and Human Rights in Lithuania* (MDAC, 2007).

[77] Keene, Kane, Kim, and Owen, 'Mental capacity – Why look for a paradigm shift?' 346.

[78] Mental Disability Advocacy Centre (MDAC), *Legal Capacity in Europe*, 20; M Keys, 'Legal Capacity Law Reform in Europe: An Urgent Challenge' in G Quinn and L Waddington (eds), *European Yearbook of Disability Law* 65 (Intersentia, 2009); L Salzman, 'Guardianship for persons with mental illness – a legal and appropriate alternative?' (2011) 4 *Saint Louis University Journal Health Law & Policy* 279.

4.4.1. Costs

The functional approach requires determinations of legal capacity in a court or administrative proceeding every time a person makes a decision to which his capacity is questioned.[79] This requires a decision-maker, an assessment of abilities, and the representation of legal interests pro and contra. To decide on somebody's legal capacity on a weekly or monthly basis can be therefore very costly.

Compared to that, the first three approaches incur costs depending on how frequently they are reviewed. A guardianship order of indefinite duration is the cheapest, because it requires only one procedure, to issue it. A less restrictive guardianship order which is reviewed on a regular basis is costlier.

Concerning the quality of assessments, the status approach is probably the cheapest, as it requires showing merely the existence of a disability. The other three less restrictive approaches require some assessment of abilities, with psychological, psychiatric or other expert involvement.[80] The more detailed and versatile the assessment, the more reliably it establishes the person's actual skills, but other than that, it is difficult to generalise any cost differences between the three approaches in this regard.

In general, the status approach is the cheapest, followed by the quasi-status and the quasi-functional approaches, internally differentiated by the frequency of reviews, and the functional approach is the costliest.

4.4.2. Legal Certainty

It is essential that parties entering into legal transactions with persons with disabilities can be confident that their agreements are definite and legally binding.[81] Some decisions of a person lacking capacity can be automatically null and void; others are voidable by court intervention or by other methods.[82] Legal certainty is not only an important abstract feature of the legal system, but it also has a direct implication on the well-being of persons with disabilities.[83] The less

[79] Turner-Stokes, Benaichouche-Motam, Goodison, Altaie, Howard, McKnight, and Alfonso, 'Improving the systematic screening'.

[80] SE Rothke, GJ Demakis, and HM Amsbaugh, 'State statutes regarding the role of psychologists in performing capacity evaluations for guardianship determinations' (2019) 50(4) *Professional Psychology: Research and Practice* 228.

[81] Bantekas, 'Mental and Intellectual Capacity and Contractual Freedom' 586.

[82] Nullity is sometimes called absolute voidness, while voidability can be called relative voidness; see Act no. IV of 1959 on the Civil Code of the Hungarian Republic, § 15/A. § (1) for nullity, and §§ 234–239 for invalidity.

[83] M Domański and B Lackoroński, 'Comparative analysis of the transposition of Article 12 of the UN Convention on the Rights of Persons with Disabilities' in M Domański and B Lackoroński (eds), *Models of Implementation of Article 12 of the Convention on the Rights of Persons with Disabilities (CRPD); Private and Criminal Law Aspects* (Routledge, 2024) 600.

certain contracts concluded with persons with disabilities appear, the less likely will be other parties to enter into transactions with them, affecting many areas, from ordinary property transactions and healthcare decisions to the ability to invest and do business.[84]

The status approach seems to promote legal certainty the most. Other parties have to be aware only of the restrictions attached to particular disabilities. Plenary guardianship is also easy to understand from this perspective. All the person's transactions are handled by her guardian. Any contract agreed to by the guardian will be valid; any contract not agreed to by the guardian (with minor exceptions)[85] will be void.[86]

Partial guardianship is more problematic. It requires a value judgment by the contracting party, and often by the person under guardianship, on whether the specific transaction the parties are contemplating is covered by the guardianship order. The broader and more general the guardianship order, the easier such a determination is. Therefore, the less restrictive (the narrower) the order, the more complications can arise with regard to legal certainty.

The functional approach is the most uncertain in this regard. Every transaction is valid but is voidable if the person's legal capacity is put in doubt and an assessment is ordered. Parties therefore have the least legal certainty about the validity of their contracts. They can be challenged even by a third party, who, for example, is concerned about the abuse and well-being of the disabled person and initiates a capacity assessment to contest the specific contract.[87] Uncertainty can be avoided only by asking for an assessment and court approval of the contract proactively at the time of signing it, which would make contracting with persons with disabilities cumbersome, time-consuming and costly. It follows that from the perspective of legal certainty, the more restrictive the approach, the better.

4.4.3. Protection from Abuse

One of the main reasons why guardianship exists is to protect persons with disability from harm caused by their decisions.[88] Harm is hard to predict, therefore incapacitation protects persons from all incompetent decisions, whether

[84] Keene, Kane, Kim, Owen, 'Mental capacity – Why look for a paradigm shift?' 346.

[85] The law can provide exceptions from this general approach, notably allowing the person to buy goods of everyday need; see for example Act no. IV of 1959 on the Civil Code of the Hungarian Republic, § 15/A. § (2).

[86] I Hoffman and G Konczei, 'Legal Regulations Relating to the Passive and Active Legal Capacity of Persons with Intellectual and Psychosocial Disabilities in Light of the Convention on the Rights' (2010) 33 *Loyola of Los Angeles International and Comparative Law* Review 168.

[87] A long list of family members, the guardianship authority, and the public prosecutor can initiate capacity assessments in Hungary; see Act no. IV of 1959 on the Civil Code of the Hungarian Republic, § 14 (2).

[88] Bigby, C and J Douglas, *Support for Decision Making – A Practice Framework* (Melbourne, Living with Disability Research Centre, La Trobe University, 2015), 7; K Mackay and P McCusker,

harmful or beneficial.[89] The golden rule of guardianship in this regard is that it is easier to prevent harm than it is to remedy it once it has happened.

From this perspective, the broader the incapacitation, the more protection it provides from self-inflicted harm because it excludes persons from a broader set of decisions. Plenary guardianship is the most protective measure as it prevents the person from entering any transaction; all are done by the guardian. Partial guardianship is narrower, therefore, it protects the person in fewer areas with regard to a narrower set of decisions. The functional approach is the least protective: it does not provide any prior protection, only ex-post voidability of select transactions. The less restrictive the approach, the less protection it provides.

However, court decisions[90] and human rights reports[91] show that not only other parties can be the sources of abuse, but also the guardian.[92] From this angle, plenary guardianship provides the least protection, as it is the most open to abuse. A plenary guardian can make decisions on behalf of the person in any area of the latter's life. Partial guardianship is less abusive in this respect, as the guardian's competencies are more limited. The functional approach provides the most protection, as there is no guardian involved; all claims of incapacity are decided by a court or by an administrative body.

Concerning protection from abuse, the picture is thus mixed. The more restrictive an approach, the more protection it provides against abuse by others, and the less protection against abuse by the guardian or other designated substitute decision-maker.

4.4.4. Ease of Administration and Oversight

This category is related to costs but is not identical to it. Substituted decision-making requires an infrastructure, with bodies involved in administering and supervising it. Incapacitation procedures have to be initiated, medical experts need to assess the person's capacity, and suitable guardians have to be found and appointed by the courts. Guardians need to be trained and supervised, which can include reviewing yearly reports or resolving complaints against them. Running

'Adult safeguarding legislation: Navigating the borderlands between mental capacity, mental health and social care law and practice' (2024) 94 *International Journal of Law and Psychiatry*.

[89] A Arstein-Kerslake and E Flynn, 'The General Comment on Article 12 of the Convention on the Rights of Persons with Disabilities: a roadmap for equality before the law' (2016) 20(4) *International Journal of Human Rights* 471, 482.

[90] *Shtukaturov v Russia*; *Stanev v Bulgaria*; *Sýkora v the Czech Republic*.

[91] Hungarian Civil Liberties Union (TASZ), *Ki a kompetens?* (TASZ, 2001) 18 (2001); Mental Disability Advocacy Centre (MDAC), *Guardianship and Human Rights in Hungary* (Hungary, 2007) 73.

[92] A-M Callus,' Removing obstacles to equal recognition for persons with intellectual disability: Taking exception to the way things are' (2018) 12 *ALTER European Journal of Disability Research* 153, 163.

a guardianship system is a challenge to the country's bureaucracy and requires significant investments in administrative capacities.

Three points can be raised regarding the administrative costs of each incapacitation approach. First, fragmentation makes running the system more complex. From the bureaucracy's perspective, concentrating different competencies on one person is therefore preferable. From this viewpoint, plenary guardianship is an ideal solution: one guardian is responsible for all decisions, they are the only one who needs to be supervised. If the person were under partial guardianship, some of her decisions would be made by a guardian, others could be reviewed under an ad hoc voidability procedure, which makes administration of the person's interests more complicated. This was raised as one of the main reasons for the preference for plenary guardianship by guardianship authorities in Hungary.[93]

Second, administrative costs are dependent on the context. If a medical decision needs to be made, the person is likely in a hospital, where an ad hoc assessment of her capacity is probably not very difficult or costly. It seems administratively more convenient to use the hospital's resources and only ensure procedural safeguards of using the functional approach for an ad hoc decision on medical procedures rather than trying to intervene with an incapacitation proceeding and using a guardian as a substitute decision-maker, who might not be present or might not be of much help regarding the incapacitated person's choices. Yet the latter is not uncommon.[94] Similarly, if a person lives in a care home, she is already under close supervision. Using the guardianship authority as a supervisory body for all her interests does not seem to be efficient. In those cases, a partial guardianship affecting only issues outside of the care home, coupled with an effective complaint mechanism for problems relating to life in the care home, seems to be the most effective solution.[95]

Third, while administrative difficulties are a valid concern, it is worrying if they become the primary or only concern. The correlation between institutionalisation and incapacitation is well-known in Central Europe:[96] placement under guardianship makes possible or immediately follows placement into institutional care.[97] Similar correlations between placements under guardianship and institutionalisation were also shown in Australia, where institutional caregivers

[93] Statement of L.B., a professional public guardian of the Budapest IV. District Guardianship Authority, at the conference organised by the Mental Disability Advocacy Centre on Guardianship and Human Rights in Hungary, 8 June 2007, Budapest.

[94] *Sýkora v the Czech Republic* 3.

[95] For a discussion of effective complaint mechanisms see J Fiala-Butora, 'Disabling Torture: the Obligation to Investigate Ill-Treatment of Persons with Disabilities' (2013) 45 *Columbia Human Rights Law Review* 214.

[96] Hungarian Civil Liberties Union (TASZ), *Ki a kompetens?*, 18.

[97] ibid, 59; In Slovakia, 93 per cent of residents of social care institutions were under plenary guardianship according to the Ministry of Social Affairs, see Ministerstvo práce, sociálnych vecí a rodiny Slovenskej republiky, 'Národný akčný plán prechodu z inštitucionálnej na komunitnú starostlivosť v systéme sociálnych služieb na roky 2011–2015' (December 2011) 18.

initiate incapacitations in order to transfer responsibility for residents' financial matters to their guardians.[98]

An in-depth study demonstrated a causal relationship between administrative capacities and plenary guardianship.[99] An investment in capacities in certain regions was shown to lead to increases in newly ordered plenary guardianships in those regions.[100] Once guardians are hired and trained and institutions are built to house persons with disabilities, persons need to be placed under guardianship to occupy the empty capacities.

4.4.5. Evaluation of the Above Approaches

The above analysis shows why the functional approach, the least restrictive incapacitation approach, is not the sole approach used around the world. Restrictiveness is not the only value determining the choice of an intervention. Generally, the more restrictive an approach, the less costly it is, the more it promotes legal certainty, the less it protects from abuse by guardians and the more from abuse by others.

The choice of a specific measure, therefore, depends on how high a priority is given to a particular value. The most appropriate guardianship system for a given jurisdiction based on the above criteria is likely to be a mix utilizing all measures or all three, except for the status approach. A functional approach can be most appropriate in situations in which capacity determinations are the easiest to administer: for example, with regard to medical decisions in hospitals, where the assessments can be done on the spot, or with regard to decisions that are very infrequent or require a court approval by default. The latter category can include disposing of property of significant value (for example, selling or buying a house) or moving into a social care home – these are unlikely to take place very often in a person's life and are of a serious nature where abuse is particularly likely and can have serious consequences. A court review on every occasion will therefore likely be worth the cost.

Plenary guardianship can be the most appropriate for persons whose condition is very severe. If they are unlikely to develop skills required for decision-making, it seems acceptable to incapacitate them with regard to all decisions without automatic review. While this can prove to be overly restrictive on particular occasions, mandating regular reviews or narrowing orders only to areas where the person is specifically shown to be incompetent can be excessively costly.

Partial guardianship can seem to be the most useful default approach for all other persons and for all other decisions. It is flexible in scope and in duration; it

[98] T Carney and D Tait, 'Caught Between Two Systems? – Guardianship and Young People with a Disability' (1997) 20 *International Journal of Law and Psychiatry* 157.

[99] T Verdes and M Tóth, *A per tárgya* (ELTE Eötvös Kiadó, 2010).

[100] ibid.

can therefore be tailored to the individual circumstances of each individual. The more protection the person needs, the more restrictive the order will be.

The above analysis is based on the assumption that the various goals pursued by incapacitation are equally worthy, and that a legislator is free to choose among them. That might not be true in practice. For example, the more cases highlight abuse by guardians as opposed to abuse by other parties, the more compelling the obligation to prevent that specific abuse becomes. Also, international human rights law's development towards less restrictive alternatives can be interpreted as a reorganisation of the values behind incapacitation. The more emphasis is placed on reducing restrictiveness, the less acceptable reliance on other values becomes. Plenary guardianship might have been defended on cost grounds thirty years ago, but in light of current human rights norms, it is much less likely to be accepted.[101]

Also, while reliance on certain values might justify choosing between incapacitation methods in the abstract, it is a different question whether the chosen measure is, in fact, pursuing the selected values in practice. Plenary guardianship might promote legal certainty if used well. However, a lot of uncertainty can be introduced in the system if persons placed under guardianship do not even know about their incapacitation because they were excluded from the proceeding[102] and the decision was not delivered to them.[103] Legal transactions made by them between the time of incapacitation and the time they found out about it would not be valid under the law but often indissoluble in practice,[104] which raises questions about these transactions' legal status, the parties' responsibility for the state of affairs, and compensation. Similarly, plenary guardianship might be less costly in theory, but if, in practice, it is overused, the system's overall costs might be higher than those of its seemingly more expensive alternatives. Similar examples could be raised with any value listed above. From a policy point of view, the choice between alternatives should not be based on values they pursue in theory but on values they are actually able to pursue in the given societal context.

It is important to emphasise at this point that the above is not a normative proposal of how incapacitation should be used. It is only a description of the assumptions behind its use in general, which are essential to understand if guardianship is to be compared with its alternatives. This assessment cannot be limited to restrictiveness alone. Only by fully understanding the functions guardianship plays in law can we assess how other approaches can fulfil those functions.

[101] *Shtukaturov v Russia.*

[102] Grisso, *Evaluating Competencies*, 317.

[103] *Sýkora v the Czech Republic.*

[104] For example, because some of the goods and services exchanged could not be returned after they were consumed.

5

The Alternative: Supported Decision-Making

GUARDIANSHIP BECAME A serious human rights concern at the end of the last century.[1] As criticism of abuses related to guardianship grew, a clear tendency arose in international law to prefer less restrictive versions of guardianship.[2] Plenary guardianship became untenable from an international law perspective and was replaced gradually or entirely by partial guardianship in several countries.[3] Other alternatives, such as enduring powers of attorney, also became popular and were introduced in more and more jurisdictions.[4]

These developments, however, have not aimed at eliminating guardianship but at improving it. While the various newly introduced legal institutions differ in their restrictiveness, safeguards, and how narrowly they are tailored to individual needs, they do not challenge guardianship as such: they are all methods of substituting the disabled person's decision with that of another person. For that reason, they seem unsatisfactory to those for whom overcoming guardianship has become the international disability rights movement's top priority at the beginning of the twenty-first century.[5] Opponents of guardianship argue

[1] O Lewis, 'Advancing Legal Capacity Jurisprudence' (2010) 6 *European Human Rights Law Review* 700, 705.

[2] A Arstein-Kerslake, *Restoring Voice to People with Cognitive Disabilities: Realizing the Right to Equal Recognition Before the Law* (Cambridge University Press, 2017) 7.

[3] For a review of the situation in Western Europe, see K Blankman, 'Guardianship Models in the Netherlands and Western Europe' (1997) 20 *International Journal of Law and Psychiatry* 47; for Canada, see RM Gordon, 'The Emergence of Assisted (Supported) Decision-Making in the Canadian Law of Adult Guardianship and Substitute Decision-Making' (2000) 23 *International Journal of Law and Psychiatry* 61; for Australia, see T Carney, 'Supported Decision-Making for People with Cognitive Impairments: An Australian Perspective?' (2015) 4 *Laws* 37; for Japan, see: M Arai and A Homma, 'Guardianship for adults in Japan: Legal reforms and advances in practice' 24 (Supplement June 2005) *Australasian Journal on Ageing* S19. For reforms in Central Europe, see Mental Disability Advocacy Centre (MDAC), *Legal Capacity in Europe* (Budapest, MDAC, 2013) 1; for an overview of the situation in the US, see L Salzman, 'Guardianship for persons with mental illness – a legal and appropriate alternative?' (2011) 4 Saint Louis University Journal Health Law & Policy 279.

[4] T Carney, 'Guardianship, Citizenship, & Theorizing Substitute-decisionmaking Law' (2012) 12/25 *Sydney Law School Research Paper* 2; I Doron, 'Elder Guardianship Kaleidoscope – a Comparative Perspective' (2002) 16 *International Journal of Law, Policy and the Family* 368.

[5] G Quinn, 'Personhood and Legal Capacity – Perspectives on the Paradigm Shift of Article 12 CRPD', Harvard Law School Project on Disability Conference presentation (2010).

that all forms of substituted decision-making, regardless of how closely tailored to the person's abilities and circumstances they may be, unjustly restrict disabled persons' autonomy.[6] Even the least restrictive form of guardianship therefore prevents persons with disabilities from exercising their legal capacity on an equal basis with non-disabled individuals.[7]

The flaws of guardianship can be tolerated if no better solution exists. However, with the negotiations of the CRPD, an alternative was proposed to guardianship that is not based on substituted decisions.[8] Representatives of the International Disability Caucus claimed that persons with disabilities are able to make decisions with support.[9] They proposed that supported decision-making replaces, to a large extent or fully, guardianship and other methods based on substituted decisions.[10]

The first part of this chapter explores what supported decision-making is. It looks into the historical origins of supported decision-making and its appearance in international and domestic legal sources. It shows that there is a discrepancy between how supported decision-making is described in the literature and the legal sources on which this description is apparently based. Supported decision-making should be understood as a theoretical model rather than as an existing legal institution. This part describes the main features of this model from the literature, which will serve as an ideal model for the analysis.

The second part explores the psychological foundations of the ideal model of supported decision-making. Scholars have made various claims about the superiority of supported decision-making.[11] Because, despite the growing empirical evidence,[12] these claims cannot be fully verified empirically,[13] I analyse in this

[6] T Minkowitz, 'Abolishing Mental Health Laws to Comply with the Convention on the Rights of Persons with Disabilities' in B McSherry and P Weller (eds), *Rethinking Rights Based Mental Health Laws* (Hart, 2010) 156.

[7] Salzman, 'Guardianship for persons with mental illness'.

[8] T Minkowitz, 'The United Nations Convention on the Rights of Persons with Disabilities and the Right to Be Free from Nonconsensual Psychiatric Interventions' (2007) 34 *Syracuse Journal of International Law and Commerce* 405, 408–11; A Dhanda, 'Legal Capacity in the Disability Rights Convention: Stranglehold of the Past or Lodestar for the Future?' (2007) 34 *Syracuse Journal of International Law and Commerce* 429, 445; M Bach and L Kerzner, 'A New Paradigm for Protecting Autonomy and the Right to Legal Capacity', paper prepared for the Law Commission of Ontario (2010).

[9] S Wildeman, 'Protecting Rights and Building Capacities: Challenges to Global Mental Health Policy in Light of the Convention on the Rights of Persons with Disabilities' (2013) 41 *The Journal of Law, Medicine & Ethics* 48, 54.

[10] L Series and A Nilsson, 'Article 12 CRPD' in I Bantekas, M Stein, D Anastasiou (eds), *The UN Convention on the Rights of Persons with Disabilities: a commentary* (Oxford University Press, 2018) 339, 345.

[11] T Carney, 'Clarifying, Operationalising, and Evaluating Supported Decision Making Models' (2014) 1(1) *Research and Practice in Intellectual and Developmental Disabilities* 46, 46.

[12] M Donnelly, 'Support Relationships in Law: Framing, Fictions and the Responsive State' in M Donnelly, R Harding, and E Taşcıoğlu (eds), *Supporting Legal Capacity in Socio-Legal Context* (Hart, 2022) 22.

[13] NA Kohn, JA Blumenthal, and AT Campbell, 'Supported Decision-Making: A Viable Alternative to Guardianship?' (2013) 117(4) *Penn State Law Review* 1111, 1114.

part whether they can be substantiated on the basis of the existing scientific knowledge about legal capacity. I assess the psychological assumptions behind the theoretical model of supported decision-making and describe whether, as a conceptual matter, these lead to any advantages compared to guardianship.

5.1. WHAT IS SUPPORTED DECISION-MAKING?

Supported decision-making is an elusive concept.[14] Although the term is widely used, it has so far not been authoritatively defined in international law.[15] Various authors have offered their own definitions in the legal literature, usually by contrasting it to guardianship.[16] In the narrowest sense, supported decision-making can be understood as a form of assistance to the disabled person that does not involve the transfer of legal decision-making power from the disabled person to the person assisting her.[17] The core feature is the support provided to exercise legal capacity:[18] according to one definition, supported decision-making is 'the process whereby a vulnerable person is enabled to make and communicate decisions with respect to personal care or his or her property and in which advice, support or assistance is provided to the vulnerable person by members of his or her support network'.[19]

A large variety of legal institutions can fit this vague description; it is therefore common to talk about supported decision-making models in the plural.[20] Some forms of supported decision-making are purely informal, while others are official and are recognised by the legal system; in the latter case, the supporting relationship can be established by a private contract[21] or by court appointment.[22] Many authors emphasise the voluntary nature of supported decision-making – a

[14] C Sinclair, J Bajic-Smith, M Gresham, M Blake, RS Bucks, S Field, JM Clayton, H Radoslovich, M Agar, and S Kurrle, S., 'Professionals' views and experiences in supporting decision-making involvement for people living with dementia' (2021) 20(1) *Dementia* 84, 85.

[15] Carney, 'Clarifying, Operationalising, and Evaluating Supported Decision Making' 46.

[16] Salzman, 'Guardianship for persons with mental illness' 306; RD Dinerstein, 'Implementing Legal Capacity Under Article 12 of the UN Convention on the Rights of Persons with Disabilities: The Difficult Road From Guardianship to Supported Decision-Making' (2012) 19 *Human Rights Brief* 4; Gordon, 'The Emergence of Assisted (Supported) Decision-Making in the Canadian Law' 68; M Bach, 'Supported Decision Making under Article 12 of the UN Convention on the Rights of Persons with Disabilities', Presentation to the Conference on Legal Capacity and Supported Decision Making, Athlone, Ireland (3 November 2007); Arstein-Kerslake, *Restoring Voice*; L Series, 'Relationships, Autonomy and Legal Capacity: Mental Capacity and Support Paradigms' (2015) 40 *International Journal of Psychiatry* 80, 85.

[17] Carney, 'Guardianship, Citizenship' 3.

[18] P Gooding, 'Supported Decision-Making: A Rights-Based Disability Concept and its Implications for Mental Health Law' (2013) 20(3) *Psychiatry, Psychology and Law* 431, 434.

[19] The Vulnerable Persons Living with a Mental Disability Act, CCSM c V90 (Manitoba, Canada).

[20] Dinerstein, 'Implementing Legal Capacity Under Article 12' 4.

[21] A Peterson, J Karlawish, and E Largent, 'Supported Decision Making With People at the Margins of Autonomy' (2021) 21(11) *American Journal of Bioethics* 4, 14.

[22] Salzman, 'Guardianship for persons with mental illness' 307.

disabled person chooses her own supporter, they cannot be appointed against the supported person's will.[23] Supporters can be drawn from family, friends, peer support groups (for example, in the case of users of mental health services), personal assistance, and community support networks.[24]

Supported decision-making empowers the supported person in expressing her wishes, and gives these wishes legal effect.[25] It is based on recognising the disabled person's autonomy and the right to make decisions on an equal basis with others.[26] The supporter only helps the person to express her decisions through facilitating communication and understanding,[27] but the decision is made by the person with the disability herself, which then must be accepted by third parties.[28]

As mentioned above, these characteristics of supported decision-making have been developed in the academic literature. They are normative descriptions of how the institution should function, they are not based on empirical observations about how supporting relationships operate in real life.[29] The following part will, therefore, look at the developments of the concept in international and domestic law to analyse whether any clarity about the content of supported decision-making can be deduced from the legal sources.

5.1.1. The Emergence of Supported Decision-Making in International Law

Supported decision-making first appeared in the international arena during the negotiations of the Convention on the Rights of Persons with Disabilities.[30] Disability advocates proposed it as a solution that could replace guardianship and other forms of substituted decisions.[31] It was heavily debated during

[23] Salzman, 'Guardianship for persons with mental illness' 306.

[24] Dinerstein, 'Implementing Legal Capacity Under Article 12' 4.

[25] Gooding 'Supported Decision-Making' 434.

[26] M Bach, 'Securing Self-Determination: Building the Agenda in Canada', TASH Newsletter (1998) 3.

[27] ibid, 5.

[28] M Rioux, J Gilmour, and N Angel, 'Negotiating capacity: legally constructed entitlement and protection' in B McSherry and I Freckelton (eds), *Coercive care: rights, law and policy* (Routledge, 2013) 51, 70.

[29] Kohn, Blumenthal, Campbell, 'Supported Decision-Making' 1128.

[30] Dinerstein, 'Implementing Legal Capacity Under Article 12' 7.

[31] Wildeman, 'Protecting Rights and Building Capacities' 56; CJ Sundram, 'A Discussion of Legal Capacity in the Draft Convention on Disability', National Disability Authority, Dublin, Ireland (15 June 2006), 15; S Trömel, 'A Personal Perspective on the Drafting History of the United Nations Convention on the Rights of Persons with Disabilities' in O M Arnadóttir and G Quinn (eds), *The United Nations Convention on the Rights of Persons with Disabilities: European and Scandinavian Perspectives* (Martinus Nijhoff, 2009) 115; D Nandini, J Bickenbach, and G Stucki, 'Moving towards substituted or supported decision-making? Article 12 of the Convention on the Rights of Persons with Disabilities' (2011) 5 *Alter European Journal of Disability Research* 259.

the negotiations, and 'support' for decisions also appears in the final text of Article 12(3).[32]

The idea that equality of persons with disabilities requires supported decision-making had little precedent before the CRPD. The Council of Europe's Recommendation R(99)4 on the legal protection of incapable adults, adopted in 1999, does not mention it.[33] Nor do the earlier soft-law instruments of the United Nations, such as the Mental Illness Principles[34] or the Standard Rules on the Equalization of Opportunities for Persons with Disabilities.[35] The concept is, to date, entirely missing from the case law of the European Court of Human Rights,[36] the Inter-American Court of Human Rights[37] and the UN Human Rights Committee.[38] The international norms of the twentieth century are fully anchored in the paradigm of substituted decision-making. The only reference to supported decision-making in international law predating the adoption of the CRPD was the Montreal Declaration on Intellectual Disabilities from 2004, a non-binding document issued during the CRPD negotiation process.[39] The emergence of supported decision-making on the international level can thus clearly be connected to the CRPD and the participation of disability advocates during the negotiations.[40]

While the CRPD is not explicit about banning all forms of substituted decisions,[41] it, without doubt, obliges states to introduce supported decision-making to their legal order.[42] The CRPD Committee has criticised States Parties frequently for relying on guardianship, and recommended that they shift to providing support instead.[43] However, the CRPD does not define the term; in

[32] R Kayess and P French, 'Out of Darkness into Light? Introducing the Convention on the Rights of Persons with Disabilities' (2008) 8(1) *Human Rights Law Review* 1, 29.

[33] Council of Europe Committee of Ministers, Recommendation R(99)4 on the legal protection of incapable adults (February 23, 1999).

[34] Principles for the Protection of Persons with Mental Illness and the Improvement of Mental Health Care, UN General Assembly Resolution A/RES/46/119 (17 December 1991).

[35] Standard Rules on the Equalization of Opportunities for Persons with Disabilities, UN General Assembly Resolution A/RES/48/96 (4 March 1994).

[36] See recent leading case-law on guardianship referring to the CRPD, but not mentioning supported decision-making: *Shtukaturov v Russia* App no 44009/05 (ECtHR 27 March 2008); *Stanev v Bulgaria*, App no 36760/06 (ECtHR 17 January 2012); *Kiss v Hungary* App no 38832/06 (ECtHR 20 May 2010).

[37] No case dealing with guardianship and legal capacity has been decided by the Inter-American Court of Human Rights to date.

[38] No communication challenging guardianship and legal capacity has been decided by the Human Rights Committee to date.

[39] The Montreal Declaration on Intellectual Disabilities, Pan-American Health Organization and World Health Organization, Montreal, Canada (adopted 6 October 2004).

[40] Sundram, 'A Discussion of Legal Capacity' 15.

[41] Dhanda, 'Legal Capacity in the Disability Rights Convention' 437.

[42] Even skeptical views as to the scope of this obligation accept that the obligation exists; see Carney, 'Guardianship, Citizenship' 8.

[43] See, for example, the Committee's recommendations to Australia (Concluding observations on the initial report of Australia, CRPD/C/AUS/CO/1, 21 October 2013) § 25, Argentina (Concluding observations on the initial report of Argentina, CRPD/C/ARG/CO/1, 8 October 2012) § 20,

its General Comment No. 1 on Article 12 of the CRPD, the Committee reiterated that support 'is a broad term that encompasses both informal and formal support arrangements, of varying types and intensity'.[44] Some States Parties to the CRPD argued that guardianship itself constitutes support within the meaning of Article 12.[45] This interpretation was rejected by the CRPD Committee, but the Committee did not offer an alternative positive definition of support.

5.1.2. Supported Decision-Making in Domestic Laws

If supported decision-making had not had a precedent in earlier international instruments, its origins must be found elsewhere. The countries often referred to as having had supported decision-making in their laws at the time of drafting the CRPD are Canada, Sweden and Germany;[46] it therefore seems a sensible suggestion that disability advocates arguing for supported decision-making during the CRPD negotiations were relying on these countries for inspiration. Indeed, the advocacy documents of disabled people's organisations refer to Canada as an, and often the only, example where supported decision-making exists.[47] According to Sundram, it was the Canadian Association for Community Living's representative who first introduced the concept during the negotiations.[48]

Hungary (Concluding observations on the initial periodic report of Hungary, CRPD/C/HUN/CO/1, 22 October 2012) § 26, and Spain (Concluding observations of the Committee on the Rights of Persons with Disabilities – Spain, CRPD/C/ESP/CO/1) § 34.

[44] UN Committee on the Rights of Persons with Disabilities, General comment No. 1 (2014) – Article 12: Equal recognition before the law, Committee on the Rights of Persons with Disabilities, CRPD/C/GC/1(19 May 2014) § 17.

[45] See, for example, the country report of Spain: Committee on the Rights of Persons with Disabilities, Initial reports submitted by States parties in accordance with article 35 of the Convention: Spain, CRPD/C/ESP/1 (5 October 2010) § 53.

[46] When describing supported decision-making in Canada, Gordon points to the Swedish origins of the concept: Gordon, 'The Emergence of Assisted (Supported) Decision-Making in the Canadian Law' 63. Herr describes Sweden and Germany as countries with alternatives to guardianship, although not using the term supported decision-making: SS Herr, 'Self Determination, Autonomy, and Alternatives for Guardianship' in SS Herr, LO Gostin, and HH Koh (eds), *The Human Rights of Persons with Intellectual Disabilities* (Oxford University Press, 2003) 429; Hoffman and Könczei argue that supported decision-making was adopted in Hungary from German law: I Hoffman and G Konczei, 'Legal Regulations Relating to the Passive and Active Legal Capacity of Persons with Intellectual and Psychosocial Disabilities in Light of the Convention on the Rights' (2010) 33 *Loyola of Los Angeles International and Comparative Law* Review 143, 168; N Devi, J Bickenbach and G Stucki, 'Moving towards substituted or supported decision-making? Article 12 of the Convention on the Rights of Persons with Disabilities' (2011) *ALTER, 5 European Journal of Disability Research* 259, 255; M Keys, 'Legal Capacity Law Reform in Europe: An Urgent Challenge' in G Quinn and L Waddington (eds), *European Yearbook of Disability Law 65* (Intersentia, 2009) 86; Kohn, Blumenthal, and Campbell, 'Supported Decision-Making' 1124; I Bantekas, 'Mental and Intellectual Capacity and Contractual Freedom: Assistive Decision-Making Matters' (2023) 21(2) *Seattle Journal for Social Justice* 569, 584; Arstein-Kerslake, *Restoring Voice to People (2017)* 210.

[47] Mental Disability Advocacy Centre (MDAC), *Legal Capacity in Europe*, 26.

[48] Sundram, 'A Discussion of Legal Capacity' 15.

The only legal journal article predating the CRPD negotiations describing supported decision-making is Robert Gordon's seminal 'Emergence of supported decision-making in Canada'.[49] According to Gordon, supported decision-making appeared in Canada through the advocacy of disability advocates, first articulated in the Canadian Association for Community Living's 1992 report on alternatives to guardianship.[50] The idea was based on earlier experiences of Scandinavian countries, particularly Sweden.[51] The Swedish model of normalisation of the lives of persons with disabilities was studied and spread in Canada through the work of Wolf Wolfensberger[52] and relied on by Canadians advocating for guardianship reform. It led to the creation of a new legal institution, different from the Swedish original.

Supported decision-making appeared in Canadian law in three main ways, according to Gordon: as a court-ordered alternative to guardianship, as a legislatively defined alternative to guardianship, and as an undefined alternative to guardianship.[53] One of the leading cases from the early period was *re: Koch*, in which the court refused to place the applicant under guardianship on the basis that if she is able to manage her affairs with support, she should not lose her legal capacity.[54] At the time of the CRPD negotiations, several provinces had adopted legislation recognising supported decision-making, such as the Representation Agreement Act in British Columbia, the Vulnerable Persons Living with a Mental Disability Act in Manitoba, the Dependent Adults Act in Saskatchewan, and the Substitute Decision Making Act in Ontario.[55]

From these models, the British Columbian was the most commonly cited by advocates as an example of a support model adopted by the CRPD.[56] However, the Canadian example differs from the description of supported decision-making offered above in important respects. According to the British Columbia Representation Agreement Act, a person with a disability can authorise another person to act on her behalf.[57] The decisions are thus legally expressed by the

[49] Gordon, 'The Emergence of Assisted (Supported) Decision-Making in the Canadian Law' 65.

[50] Canadian Association for Community Living (CACL), Report of the Task Force on Alternatives to Guardianship (1992), cited in Gordon, 'The Emergence of Assisted (Supported) Decision-Making in the Canadian Law' 65.

[51] Gordon, 'The Emergence of Assisted (Supported) Decision-Making in the Canadian Law' 63.

[52] W Wolfensberger, *The principle of normalization in human services* (Downsview, National Association for Mental Retardation, 1972).

[53] Gordon, 'The Emergence of Assisted (Supported) Decision-Making in the Canadian Law' 65.

[54] Rioux, Gilmour, and Angel, 'Negotiating capacity: legally constructed entitlement and protection' 70.

[55] M Bach, 'Overview of the Supported Decision-Making Model and Legal Provisions in Canada', Include 1/2007, Inclusion Europe Newsletter (2007).

[56] NA Kohn, JA Blumenthal, 'A critical assessment of supported decision-making for persons aging with intellectual disabilities' (2014) 7 *Disability and Health Journal* S40; SA Crane, 'Is Guardianship Reform Enough? Next Steps in Policy Reforms to Promote Self-Determination among People with Disabilities' (2015) 8 *Journal of International Aging Law and Policy* 177, 195; Bach and Kerzner, 'A New Paradigm' 34.

[57] Representation Agreement Act, [RSBC 1996] CHAPTER 405, § 7(1).

representative, who is under a duty to consult with the represented person 'to the extent reasonable' and to execute her wishes 'if it is reasonable to do so'.[58] The legal powers of the representative are thus not significantly different from that of guardians, who are often also under a similar duty to consult the represented person to establish her wishes.[59] Also, while the represented person does not lose her legal capacity and is thus able to enter into transactions on her own, in some situations, if she fails to consult with her representative, her contracts can be declared void on this ground.[60] These described features make the British Columbian law similar to a limited form of guardianship.

Similar conclusions can be reached by examining the other two countries besides Canada that had also experimented with alternatives to guardianship before the adoption of the CRPD. Sweden adopted a new legal institution arguably based on support already in 1972, and so did Germany in 1991.[61] Although neither is named supported decision-making, they can be seen as a predecessor of the concept, and disability advocates frequently refer to them as such.[62]

The Swedish system consists of two institutions: administratorship and God Man (Good Man or Mentor).[63] The former is based on a court-appointed administrator to manage the disabled person's property, which are the classic features of guardianship.[64] While some claim that administratorship is different than guardianship because it does not lead to the represented person's disenfranchisement,[65] surely this difference in itself does not make it a different legal institution. The God Man, on the other hand, is based on appointing a mentor of the person's choosing, who is supposed to consult the represented person and execute his wishes. This obligation, however, is not absolute. The mentor can make independent decisions on behalf of the person in certain circumstances,[66] which makes this institution similar to substitute

[58] Representation Agreement Act, [RSBC 1996] CHAPTER 405, § 16(2).

[59] Provisions mandating consultation formally exist also in legislations where they are widely disregarded in practice; see, for example, the Hungarian Civil Code, Act no. IV of 1959 on the Civil Code of the Hungarian Republic, § 20/C, which unconditionally requires the guardian to consult the represented person; in practice, this provision is widely ignored by guardians, as reported in: Mental Disability Advocacy Centre (MDAC), *Guardianship and Human Rights in Hungary* (MDAC, 2007) 73.

[60] Gordon, 'The Emergence of Assisted (Supported) Decision-Making in the Canadian Law' 65.

[61] Herr, 'Self Determination' 429.

[62] Keys, 'Legal Capacity Law Reform in Europe'; Devi, Bickenbach, Stucki, 'Moving towards substituted or supported decision-making?' 255; Arstein-Kerslake, *Restoring Voice to People (2017)* 210; Bantekas, 'Mental and Intellectual Capacity and Contractual Freedom' 584.

[63] TF Montoya, 'Supported Decision-Making in Swedish Law – Is the "Good Man" a Good or Bad Guy in Light of the CRPD?', English translation of 'Unterstützte Entscheidungsfindung im schwedischen Recht – der "Gute Mann": Held oder Schurke im Licht der UN-BRK?" in M Zinkler, C Mahlke, R Marschner (eds), *Selbstbestimmung und Solidarität Unterstützte Entscheidungsfindung in der psychiatrischen Praxis* (Psychiatrie Verlag, 2019) 227.

[64] Herr, 'Self Determination' 435–36.

[65] ibid.

[66] T Mattsson, 'Autonomy, Capacity, and Vulnerability: Making Decisions on Social Services for Persons with Dementia in Sweden' in M Donnelly and R Harding, and E Taşçıoğlu (eds), *Supporting Legal Capacity in Socio-Legal Context* (Hart, 2022) 238.

decision-making.[67] Mentors acting in restrictive ways is not only a theoretical possibility – one author notes that complaints about mentors' actions had risen by 2007 compared to earlier periods.[68]

The German Betreung system is similar to the Swedish God Man.[69] Since 1992, formal judgments on incapacity are not needed for a representative's appointment.[70] Instead, the court can appoint a Betreuer to the person with a disability, who is assisting her in making her decisions.[71] However, the Betreuer can make decisions on behalf of the person if it is necessary.[72] Also, although the represented person can make decisions alone, without the support of the Betreuer, her decisions can be declared void by the courts.[73] The courts can also impose restrictions on her ability to make some types of decisions, called Einwilligungsvorbehalt (Reservation of consent), which is essentially partial incapacitation – in the affected areas, the Betreuer alone will make all decisions, acting like a (partial) guardian.[74]

5.1.3. The Ideal and Existing Models of Supported Decision-Making

The overview of the three models, which served as a reference for adopting supported decision-making in the CRPD, shows that, as a legal matter, they are different from the descriptions put forward in the literature – none of them conforms to the ideal model described by scholars and advocates. They have features that bring them close to guardianship or can also be characterised as co-decision-making procedures.[75] Of course, this is not to suggest that these legal institutions function the same way in practice as guardianship elsewhere – indeed, advocates relying on the experiences of these three countries during

[67] Montoya, 'Supported Decision-Making in Swedish Law' 230.

[68] K Grunewald, 'The Swedish System of Legal Capacity and Supported Decision Making Concerning Adults with Intellectual Disabilities', Inclusion Europe, Europe in Action, Citizen's Right for All, Warsaw (10–12 May 2007) 3.

[69] G Szmukler, 'The UN Convention on the Rights of Persons with Disabilities: 'Rights, will and preferences' in relation to mental health disabilities' (2017) 54 *International Journal of Law and Psychiatry* 90, 92.

[70] Herr, 'Self Determination' 435.

[71] T Henking and M Scholten, 'Respect for the Will and Preferences of People with Mental Disorders in German Law'. in: C Kong, J Coggon, P Cooper, M Dunn, and AR Keene (eds), *Capacity, Participation and Values in Comparative Legal Perspective* (Policy Press, 2023) 212.

[72] U Hellmann, 'Civil Rights for Everybody!' (2007) Include 1/2007, Inclusion Europe Newsletter, 11.

[73] German Civil Code – Bürgerliches Gesetzbuch (BGB) Federal Law Gazette [Bundesgesetzblatt] I page 42, 2909; 2003 I page 738, § 105.

[74] ibid, § 1903.

[75] For a discussion of co-decision-making procedures in Canada, see L Kerzner, 'Paving the way to Full Realization of the CRPD's Rights to Legal Capacity and Supported Decision-Making: A Canadian Perspective', Prepared for In From the Margins: New Foundations for Personhood and Legal Capacity in the 21st century (April 2011).

the CRPD negotiation process considered that there are important differences between them and guardianship.[76] From the available descriptions, they seem to be working very efficiently and are more respectful of disabled person's autonomy than traditional guardianship systems.[77] Instead, the above analysis only shows that differences between guardianship and the legal capacity systems of the three examined jurisdictions are not caused merely by the laws. There is a difference between how supported decision-making is described in theory and the way it is codified in British Columbia, Germany, and Sweden. If these countries were the inspiration for the introduction of supported decision-making into the CRPD and later in other countries, the sources of examples were the idealised descriptions of how these models operate in practice rather than the respective laws.[78]

Since the adoption of the CRPD, a number of countries have revised their guardianship legislation and have adopted less restrictive alternatives to guardianship.[79] Some of these attempts seem to be much closer to the theoretical definition of supported decision-making in that they do not transfer any decision-making powers to the supporter, for example, in Ireland,[80] Hungary,[81] and the Czech Republic.[82] Guardianship is retained for situations in which the supported person cannot make a decision, and it needs to be made on her behalf.[83] Legal reform in Latin America seems to have progressed the furthest,

[76] Devi, Bickenbach, Stucki, 'Moving towards substituted or supported decision-making?'.

[77] Herr, for example, notes how the proportions in Sweden have changed since the adoption of the God Man, see Herr, 'Self Determination' 435.

[78] For example, advocates have frequently relied on the Swedish, German and Canadian experience of supported decision-making in the course of legal reform in Hungary, Czech Republic, Slovakia, and Croatia. For Hungary, see: Guardianship reform coalition of 15 Hungarian organisations, 'A gondnoksági rendszer módosításának javasolt alapelvei' (22 June 2007) 3; for the Czech Republic, see: Liga lidských práv, 'Zásady pro poskytování asistence při rozhodování osobám s duševní poruchou' (2007) 5; for Slovakia, see: Združenie na pomoc ľuďom s mentálnym postihnitím (ZPMP), 'Osnova návrhu reformy opatrovníctva v Slovenskej republike' (2011) 3; for Croatia, see: Disability Rights Centre, 'Proposal for implementing Article 12 of the Convention on the Rights of Persons with Disabilities in Croatia' (9 February 2013) 24.

[79] M Domański and B Lackoroński, *Models of Implementation of Article 12 of the Convention on the Rights of Persons with Disabilities (CRPD); Private and Criminal Law Aspects* (Routledge, 2024); C Kong, J Coggon, P Cooper, M Dunn, and AR Keene, *Capacity, Participation and Values in Comparative Legal Perspective* (Policy Press, 2023).

[80] M Donnelly, 'Deciding in dementia: The possibilities and limits of supported decision-making' (2019) 66 *International Journal of Law and Psychiatry* 101466.

[81] J Fiala-Butora, 'The CRPD and legal capacity reform in Hungary: Compromise of what?' in C O'Mahoney and G Quinn (eds), *Disability Law and Policy – An Analysis of the UN Convention* (Clarus Press, 2017) 127.

[82] D Frintová, 'Implementation of Article 12 of the UN Convention on the Rights of Persons with Disabilities in the Czech Republic' in M Domański and B Lackoroński (eds), *Models of Implementation of Article 12 of the Convention on the Rights of Persons with Disabilities (CRPD); Private and Criminal Law Aspects* (Routledge, 2024) 145.

[83] For example, the Hungarian Civil Code of 2009 (Act no. CXX of 2009) § 2:22; the Czech Civil Code of 2012 (Act no. 89/2012 Col.) § 55.

with the lead of Peru, Colombia, Costa Rica, and Argentina.[84] Peru is sometimes especially appraised as having abolished guardianship and becoming compliant with the CRPD,[85] although these claims are disputed by other authors.[86] These newer proposals are influenced by the CRPD and theoretical writings on supported decision-making and are apparently going further in securing disabled persons' autonomy than the three original models predating the CRPD. However, the evaluation of these laws is not the aim of this book.

The above analysis shows that supported decision-making as a legal institution does not originate in the three models that served as an example during the CRPD negotiation process. Since there is no other real-life example the advocacy documents refer to, supported decision-making as described in the literature must originate in this literature itself. It is a theoretical model, which aims to prescribe normatively how the systems should operate.

This theoretical model of supported decision-making should serve as the basis for future analysis. There are more models described in the literature,[87] but they share some essential features:

1. The disabled person's decisions are accepted as valid by third parties;[88]
2. The relationship between the supporter and the supported person is based on trust; the supporter is chosen by the supporter, they cannot be appointed against the supported person's will;[89]
3. The supporter's role is only to facilitate the supported person's decision-making; the supporter cannot substitute the disabled person's decision with their own.[90]

These core features will constitute the ideal model of supported decision-making for the purposes of our analysis, to be later contrasted with a legal model. A fourth feature also appears in the literature, namely that support is available to all persons with disabilities, including those with the most severe disabilities.[91] That claim is not universally shared,[92] therefore, I will not analyse it here. I will return to it in chapter seven.

[84] P Marshall, P Vasquez, V Purin, and L Godoy, 'Are We Closing the Gap? Reforms to Legal Capacity in Latin America in Light of the Convention on the Rights of Persons with Disabilities' (2023) 56(1) *Vanderbilt Journal of Transnational Law* 119.

[85] A Martinez-Pujalte, 'Legal Capacity and Supported Decision-Making: Lessons from Some Recent Legal Reforms' (2019) 8(1) *Laws* 1.

[86] RAB Lazarte and RAC Caycho, 'Legal Capacity in Peruvian Law. Qualitative Analysis of Court Ruling of Restitution on Legal Capacity and Designation of a Support Person under the Framework of the Legislative Decree 1384' (2023) 44 *Revista de Derecho Privado* 15, 26; RAC Caycho, 'The flag of imagination: Peru's new reform on legal capacity for persons with intellectual and psychosocial disabilities and the need for new understandings in private law' (2020) 14 *Age of Human Rights Journal* 155, 169.

[87] Salzman, 'Guardianship for persons with mental illness' 306–307.

[88] Gooding 'Supported Decision-Making' 434.

[89] Donnelly, 'Support Relationships in Law: Framing, Fictions and the Responsive State'.

[90] Salzman, 'Guardianship for persons with mental illness' 306–307.

[91] Dhanda, 'Legal Capacity in the Disability Rights Convention' 445.

[92] For a range of opinions, see Carney, 'Guardianship, Citizenship' 4.

5.2. THE PSYCHOLOGICAL ASSUMPTIONS BEHIND SUPPORTED DECISION-MAKING

Since the ideal version of supported decision-making is a theoretical model for the purposes of our analysis, there is little evidence about how it works in real life.[93] Several of the claims on which it is based therefore cannot be backed up by empirical evidence. However, that does not mean that these claims cannot be verified by different methods. The following part analyses whether the most important assumptions behind supported decision-making as a theoretical model can be supported by the newest developments in psychology and the science of capacity assessments.

5.2.1. Interdependent Decision-Making

Supported decision-making rests on a simple idea: although persons with disabilities can have difficulties in making decisions alone, they are able to perform much better if they are supported.[94] This is common sense, but its implications for legal capacity are radical. Guardianship laws have failed to incorporate this basic idea. They are built on a false dichotomy of competent and non-competent individuals.[95] Non-disabled persons are considered capable decision-makers – their legal capacity and their psychological ability to make decisions cannot be questioned under the law.[96] Persons with disability, on the other hand, have legal capacity only if they possess the necessary mental capacity required by guardianship laws.[97] There is a cut-off point in the assessment of abilities, below which a person will be considered incompetent and will lose the right to make legally valid decisions.[98] Instead, another person will make that decision on her behalf.

According to theoretical descriptions of supported decision-making, persons with and without disabilities are not that different with regard to making

[93] Kohn, Blumenthal, Campbell, 'Supported Decision-Making' 1114; there are some empirical studies about supported decision-making: P Gooding, 'Psychiatrists' Perceptions of Supported Decision-Making: A Victorian Empirical Study' (2014) 22 *Psychiatry, Psychology and Law* 701; G Gombos, I Hoffman, G Könczei, Z Nagy, and G Szabó, *A támogatott döntéshozatal elmélete és gyakorlata* (Eötvös Lóránd University Bárczi Gusztáv Faculty of Special Education, 2009); W Harrison, 'Representation Agreements in British Columbia: Who is Using Them and Why?' (M.A. thesis, Simon Fraser University 2008).

[94] Rioux, Gilmour, Angel, 'Negotiating capacity: legally constructed entitlement and protection' 71.

[95] J Moye and DC Marson, 'Assessment of decision-making capacity in older adults: An emerging area of practice and research' (2007) 62(1) *Journal of Gerontology: Psychological Sciences* P3, P3.

[96] W Martin, S Michalowsky, T Jütten, and M Burch, 'Achieving CRPD Compliance, Is the Mental Capacity Act of England and Wales Compatible with the UN CRPD? If not, what next?', Essex Autonomy Project, Essex University (2014).

[97] Salzman, 'Guardianship for persons with mental illness' 286.

[98] Bantekas, 'Mental and Intellectual Capacity and Contractual Freedom' 580.

decisions.[99] Many decisions a person makes in her life are not independent but interdependent – that is, they are made through interaction with the person's environment.[100] Autonomy itself should be understood as relational, as not being vested in the individual but in her social relations.[101] Support is an integral part of that environment. All persons utilise support, even persons without disabilities.[102] The more complicated the decision, the higher the stakes, or the more limited the person's knowledge about or experience in the given area, the more likely she is to seek advice from others.[103] An average person might not need help with her weekly shopping or deciding whether to open a new credit account. She, however, might have difficulties in choosing computers or cars and could require substantial advice from sales representatives or trusted persons. With complicated financial decisions, such as investing a large sum of money or deciding whether to sell her house and move to a nursing home, she might turn to professional advisors and involve her family in the decision-making process.[104] These are examples of support that do not result in questioning her legal capacity. The law presumes that she can decide what support to use, and is ultimately making the decision herself and is taking responsibility for it.

Persons with disabilities utilise support in a similar way.[105] The difference is the type of tasks they need support for: while an ordinary person might need help with buying a car but not for her daily shopping, a person with an intellectual disability might need it for both tasks. If her disability is severe and her skills minimal, she might need support with even more basic decisions, such as what to wear and what to eat. Nevertheless, the claim is that the nature of the support remains similar across all areas, both for persons with and without disabilities.[106]

Law reacts very differently to the decision-making difficulties of persons with disabilities. If they cannot make a decision alone, another person (i.e., a guardian) is appointed to make it on their behalf.[107] While non-disabled persons in need of support are considered fully capable, disabled individuals are legally incapacitated for the same reason. The law thus treats similar situations very differently, unjustly discriminating against persons with disabilities. Instead,

[99] Gordon, 'The Emergence of Assisted (Supported) Decision-Making in the Canadian Law' 65.

[100] G de Beco, *Disability in International Human Rights Law* (Oxford University Press, 2021) 101.

[101] C Mackenzie, 'The Importance of Relational Autonomy and Capabilities for an Ethics of Vulnerability' in C Mackenzie, W Rogers, and S Dodds (eds), *Vulnerability: New Essays in Ethics and Feminist Philosophy* (Oxford University Press, 2014) 30.

[102] M Hamilton, 'Supported Decision-making as an Alternative to Guardianship' (2023) *Trends in State Courts* 87, 89.

[103] Dhanda, 'Legal Capacity in the Disability Rights Convention' 445.

[104] Gordon, 'The Emergence of Assisted (Supported) Decision-Making in the Canadian Law' 65.

[105] de Beco, *Disability in International Human Rights Law*, 101.

[106] Gordon, 'The Emergence of Assisted (Supported) Decision-Making in the Canadian Law' 65.

[107] MB Kapp, 'Assessing Assessments of Decision-Making Capacity: A Few Legal Queries and Commentary on "Assessment of Decision-Making Capacity in Older Adults"' (2007) 62B(1) *Journal of Gerontology: Psychological Sciences* P12.

it should incorporate the higher level of support they need for the concept of autonomous decisions.[108] It should not lead to the loss of their legal capacity but to the recognition of the supported person's decisions as autonomous ones.

5.2.2. The Psychological Basis of Supported Decision-Making

Supported decision-making challenges the binary concept of legal capacity laws, according to which somebody is either competent or not competent to make a particular decision.[109] Instead, it proposes that persons with disabilities are able to make decisions with support, and in this respect, they are not different from the general population.[110] This claim does not rest on a fully developed psychological theory of how persons with disabilities utilise support. The psychological literature concerning disability concentrates on the question of incapacity, not on support.[111] It is thus difficult to do justice to the claim that all forms of support are similar, that there are no qualitative differences between supporting a person with a disability on daily hygiene and advising a non-disabled person on selling his property. However, the existing psychological literature on capacity assessments upholds some arguments in favour of supported decision-making.

Capacity assessment has recently emerged as a distinct field of research.[112] Its origins lie in the studies on the capacity of psychiatric patients to consent to treatment led by Paul Appelbaum in the early 1980s.[113] The development of standardised instruments to measure capacity in various areas, such as voting, consent to treatment, competency to stand trial, or managing finances, is an important contribution to this body of research. These instruments are much more reliable indicators of capacity than diagnosis or clinical judgment,[114] which was the primary method of assessment earlier and still is in many parts of the world.[115] As Thomas Grisso explains, earlier methods often led to the phenomenon known as 'diagnostic testimony', in which the person's capacity is presumed on the basis of the general characteristics of her particular diagnosis – if she is found to have schizophrenia, the clinician would consider on that basis alone that she is, for example, incompetent to stand for trial.[116] Empirical research discovered that 22 out of 23 known pitfalls and misunderstandings

[108] Dhanda, 'Legal Capacity in the Disability Rights Convention' 445.

[109] Moye and Marson, 'Assessment of decision-making capacity in older adults' P3.

[110] Gordon, 'The Emergence of Assisted (Supported) Decision-Making in the Canadian Law' 65.

[111] KC Glass, 'Refining definitions and devising instruments: Two decades of assessing mental competence' (1997) 20 *International Journal of Law and Psychiatry* 5.

[112] Moye and Marson, 'Assessment of decision-making capacity in older adults' P4.

[113] PS Appelbaum, SA Mirkin, and AL Bateman, 'Empirical assessment of competency to consent to psychiatric hospitalization' (1981) 138 *American Journal of Psychiatry* 1170.

[114] T Grisso, *Evaluating Competencies: Forensic Assessments and Instruments,* Perspectives in Law and Psychology 16 (Kluwer Academic Plenum Publishers, 2nd Edition, 2003) 12.

[115] Moye and Marson, 'Assessment of decision-making capacity in older adults' P4.

[116] Grisso, *Evaluating Competencies*, 12.

are 'common' among professionals conducting capacity assessments.[117] This is confounded by the fact that in many jurisdictions, capacity assessments are conducted only by psychiatrists, not relying on psychological expertise.[118]

The Macarthur studies conducted by Appelbaum and Grisso are among the most well-known and authoritative studies on capacity assessments. Grisso provides a comprehensive summary of them and the most developed, state-of-the-art capacity assessment tools in his *Evaluating Competencies: Forensic Assessments and Instruments*.[119] Reading the descriptions of tools most relevant for guardianship (competence to decide on property matters and care of the person) with a critical eye, it appears that capacity assessments do not incorporate some crucial insights of supported decision-making: the overreliance on abstract thinking for evaluations, the existence of other dimensions of intelligence, the notion of support, and the relationship between legal and clinical incompetence. I will address these in turn.

5.2.2.1. Abstract Thinking and Context

Capacity assessments are based on abstract thinking. They are conducted in the form of interviews: the disabled person has to explain how she does certain things, how she makes certain decisions. The assessment is a set of questions that she needs to answer.[120]

However, there is a difference between being able to do certain things and being able to explain in the abstract how one does them. Many people who are able to do the latter cannot do the former. As explained by Allen Buchanan and Dan Brock, a lot depends on the context in which capacity is exercised: a person may be able to make a decision about treatment if she is asked about it in her home by her relatives whom she trusts and may be found incompetent to perform the same task in a hospital responding to the doctor, if the place and the person are unfamiliar to her.[121] Guardianship proceedings provide many examples of persons who were able to cook, shop, clean themselves, etc., but failed to explain to the doctor or in the courtroom how they do these things.[122] The latter requires a higher standard of competence.

[117] L Ganzini, W Nelson, and A Derse, 'Pitfalls in Assessment of Decision-Making Capacity' (2003) 44(3) *Psychosomatics* 237.

[118] SE Rothke, GJ Demakis, and HM Amsbaugh, 'State statutes regarding the role of psychologists in performing capacity evaluations for guardianship determinations' (2019) 50(4) *Professional Psychology: Research and Practice* 228.

[119] Grisso, *Evaluating Competencies.*

[120] For an overview of assessment tools, see Grisso, *Evaluating Competencies.*

[121] AE Buchanan and DW Brock, *Deciding For Others: The Ethics of Surrogate Decision Making* (Cambridge University Press, 1989) 20.

[122] This observation is based on my practice as an attorney in guardianship proceedings. I have been representing clients in guardianship proceedings since 2004.

5.2.2.2. *Logical/Linguistic Intelligence*

Howard Gardner's theory of multiple intelligences provides another insight into the deficiencies of assessment tools.[123] Gardner argues that intelligence is not one-dimensional, it cannot be measured on a single axis. Instead, people use a variety of skills or 'intelligences' to solve problems, to make decisions. He originally listed seven such intelligences,[124] later expanding the list.[125] A person's abilities can vary: she can have very high logical intelligence, low musical intelligence, and average spatial intelligence, or the other way round. Western culture emphasises logical and linguistic intelligences to the detriment of others.[126] The IQ tests used for assessing children's educational potential almost exclusively measure logical and linguistic skills and, therefore, provide a very limited understanding of 'intelligence'.[127]

Capacity assessments also measure logical and linguistic intelligence to the detriment of other forms of decision-making skills.[128] These are the areas in which persons with some types of disabilities have, by definition, lower skills.[129] However, this only means that they will do poorly on the assessment, not that they have a lower comprehensive 'intelligence' in the Gardnerian sense. They might use other skills to perform tasks that the average person would approach rationally.[130]

Gardner did not apply his theory to persons with disabilities. It will therefore be a task for future researchers to show how exactly persons with disabilities can utilise other intelligences to solve tasks. One example can be the use of interpersonal skills.[131] One of the reasons for incapacitating persons with disabilities is

[123] H Gardner, *Frames of Mind. The Theory of Multiple Intelligences,* 10th edn (Basic Books Publisher, 1993).

[124] These are: 1. Linguistic, 2. Musical, 3. Logical-mathematical, 4. Spatial (recognising special dimension of objects, for drawing, orientation, map-reading,) – artists, designers, architects, 5. Bodily-kinesthetic (dancing, sports, acting, surgeons, soldiers), 6. Personal intelligences-intrapersonal, 7. Personal intelligences-interpersonal, see in: Gardner, *Frames of Mind.*

[125] These are: Naturalist, Spiritual, Existential, Moral intelligences; see in: Gardner, *Frames of Mind.*

[126] D O'Connor, J Braun, N Marriette, and K Purser, 'Assessing mental capacity in the context of abuse and neglect: A relational lens' (2024) 97 *International Journal of Law and Psychiatry.*

[127] LL Cavalli-Sforza, *The Great Human Diasporas: the history of diversity and evolution* (Perseus Books, 1995) 270.

[128] G Kelemen, 'A fogyatékosság jelensége a pszichiátriában' in P Zászkaliczky and T Verdes (eds), *Tágabb értelemben vett gyógypedagógia* (ELTE Eötvös Kiadó, 2004) 135.

[129] S O'Keeffe, 'Functional Capacity Assessments by Healthcare Professionals: Problems and Mitigating Strategies' in M. Donnelly, R. Harding, and E. Taşcıoğlu (eds), *Supporting Legal Capacity in Socio-Legal Context* (Hart, 2022) 79.

[130] L Badenhoop, S Baisch, S Penger, and J Haberstroh, 'The Role of Different Aspects of Communication Behavior in the Assessment of Capacity to Consent' (2023) 36(4) *GeroPsych: The Journal of Gerontopsychology and Geriatric Psychiatry* 227, 227.

[131] U Neisser, G Boodoo, TJ Bouchard, AW Boykin, N Brody, SJ Ceci, DF Halpern, JC Loehlin, R Perloff, RJ Sternberg, and S Urbina, *Intelligence: Knowns and Unknowns* (1996) 51 American Psychologist 77, 79.

that they are thought to be susceptible to abuse by others.[132] Interpersonal skills are one of Gardner's intelligences. There is no reason why a person with low linguistic and logical skills could not be a good judge of character, who could tell better than most if somebody wants to trick her or harm her in a different way.[133] Perhaps a particular person with a disability has very low interpersonal skills and is in greater danger of abuse than others.[134] That, however, cannot be established by an assessment that concentrates only on her logical and linguistic intelligence, as capacity assessments currently do.[135]

5.2.2.3. *No Support*

Capacity assessments are based on a binary conception of competence/incompetence.[136] Everybody ends up in one of these two categories. Of course, there are persons in the grey zone between the two who cannot be assigned with sufficient precision to any. They are, however, not a qualitatively different category, it is just uncertain as to which of the two categories they belong.[137] Therefore, everybody is tested on whether they can make decisions alone.[138] For decisions made with help, points are subtracted.[139]

However, according to the theory of interdependent decision-making that approach is incorrect.[140] Persons who can make decisions with support are not qualitatively different from those who do not need help. The dichotomy of competence was also challenged in the psychological literature. Kapp argues that the dichotomy rests on the dubious proposition that for every decision, there is one decision-maker: either the person with a disability or a substitute decision-maker.[141] However, many decisions can be made with the informal input of family and friends.[142] If decisions are indeed shared in this way, according to Kapp, further studies will need to develop tools about how to take this support into account in assessing capacity.[143]

[132] Moye and Marson, 'Assessment of decision-making capacity in older adults' P8.

[133] D O'Connor, J Braun, N Marriette, and K Purser, 'Assessing mental capacity in the context of abuse and neglect: A relational lens' (2024) 97 *International Journal of Law and Psychiatry* 4.

[134] Bantekas, 'Mental and Intellectual Capacity and Contractual Freedom' 586.

[135] Kelemen, 'A fogyatékosság jelensége a pszichiátriában' 131.

[136] Moye and Marson, 'Assessment of decision-making capacity in older adults' P3.

[137] Hurme and Appelbaum talk about the gray zone between competent and incompetent persons; see in SB Hurme and PS Appelbaum, 'Defining and Assessing Capacity to Vote: The Effect of Mental Impairment on the Rights of Voters' (2007) 38 *McGeorge Law Review* 931, 962.

[138] Kapp, 'Assessing Assessments of Decision-Making Capacity' P12.

[139] Grisso, *Evaluating Competencies*, 335.

[140] Gordon, 'The Emergence of Assisted (Supported) Decision-Making in the Canadian Law' 65.

[141] Kapp, 'Assessing Assessments of Decision-Making Capacity' P12.

[142] ibid.

[143] ibid, P13.

5.2.2.4. *Legal and Clinical Incompetence*

Grisso emphasises the difference between a clinical and judicial finding of incompetence.[144] The legal response is not determined by the clinical assessment itself.[145] Whether a person needs to be incapacitated is a different question from whether she is psychologically incompetent. However, the clinical and legal findings seem to be circular.[146] If the clinical assessment fails to recognise the value of support in making decisions, the law follows suit by assigning people into one of two categories: competent or incompetent. Since only these two legal categories exist, the clinical assessments are concerned only with them.

This circularity can be changed if the law introduces a new category. Indeed, this proposal seems to be well-founded, based on the findings above. Capacity assessments do not recognise the full skillset of persons with disabilities, they penalise them for the support they make use of, and expect them to meet a higher threshold than necessary to perform a certain task. In this respect, they are treated unfairly compared to non-disabled persons, who do not have to undergo a similar assessment.

The conclusion of the above analysis is not that capacity assessments are unreasonable but instead that they are deficient in a certain way. A different legal response to the need for support, distinct from the current incapacitation, is therefore worth exploring. Unfortunately, psychological studies of how persons with disabilities can make decisions with and without support are few.[147] More research in this area could be very beneficial for the development of our understanding of supported decision-making, as has been noted by others.[148] However, a change in legal capacity laws is not conditioned on such research; the existing knowledge is sufficient for considering and exploring alternatives. Indeed, as the circularity between the legal and clinical understanding of incapacity highlights, the proliferation of supported decision-making as a legal category would most likely lead to more studies into how persons with disabilities utilise support.[149] Deferring the establishment of supported decision-making as a legal category would hinder the conduct of empirical analysis about its use in practice.

[144] Grisso, *Evaluating Competencies*, 310; see also Moye and Marson, 'Assessment of decision-making capacity in older adults' P18–P19.

[145] LA Schaefer, and TJ Farrer, *A Casebook of Mental Capacity in US Legislation. Assessment and Legal Commentary* (Routledge, 2022) 4.

[146] Kapp, 'Assessing Assessments of Decision-Making Capacity' P13.

[147] Kohn and Blumenthal, 'A critical assessment of supported decision-making for persons aging with intellectual disabilities' S42.

[148] Kohn, Blumenthal, Campbell, 'Supported Decision-Making' 1114.

[149] E Flynn, A Arstein-Kerslake, C de Bhailís, and ML Serra, *Global Perspectives on Legal Capacity Reform Our Voices, Our Stories* (Routledge, 2019).

5.3. FORMS OF SUPPORTED DECISION-MAKING

Having established that existing capacity assessments and legal capacity laws fail to incorporate the support persons with disabilities receive to make their decisions, this part looks at what forms supported decision-making can take. Various forms of support can be derived from the theoretical model described above and supported decision-making as a term is used to describe all of them.[150] We have to limit the inquiry to supports that can serve as the basis for legal regulation. Supported decision-making as a term is used in three different ways: as the ordinary way of making decisions, as a principle of legal capacity laws, and as an alternative to guardianship.

5.3.1. Supported Decision-Making as the Natural Way of Making Decisions

In the broadest sense, supported decision-making is the ordinary way of how persons with and without disabilities make decisions.[151] It is not a new invention, people have been utilising support since the dawn of time.[152] Persons with disabilities rely on informal support networks of their family, friends, caregivers and other trusted persons.[153] Currently this support is not recognised or regulated by law, neither in the case of disabled nor in the case of non-disabled persons.[154]

This broad understanding of supported decision-making highlights its organic development: it is not an artificial construct but a natural order of things.[155] It is, however, too vague for legislative purposes. It is difficult to imagine what recognising this support would mean and how it could replace guardianship. Informal, unregulated support nevertheless can have a role in the legal framework of supported decision-making:[156] in certain situations, courts can take natural support networks indirectly into account when deciding about the necessity of placing a person under guardianship.[157]

[150] Carney, 'Clarifying, Operationalising, and Evaluating Supported Decision Making' 46.

[151] Peterson, Karlawish, Largent, 'Supported Decision Making With People at the Margins of Autonomy' 15.

[152] Gordon, 'The Emergence of Assisted (Supported) Decision-Making in the Canadian Law' 65.

[153] Kapp, 'Assessing Assessments of Decision-Making Capacity' P12.

[154] de Beco, *Disability in International Human Rights Law*, 101.

[155] NA Kohn, 'Legislating Supported Decision-Making' (2021) 58 *Harvard Journal on Legislation* 313, 319.

[156] M Hamilton, 'Supported Decision-making as an Alternative to Guardianship' (2023) *Trends in State Courts* 87, 89.

[157] Gordon, 'The Emergence of Assisted (Supported) Decision-Making in the Canadian Law' 65.

5.3.2. Supported Decision-Making as a Principle

Supported decision-making can also be understood as a principle relevant to all types of decision-making processes, including substituted decision-making:[158] to the extent possible, one should help the disabled person formulate her own wishes and use these wishes as a starting point for making decisions.[159] If this principle were incorporated into guardianship laws, the guardian would have to establish first what the represented person's decision would be, before making their own.[160] The guardian is free to depart from the disabled person's decisions, but perhaps not without cause. This is the model adopted recently by the Mental Capacity Act of England and Wales[161] and the earlier German and Swedish legal capacity laws described above.[162]

A guardianship system that incorporated the support principle would be an improvement but still be far from supported decision-making as ordinarily understood. The idea that the guardian's decisions should be somehow constrained and that he should consult the represented person is not new in guardianship laws.[163] Notwithstanding the communication between the guardian and the represented person, the decision is nevertheless ultimately made by the guardian, who formally expresses it, for example, by signing the contract and also by taking responsibility for it.[164] In the case of disagreement between the guardian and the represented person, it is, therefore, common for the guardian's will to prevail, which is antithetical to the idea of supported decision-making.[165]

Also, as a practical matter, it is difficult to turn this principle into a legal obligation. It is often no doubt advantageous for the guardian to know what the represented person's wishes are.[166] However, in the case in which he is not interested, or when he already made up his mind, communication between them is a meaningless exercise, if it happens at all.[167] Court decisions and human rights reports provide ample examples of public guardians who make decisions

[158] GG Enck, 'Healthcare Decisions Are Always Supported Decisions' (2021) 21(11) *American Journal of Bioethics* 29.

[159] S-N Then, H Patrick, and N Smith, 'Reinforcing guardianship regimes through assisted decision-making: a Scottish perspective' (2014) *The Juridical Review* 263, 266.

[160] Kohn, 'Legislating Supported Decision-Making' 327.

[161] Martin, Michalowsky, Jütten, Burch, 'Achieving CRPD Compliance' 27.

[162] See chapter 5.1.2 above.

[163] See, for example, the Hungarian Civil Code, Act no. IV of 1959 on the Civil Code of the Hungarian Republic, § 20/C.

[164] AM McCarthy and D Howard, 'Supported Decision-Making: Non-Domination Rather than Mental Prosthesis' (2023) 14(3) *AJOB Neuroscience* 227, 228.

[165] In fact, it is typical for persons under guardianship not to have any legal remedy against their guardian's decisions; see A-M Callus, 'Removing obstacles to equal recognition for persons with intellectual disability: Taking exception to the way things are' (2018) *ALTER, 12 European Journal of Disability Research* 153, 163.

[166] PS Appelbaum and M Trachsel, 'The Doctrine of Informed Consent Doesn't Need Modification for Supported Decision Making' (2021) 21(11) *American Journal of Bioethics* 27, 29.

[167] Salzman, 'Guardianship for persons with mental illness' 291.

on behalf of persons whom they have not met before, despite that being a legal obligation.[168]

5.3.3. Supported Decision-Making as an Alternative to Guardianship

To explore how supported decision-making can be thought of as a legal institution, the role of the supporter has to be compared to that of the guardian. If a disabled person is faced with a decision she is unable to make alone, a guardian would make that decision on her behalf. A supporter, on the other hand, would only ensure that the person is able to make the decision. The supporter needs to explain the circumstances, the various options and their consequences and let the supported person decide. If the supporter does not agree with the decision, he still has to respect it. He cannot overrule it, contrary to the guardian, who substitutes the represented person's decision with his own.

The supporter's role is, therefore, to facilitate the decision-making process. The content of this facilitation is not set in law or theory, but we can contrast it with the breakdown of capacity as understood by guardianship laws. To make a competent decision, the person has to satisfy various criteria broken down into four or five categories:[169]

a) She has to understand information relevant to the decision
b) She has to understand what the available alternatives are
c) She has to understand what their consequences are
d) She has to be able to communicate a decision
e) She has to be able to maintain consistency and stick to the decision (that is, answer the same question similarly over time)

The supporter's role is to help with all these tasks, which could be classified into two main areas. One of them relates to assisting with communication. The supporter needs to ensure that the supported person receives information in a way she understands and that her decisions are correctly interpreted by the other contracting parties. Persons with disabilities can have difficulties communicating in an ordinary way, they might use methods that are hard to understand to persons unfamiliar with them.[170] Information in the usual formats might be inaccessible for them, they might need pictures or easy-to-read language to

[168] For a good example, see *Sýkora v the Czech Republic* App no 23419/07 (ECtHR 22 November 2012); the Mental Disability Advocacy Centre's report found two guardians responsible for 350 persons in one Hungarian institution, which makes meaningful communication between the guardians and represented persons impossible: Mental Disability Advocacy Centre (MDAC), *Guardianship and Human Rights in Hungary*, 73.

[169] O'Connor, Braun, Marriette, Purser, 'Assessing mental capacity in the context of abuse' 2.

[170] Badenhoop, Baisch, Penger, Haberstroh, 'The Role of Different Aspects of Communication' 228.

process it.[171] In the case of severe communication difficulties, it is hard for an outsider to differentiate between the incompetence to make a decision and the inability to communicate it.[172] A supporter can act essentially as a translator, breaking down communication barriers between the disabled person and her environment.[173] This is an important task, which would significantly enhance the exercise of capacity by persons who are incapacitated because others cannot communicate with them.[174] According to the communication theories of persons with severe disabilities, everybody communicates, even if only through the change of pace of their breathing, and it is society's task to recognise this communication.[175] The supporter can play a major role in making this happen.

Another crucial part of the supporter's role relates to ensuring that the disabled person has reasonable alternatives to choose from. That can only happen if the supporter knows what the various options and their consequences are. It is the supporter's duty to present these to her in order to avoid or curtail arbitrariness. If a disabled person wants to spend her money on comic books, cinema tickets, or something else which others would find unreasonable, a guardian can prevent that by overruling her wishes or simply by withholding money from her.[176] A supporter would only have to make sure that the supported person understands the consequences: she knows how much money she has and what she can and cannot afford to buy if she buys, for example, three cinema tickets a week. If the supported person still prefers the cinema over eating a nice meal, it is her choice.

To make this clear with another, more complicated example: critics of supported decision-making might object that some decisions have complicated financial consequences, which a person with a disability might not be able to comprehend. If she has to choose between living in her house or moving to an institution, she could prefer to live at home even though she might not afford it, or her standard of living might be much lower than in the institution. Therefore, if simply asked where she wants to live, she might not give an answer reflecting all the consequences – a guardian might be a better decision-maker because he would be able to comprehend the issue in its complexity.

[171] SN Skarsaune and HM Hanisch, 'Holding and Professional Care: On Self-Determination for Persons With Profound Intellectual and Multiple Disabilities' (2023) 48 (1) *Research and Practice for Persons with Severe Disabilities* 25, 27.

[172] G Quinn, 'An Ideas Paper', Eur. Foundation Centre, Seminar on Legal Capacity, Brussels (4 June 2009) 7.

[173] AJ Jackson, 'Between us: Facilitated decision-making in the relational experience of profound intellectual disability' (2023) 51(4) *Ethos* 370, 372.

[174] Flynn and A Arstein-Kerslake, 'The Support Model of Legal Capacity: Fact, Fiction, or Fantasy?' (2014) 31(1) *Berkeley Journal of International Law* 124, 131.

[175] Inclusion Europe, 'Key Elements of a System of Supported Decision-Making: Position Paper of Inclusion Europe' (Inclusion Europe, 2008).

[176] A large part of professional guardians' workload in Hungary consists of approving the spending and allocating money of the persons they represent; see Mental Disability Advocacy Centre (MDAC), *Guardianship and Human Rights in Hungary*, 74.

The problem with this example is that the disabled person's decision is separated from its consequences. The supporter's task is to make sure that the person is choosing between real alternatives and is aware of their implications. If the person cannot afford to live at home, this is not an option she can choose, and that is how it should be explained to her. If living at home is more expensive than in the institution, it should be made clear to her what her standard of living in one and the other place would be so that she can choose from these complex alternatives, not simply from the two places of abode. Or, perhaps other options should be explored, such as moving to a smaller house in the community with lower costs. The supporter should explore all the possible scenarios and see them in all their complexity. In that regard, his task is similar to what a guardian would do. However, the supporter then has to boil down all the complexity into a few realistic options and present them to the supported person in a way she can understand and be able to choose from.

Juxtaposing the role of the supporter and the guardian in exercising the disabled person's legal capacity allows us to identify what supported decision-making as a legal institution should be concerned with. Concentrating on the tasks necessary for making a competent decision, supported decision-making as an object of regulation can be separated from its other forms, which rely on a much broader understanding of the concept.

6

Supported Decision-Making as a Legal Institution

TO ENSURE THAT persons with disabilities can utilise support for making decisions similarly to non-disabled persons, the law has to incorporate that support into a framework of full legal capacity. That is a very different task than simply enacting the ideal model of supported decision-making into law. The aim of this chapter is to understand the trade-offs behind adopting supported decision-making as a legal institution.[1]

6.1. IDEAL v LEGAL FORMS OF SUPPORTED DECISION-MAKING

The ideal version of supported decision-making described earlier is normative: it explains how support works and how supporters should behave.[2] It was proposed in that form as a blueprint for legislation on supported decision-making.[3] That is surprising, given that it seems to be inappropriate as a source of legal regulation. Most proposals of supported decision-making are of this nature. They describe how supporters should behave in a specific situation.[4] This book addresses a different question: what general rules should govern the supporters' behaviour to operationalise the ideal model? The difference is small but important. States cannot be expected to achieve perfect outcomes in each case of supported decision-making situation. There are limits on what general

[1] M Donnelly, 'Deciding in dementia: The possibilities and limits of supported decision-making' (2019) 66 *International Journal of Law and Psychiatry* 101466, 4.

[2] NA Kohn, JA Blumenthal, AT Campbell, 'Supported Decision-Making: A Viable Alternative to Guardianship?' (2013) 117 *Penn State Law Review* 1111, 1128.

[3] T Minkowitz, 'Legal Capacity: Alternatives to Functional Capacity' in O'Mahoney, C and G Quinn (eds), Disability Law and Policy: An Analysis of the UN Convention (Clarus Press, 2017) 103, describes a proposal for a legal capacity law in India based on the wording of Article 12.

[4] T Minkowitz, 'The United Nations Convention on the Rights of Persons with Disabilities and the Right to Be Free from Nonconsensual Psychiatric Interventions' (2007) 34 *Syracuse Journal of International Law and Commerce* 405; A Dhanda, 'Legal Capacity in the Disability Rights Convention: Stranglehold of the Past or Lodestar for the Future?' (2007) 34 *Syracuse Journal of International Law and Commerce* 429; C Kong, *Mental Capacity in Relationship: Decision-Making, Dialogue, and Autonomy* (Cambridge, Cambridge University Press, 2017); E Flynn and A Arstein-Kerslake, 'Legislating personhood: realising the right to support in exercising legal capacity' (2014) 10(1) *International Journal of Law in Context* 81.

rules can achieve, what differences in expected behaviour they can enforce.[5] An elaborate framework distinguishing between permissible and impermissible influence in the abstract might therefore not be an adequate source of regulation if it cannot be implemented in practice.[6] States can only be required to adopt general rules that should strive to achieve the desired behaviour from supporters, but with the trade-offs characteristic of law, which is an imperfect tool.[7]

If the ideal version is enacted into law, it would require supporters to help supported persons make decisions and would detail the nature and rules of this support. It would mandate what supporters should take into account and what they should refrain from. It is difficult to see how this regulation in itself would achieve the required result. Support emanates from an intimate relationship between a person with a disability and her supporter(s).[8] If it works well, the law is irrelevant. However, if the supporter misunderstands his role or openly abuses it, the law is of no help either. There is no outside supervision over the supporters. An outside person cannot intervene in the intimate relationship between supporters and the supported person, as that would require second-guessing the quality of support and the decisions reached by it. Mandating such a review would defeat the whole purpose of supported decision-making since it would require disabled persons to justify their decisions to an outside body for approval. That is not how non-disabled persons make their decisions.

We can illustrate the shortcomings of such an approach by contrasting it with guardianship. Guardians are required to base their decisions on the represented person's best interests or some other similar standard.[9] As amply illustrated in the previous chapters, guardians often fail to meet their obligations.[10] Those who abuse their position are seldom held accountable.[11] Even though it is possible, it is very difficult to intervene in the relationship between a guardian and the person they represent. The fact that the law certifies somebody as legally incompetent and entrusts the guardian to represent her interests creates a massive imbalance of power between them. This imbalance makes it very hard, and in many legal systems impossible, for the disabled person to challenge her

[5] T Carney, 'Globalisation and Guardianship – Harmonisation or Postmodern Diversity?' (2001) 24 *International Journal of Law and Psychiatry* 95, 104.

[6] Flynn and Arstein-Kerslake, 'Legislating personhood' 98; Kong, *Mental Capacity in Relationship*, 230.

[7] V Perju, 'Constitutional Transplants, Borrowing, and Migrations' 2011, *Boston College Law School Faculty Papers* Paper 360, 36.

[8] M Donnelly, 'Support Relationships in Law: Framing, Fictions and the Responsive State' in M Donnelly, R Harding, and E Taşcıoğlu (eds), *Supporting Legal Capacity in Socio-Legal Context* (Oxford, Hart, 2022) 24.

[9] M Scholten and J Gather, 'Adverse consequences of article 12 of the UN Convention on the Rights of Persons with Disabilities for persons with mental disabilities and an alternative way forward' (2018) 44 *Journal of Medical Ethics* 226, 231.

[10] I Bantekas, 'Mental and Intellectual Capacity and Contractual Freedom: Assistive Decision-Making Matters' (2023) 21(2) *Seattle Journal for Social Justice* 569, 586.

[11] L Salzman, 'Guardianship for persons with mental illness – a legal and appropriate alternative?' (2011) 4 *Saint Louis University Journal Health Law & Policy* 279.

guardian's actions.[12] Automatic oversight by an outside body of all decisions would make the system very complicated and costly, with unsure prospects of improving the disabled person's position.

If the guardian were required to base his decisions on the represented person's wishes instead of the best interest standard, the situation would not improve.[13] Without oversight, we would still have no way of knowing which guardian is acting according to his duties and which is abusing his position.

The ideal version of supported decision-making suffers from the same problem: it lets malfunctioning supporters off the hook. It has no possibility of separating them from well-functioning supporters and of taking action against the former. The system may work better in practice than guardianship. Perhaps the proportion of abuses would be much lower than currently. That, however, would not be the result of the rules but of extra-legal factors.[14]

6.2. THE FUNCTIONS OF THE LEGAL REGULATION OF SUPPORTED DECISION-MAKING

To understand how legal regulation can establish a proper supporting framework, we cannot simply read the ideal version of supported decision-making as a legal blueprint. Instead, we have to look into the functions that guardianship currently fulfils, or should fulfil, in the legal order. I suggest how these functions could be achieved by an alternative legal framework based on the ideal version of supported decision-making. The aim is to explore the possible solutions and their advantages and disadvantages so that they can be compared with an ideal version of guardianship and their strengths and weaknesses evaluated in light of the values identified previously.

6.2.1. The Guardian's Right to be Present and to Access Information

To be able to give support, supporters have to be present at the time of concluding a legal transaction. This does not cause complications in informal settings, such as shopping or at the hairdresser. However, with more formalised transactions, the presence of third parties may ordinarily not be permitted.[15]

[12] A-M Callus, 'Removing obstacles to equal recognition for persons with intellectual disability: Taking exception to the way things are' (2018) *12 ALTER European Journal of Disability Research* 153, 163.

[13] N Devi, 'Supported Decision-Making and Personal Autonomy for Persons with Intellectual Disabilities: Article 12 of the UN Convention on the Rights of Persons with Disabilities' (2013) 41(4) *Journal of Law Medicine and Ethics* 792, 803.

[14] T Carney and D Tait, 'Adult Guardianship: Narrative Readings in the "Shadow" of the Law?' (1998) 21(2) *International Journal of Law and Psychiatry* 147, 149.

[15] RM Gordon, 'The Emergence of Assisted (Supported) Decision-Making in the Canadian Law of Adult Guardianship and Substitute Decision-Making' (2000) 23 *International Journal of Law and Psychiatry* 64.

A bank giving a loan, an estate agent selling a house, or a police officer inquiring about an incident might all raise concerns about a supporter's presence and his influencing the person with a disability with whom they want to deal directly. Some decisions and transactions also involve sensitive information to which a supporter might not have access. A doctor, for example, might refuse to disclose the patient's medical history to a supporter, which can be crucial to reaching a decision about a course of treatment.

The right of the supporter to be present and his right to access information are important reasons for formalising supported decision-making.[16] By certifying supporters, the law makes apparent to other persons what the supporters' rights and obligations are and why they are present in discussing transactions to which they are not a party.[17]

Some authors argue that certification is unnecessary to utilise supported decision-making,[18] and formalised supported decision-making can even have disadvantages[19] because it may increase the risk of abuse.[20] That can be true in some contexts, but certification nevertheless has the advantages described above, and courts are more likely to take formal agreements into account when deciding on guardianship. In any case, certification and informal support are not mutually exclusive. A person can utilise the aid from any number of informal supporters in areas where this is possible and rely on certified supporters in more formal contexts.

Guardianship fulfils similar essential functions of making clear where the guardian can be present and what information he can access.[21] Guardians are appointed by court or administrative proceedings, where the decision and the law clarify the areas in which they represent the disabled person, those in which they act together, and those that remain in the competence of the person herself. A similar appointment procedure can also be used for supporters, with a significant modification: if supported decision-making is based on a relationship of trust, no supporter can be appointed without the person's consent.[22] This means an agreement must be reached between the supporter and the supported person. The role of the appointing body is not to decide who the supporter will be but merely to certify to the public that a supporter has been validly chosen.

[16] S-N Then, H Patrick, and N Smith, 'Reinforcing guardianship regimes through assisted decision-making: a Scottish perspective' (2014) *The Juridical Review* 263, 269.

[17] A Peterson, J Karlawish, and E Largent, 'Supported Decision Making With People at the Margins of Autonomy' (2021) 21(11) *American Journal of Bioethics* 4, 6.

[18] NA Kohn, 'Realizing Supported Decision-Making: What It Does – and Does Not – Require' (2021) 21(11) *American Journal of Bioethics* 37, 38.

[19] Peterson, Karlawish, Largent, 'Supported Decision Making with People at the Margins' 1.

[20] MS Wright, 'Implementing Ethical and Legal Supported Decision Making: Some Unresolved Issues' (2021) 21(11) *American Journal of Bioethics* 40, 41.

[21] AR Keene, NB Kane, SYH Kim, GS Owen, 'Mental capacity – Why look for a paradigm shift?' (2023) 31(3) *Medical Law Review* 340, 346.

[22] C de Bhailís and E Flynn, 'Recognising legal capacity: commentary and analysis of Article 12 CRPD' (2017) 13(1) *International Journal of Law in Context* 6, 15.

As an effect of the certification, the supporter is recognised by law to support the person in various circumstances. This allows him access to situations to which a third party generally would not have access.[23] The certification also signals to the other parties of the transaction that they can trust the process, that they do not have to be afraid that the supporter's presence constitutes a defect of the transaction, which could lead to its annulment.

The process of appointing guardians allows screening out persons unfit for this role.[24] A similar function seems permissible for supported decision-making as well.[25] The certifying body could reject certain candidates, even though they are validly chosen by the supported person. Since supporters' rights and their possibility to abuse their position are much narrower compared to guardians, supporters should be rejected only on narrow grounds, such as a history of abuse of their position.

It is an interesting question whether certifying bodies should interfere with the quality of the agreement between the supporter and the supported person.[26] Bach and Kerzner propose that the threshold for capacity for this agreement should be very low: any indication of consent should be accepted as valid.[27] However, should the supporter be certified if the agreement is not confirmed before the certifying body or if consent is expressed in a form which only the supporter can interpret? At this point, it is sufficient to mention that some jurisdictions, such as Hungary, have optional but explicit provisions for the assessment of the capacity to choose one's supporters.[28] In British Columbia, the law requires a lower threshold of capacity specifically for appointing a supporter.[29] At the other end of the informality spectrum, supporters in India under the proposed legislation are appointed by a private agreement, which is later certified by an administrative body without contesting or assessing capacity.[30] Both approaches, and others in between, are thus possible.

6.2.2. The Role of Supporters

A guardian makes decisions on behalf of legally incapacitated persons. On the other hand, a supporter merely facilitates a supported person's own decisions.

[23] K Mackay, P McCusker, 'Adult safeguarding legislation: Navigating the borderlands between mental capacity, mental health and social care law and practice.' (2024) 94 *International Journal of Law and Psychiatry* 5.

[24] See, for example, Act no. IV of 1959 on the Civil Code of the Hungarian Republic, § 19/C.

[25] Act No. CXX of 2009 on the Civil Code of Hungary, § 2:18 (5).

[26] Donnelly, 'Support Relationships in Law' 24.

[27] M Bach and L Kerzner, 'A New Paradigm for Protecting Autonomy and the Right to Legal Capacity', paper prepared for the Law Commission of Ontario (2010) 48.

[28] Act No. CXX of 2009 on the Civil Code of Hungary, § 2:18 (1).

[29] Peterson, Karlawish, Largent, 'Supported Decision Making With People at the Margins of Autonomy' 14.

[30] Minkowitz, 'Legal Capacity: Alternatives to Functional Capacity' 103.

Commentators have raised the concern that the two might sometimes be different in name only.[31] They warn that support in practice can turn into substitution, which may lead to a new type of paternalism.[32]

Indeed, the conflation of support and substitution is inevitable if supporters have the right to express the supported person's decision. The Swedish God Man, the German Betreuer, and the person's chosen representative in British Columbia can all make legal transactions binding the disabled person.[33] In principle, they are only communicating and executing her decisions, but an outsider might not be able to tell whose will the decision represents.[34]

This uncertainty can be avoided if the supported person is required to express her own wishes herself. The supporter can help her formulate her decision, but only the supported person will communicate it to the other contracting parties. This is the norm adopted in Hungary[35] and the Czech Republic,[36] where guardianship was retained and is applicable to situations where the person cannot express their wish in a way that third parties would understand.

This solution conflicts with the ideal version of supported decision-making in an important way. It restricts the use of support to persons who are able to communicate a decision in a way that is intelligible to the other contracting parties. If their wishes can only be understood by the supporter, other persons learn about their content only through the supporter's interpretation. This allows the supporter to substitute his judgment for that of the supported person without other persons' knowledge.[37]

This problem plays out differently for various sub-groups of supported persons. Persons able to communicate a preference, but not in the required form, can be accommodated similarly to other persons with communication difficulties. For example, if selling a house requires a written contract, but the supported person is unable to write, witnesses can testify with their signature that she indeed expressed consent with the contract. If the supported person is unable to speak, persons experienced in her form of communication can help to interpret her wish.

The supporter can play a significant role in making the disabled person understood. However, he should not be the only one able to ascertain her wishes. If he

[31] Kohn, Blumenthal, and Campbell, 'Supported Decision-Making' 1114.

[32] P Skowron, 'Giving substance to 'the best interpretation of will and preferences' (2019) 62 *International Journal of Law and Psychiatry* 125, 129.

[33] See chapter 5.2.2 above.

[34] A Ward, 'Abolition of Guardianship? "Best Interests" versus "Best Interpretation"' (2015) 32 *Scots Law Times* 150, 153.

[35] Act No. CXX of 2009 on the Civil Code of Hungary, § 2:19 (2). This act never entered into force, as it was repealed by Act No. V. of 2013 on the Civil Code of Hungary, currently in force. The Civil Code of 2013 regulates the relationship between supporters and supported persons in § 2:38 (3) the same way as the Civil Code of 2009.

[36] Act No. 89/2012 Col. on the Civil Code of the Czech Republic, § 47 (2).

[37] L Barclay, 'Paternalism, Supported Decision-Making and Expressive Respect' (2024) 27(1) *Journal of Ethics and Social Philosophy* 121, 138.

is, he has the power to substitute his wish for that of the supported person, either consciously or by projecting his expectations into the person's communication.[38] From this perspective, the supporter is no different from a guardian.[39] To recall, the guardian can also respect the represented person's wishes and act according to them – indeed, no doubt some guardians sometimes do. What sets them apart from supporters is that guardians have the legal power to overrule the represented person's decision if they do not like it. If supporters are the only ones able to express what the disabled person's wish is, they gain a similar power.

Of course, how supporters and guardians act in practice depends on many other factors besides law. Perhaps it is perfectly reasonable for the Swedish legislator to allow the God Man to make transactions on behalf of the person they support because God Men tend not to abuse their powers. I would merely like to highlight a trade-off in enacting supported decision-making. If the law wants to ensure that support does not become substitution, only the supported person herself should be allowed to express her decisions, to make the formal act of consenting to a legal transaction. Persons with communication difficulties can be accommodated, but those who can be understood solely by their supporters are unfortunately left out. On the other hand, if these persons are included in the support framework, the law cannot differentiate between support and substitution. In either case, the legal framework falls short of the aspirations of the ideal version of supported decision-making.

6.2.3. Legal Certainty

Guardianship makes it possible for persons with diminished capacity to enter into valid legal transactions.[40] It allows other parties to conclude agreements with the guardian, whose legal capacity is uncontested.[41] In the absence of a guardian, other parties would have to transact with the disabled person instead, which carries a certain risk. The contract thus concluded could be declared null and void if the person is found not to have had the capacity to enter into it.[42] This incapacity defence protects the disabled person from being bound by obligations to which she could not have validly consented due to her lack of capacity at the time of concluding the agreement. The affected person herself can challenge the contract, or others can do that on her behalf. Contracting through a guardian

[38] L Series, 'Relationships, Autonomy and Legal Capacity: Mental Capacity and support Paradigms' (2015) 40 *International Journal of Law and Psychiatry* 80, 85.

[39] Ward, 'Abolition of Guardianship?' 153.

[40] Bantekas, 'Mental and Intellectual Capacity and Contractual Freedom' 570.

[41] M Domański and B Lackoroński, 'Comparative analysis of the transposition of Article 12 of the UN Convention on the Rights of Persons with Disabilities' in M Domański and B Lackoroński (eds), *Models of Implementation of Article 12 of the Convention on the Rights of Persons with Disabilities (CRPD); Private and Criminal Law Aspects* (Routledge, 2024) 600.

[42] See, for example, Act No. CXX of 2009 on the Civil Code of Hungary, § 2:23 and § 2:29.

avoids such risks, therefore it strengthens the agreement's legal certainty. If the guardian is acting within his legal powers, the agreement cannot be contested on the grounds of the represented person's lack of legal capacity.[43]

The legal certainty of transactions made with support is less clear. If supported decision-making aspired for the clarity of guardianship, the law could mandate that the supported person's decision is only valid if it is co-signed by her supporter.[44] That, however, would take away the disabled person's right to make decisions alone and would give supporters power to influence her decisions simply by withholding consent if they did not like the outcome. This is the logic of the German Einwilligungsvorbehalt and British Columbia's representation agreements, as explained in the previous chapter.[45] This is too close to the idea of guardianship and contrary to the principles on which supported decision-making is built.

If supporters' consent to transactions cannot be mandatory, the person with a disability is running the risk of making a decision which will harm her.[46] Some safeguards to correct the most serious mistakes are thus desirable. However, any possibility of overruling the disabled person's decisions, in addition to limiting the person's autonomy, also decreases the other party's legal certainty. As a result, a too widely construed safeguard can be a disservice to persons with a disability. If a transaction can be declared void on a large number of grounds, in a procedure initiated by a broad group of persons, it can discourage other parties from contracting with the supported person. Therefore, any safeguard mechanism chosen should carefully strike a balance between protecting the disabled person from abuse, respecting her autonomy, and protecting legal certainty.[47] Guardianship maximises both at the expense of suppressing the person's own decisions. Supported decision-making should also provide reasonable protection to these interests. Otherwise, it cannot be considered an effective alternative to it.

6.2.4. Protection from Harmful Decisions

Guardianship protects persons with diminished capacity from abuse by other parties. By making decisions on her behalf, the guardian ensures that the person

[43] Needless to say, the agreement also cannot be contested on the ground of the guardian's lack of legal capacity, as guardians have to be persons of full legal capacity. If the guardian loses his legal capacity, for example due to a sudden psychiatric episode, he loses his position as a guardian as well; see, for example, Act No. CXX of 2009 on the Civil Code of Hungary, § 2:33 (2)c).

[44] The Czech Civil Code of 2012, Act no. 89/2012 Col. on the Civil Code of the Czech Republic, § 47 (2) mentions this possibility, but it is optional, not mandatory – the contract is valid also without the supporter's signature.

[45] See chapter 5.1.2 above.

[46] A Arstein-Kerslake and E Flynn, 'The General Comment on Article 12 of the Convention on the Rights of Persons with Disabilities: a roadmap for equality before the law' (2016) 20(4) *The International Journal of Human Rights* 471, 482.

[47] Donnelly, 'Deciding in dementia' 4.

he represents does not enter into transactions which are not in her interest. This approach seriously limits the disabled person's right to make her own decisions.[48] Those can only prevail if the guardian agrees with them. If the guardian does not, he can overrule them.[49] It is possible that the guardian's decision will be less advantageous to the person than her own would be. The aim of guardianship is, therefore, not to achieve the best outcome for the disabled person. Instead, it safeguards her best interests as perceived by the guardian.[50] That, however, it does very effectively: no legal transaction of the represented person is valid without the guardian's consent,[51] and all those he consented to are. Guardianship, therefore, rests on the assumption that, overall, guardians' decisions are better and lead to less harm than the disabled persons' own decisions would be.

Supported decision-making values disabled persons' autonomy much more than guardianship. It accepts that persons with diminished capacity would have difficulty making decisions alone and that this could lead to their abuse by others.[52] However, it presumes that they are much better at making decisions with support. There seems to be a lot of wisdom in this thought. Many decisions are of a highly personal nature, which another person cannot substitute.[53] With regard to others, reasonable persons may disagree as to what serves a person's best interests, and there is no reason why the guardian's preferences should prevail over that of the represented person's wishes.[54] After all, everybody makes decisions in their life that could be regarded by outsiders as not in their interests, but the law does not intervene in their lives.[55] Why should it in the case of persons with disabilities? Even with regard to decisions that are clearly harmful to the person, there is value in making mistakes, taking responsibility and learning from them.[56] It is part of the natural development of decision-making skills, which is crucial for everybody. Disabled people should not be exempt from this experience – perhaps they need it even more than their non-disabled peers.[57]

Although the argument for valuing one's mistakes is powerful, it cannot be denied that some errors are particularly harmful. Persons with disabilities can and do fall prey to abuse by others, who take advantage of their diminished capacity and trick them into transactions that can cost them their homes or

[48] AM McCarthy and D Howard, 'Supported Decision-Making: Non-Domination Rather than Mental Prosthesis' (2023) 14(3) *AJOB Neuroscience* 227, 228.

[49] Act no. IV of 1959 on the Civil Code of the Hungarian Republic, § 15/A. (1).

[50] McCarthy and Howard, 'Supported Decision-Making: Non-Domination' 228.

[51] Obviously, the argument relates to areas where the person is declared legally incapable. In areas where her legal incapacity is intact, she can make decisions freely without the consent of the guardian.

[52] Flynn and Arstein-Kerslake, 'Legislating personhood' 96.

[53] MA Field and VA Sanchez, *Equal Treatment for People with Mental Retardation* (Harvard University Press, 1999) 158.

[54] Dhanda, 'Legal Capacity in the Disability Rights Convention' 436.

[55] P Gooding, 'Supported Decision-Making: A Rights-Based Disability Concept and its Implications for Mental Health Law' (2013) 20(3) *Psychiatry, Psychology and Law* 431, 440.

[56] Gordon, 'The Emergence of Assisted (Supported) Decision-Making in the Canadian Law' 63.

[57] Field and Sanchez, *Equal Treatment for People with Mental Retardation*, 18.

property.[58] It is hard to consider these events as valuable learning experiences. Can supported decision-making protect persons from these types of harmful decisions? To answer this question, I will consider separately harmful decisions benefitting others, decisions not benefitting anybody, and decisions benefitting the supporters.

6.2.4.1. Abuse by Others

Guardianship protects efficiently from abuse by others: the malevolent party would have to trick the guardian, a person of full legal capacity, to take advantage of the represented person. As explained, this has its disadvantages: by trying to protect the person from all possible harm, it denies her autonomy and sacrifices her potential to develop her skills by making mistakes. Overprotection can cause harm as well.

Supported decision-making, at first sight, seems to be incompatible with safeguards that are based on overruling a person's wishes. In this ideal understanding of supported decision-making, the only safeguard possible is the support itself.[59] That should ensure that persons do not enter into disadvantageous transactions. While some inevitably make harmful decisions, their number does not justify a departure from an absolute rule of respect to the disabled person's expressed wishes. This position, therefore, rests on the assumption that abuses will not be prevalent, and the harm caused by them will be lower than the advantage of maximising the autonomy of persons with disabilities.

However, this is not the only possible formulation of supported decision-making. Other strong proponents of supported decision-making admit that in some circumstances, intervention to overturn the person's decisions might be necessary. Anna Arstein-Kerslake suggests that if a decision harms a person, it will not be implemented.[60] She and Eilionóir Flynn propose that overturning decisions to protect from serious harm might be acceptable.[61] A similar approach is taken by Michael Bach and Lara Kerzner in the case of serious adverse effects.[62] Camilla Kong approaches the same problem from the perspective of abusive relationships and suggests interventions when relationships influencing decision-making deteriorate.[63] These are all valuable proposals and

[58] Bantekas, 'Mental and Intellectual Capacity and Contractual Freedom' 586.

[59] T Minkowitz, 'Abolishing Mental Health Laws to Comply with the Convention on the Rights of Persons with Disabilities' in B McSherry and P Weller (eds), *Rethinking Rights Based Mental Health Laws* (Hart, 2010) 156.

[60] A Arstein-Kerslake, *Restoring Voice to People with Cognitive Disabilities* (Cambridge University Press, 2017) 201.

[61] E Flynn and A Arstein-Kerslake, 'State intervention in the lives of people with disabilities: the case for a disability-neutral framework' (2017) 13(1) *International Journal of Law in Context* 39, 40.

[62] Bach and Kerzner, 'A New Paradigm' 133.

[63] Kong, *Mental Capacity in Relationship*.

good bases for developing norms, but their impact is difficult to assess without the rules necessary to operationalise them.[64]

I agree with Flynn and Arstein-Kerslake that any such safeguards must be disability-neutral, both in form and in their application, to be compliant with the CRPD.[65] However, contrary to some views, I do not believe that the person's decision must always be respected, and support is the only possible form of intervention.[66] That is a standard not applicable to anyone to my knowledge, and if it is chosen as the standard of equality under the CRPD, it subjects persons with disabilities to an unfair disadvantage. In my opinion, some of the assumptions inherent in the paradigm shift, as it is described by some authors, are flawed.[67] The imagined rational man, the standard to which persons with disabilities should aspire, is not, in fact, the basis of modern law.[68] It is criticised, quite rightly, by authors relying on a relational autonomy approach for how decisions are, in fact, made: they point out that while the imagined rational man is individualistic, decisions in real life are taken in a relational way.[69] I second that opinion, but the critique does not go far enough in that it does not challenge another assumption behind the rational man: that his decisions are always accepted by law as final and binding on him. Contrary to that view, law protects all victims[70] of fraud, error, deceit, duress, misguidance, abuse of position by another party, and other unfortunate situations in various ways, including by setting aside their decisions.[71] Persons with full legal capacity who fall victim to exploitation are protected by their expressed decisions being set aside in some circumstances. These mechanisms could be used to protect supported persons as well.

The Hungarian Civil Code of 2009 provides an interesting solution to protecting persons with diminished capacity through formally disability-neutral provisions. The wording of the general voidability clause for contracts was modified to include situations where the contract was entered into by one of the parties with the intention of taking advantage of the other's personal circumstances.[72] This is broad enough to include a person's lack of experience and adverse financial situation. The law contains a special procedural rule

[64] Kong, *Mental Capacity in Relationship*, 230.

[65] Flynn and Arstein-Kerslake, 'State intervention in the lives' 40; Arstein-Kerslake and Flynn, 'The General Comment on Article 12' 482.

[66] T Minkowitz, 'CRPD and transformative equality' (2017) 13(1) *International Journal of Law in Context* 77, 82.

[67] Dhanda, 'Legal Capacity in the Disability Rights Convention' 448.

[68] G Quinn and A Rekas-Rosalbo, 'Civil Death: rethinking personhood for persons with a disability' (2019) 56 *Irish Jurist* 286, 292.

[69] JE Lord and MA Stein, 'Contingent participation and coercive care: feminist and communitarian theories of disability and legal capacity' in B McSherry and I Freckelton (eds), *Coercive care: rights, law and policy* (Routledge, 2013) 31.

[70] Bantekas, 'Mental and Intellectual Capacity and Contractual Freedom' 586.

[71] See, for example, Act No. CXX of 2009 on the Civil Code of Hungary, §§ 5:69–5:84 for a long list of incapacity clauses.

[72] Act No. CXX of 2009 on the Civil Code of Hungary, §§ 5:78 for a long list of incapacity clauses.

which makes it easier for persons with disabilities to invoke this substantive rule: besides the supported person, any of their supporters can also initiate the court proceedings to review the decision.[73] The general rule, which applies to everyone, thus accommodated the interests of persons with disabilities, who were until then not allowed to enter into any contract for fear of exploitation. The clause does not even contain a reference to disability; after all, in addition to fraud, error, abuse of unequal bargaining power, and all the other conditions listed, people with disabilities have no additional interest in having an 'incapacity defence'; all they need is protection from these evils.

Lack of capacity is thus not the only ground for protection against abuse by others, nor is it a necessary basis for intervention.[74] Somebody profits from such an abuse, and/or it is carried out in an illicit manner, taking advantage of the other person's weakness. These harms arguably cover most, if not all, scenarios of abuse of persons due to their diminished capacity. If the law can protect against these harms, there is no need for protection based on incapacity.

The Hungarian solution is not the only way that supported decision-making can incorporate a safeguard for declaring transactions void. The Civil Code's provision is phrased in a disability-neutral way. To strengthen it, disability could be explicitly mentioned as a circumstance which can be abused by the other party. If even that was insufficient, the status of a protected person can be explicitly listed as a circumstance.

Besides the substantive ground for voiding transactions, the second variable in the safeguard is the supporter's role. The Hungarian example allows any supporter to ask the courts to declare the transaction void. Some might argue that the supporter's right to initiate the proceeding alone gives him too much power to contest the supported person's decision. The supporter cannot overrule them himself like a guardian, but he can achieve the same result by turning to the courts. This claim is far-fetched for two reasons. First, it is much more challenging to achieve the same result for a supporter than for a guardian because court proceedings are lengthy and costly – in any case, more burdensome than simply having the power to overrule the decision as the guardian does. Second, while a guardian can overrule the represented person's wishes for any reason, the supporter has to convince the court that abuse has taken place. Supporters are therefore likely to exercise this power much less frequently than guardians. Nevertheless, if it did turn out that they overused it, the right to initiate the proceeding to void the transaction can be limited to the supported person. If a supporter felt the person was abused, it would have to convince her to sign the court petition.

[73] More specifically, it allows their supporters to apply to the court with a motion to void the contract. This is the only right the supporters have for themselves; all their other powers are related to facilitating the supported person's actions. See Act No. CXX of 2009 on the Civil Code of Hungary, § 2:20 (3).

[74] Flynn and Arstein-Kerslake, 'State intervention in the lives' 45.

A middle approach can also be imagined, whereby only supporters who were not present at the time of concluding the transaction could initiate the voidability proceeding alone. This would provide more certainty to the other party, as by witnessing the transaction, supporters would forfeit their right to contest it on their own.

No safeguard is able to provide complete protection. Plenary guardianship is probably the most effective in preventing abuse by others, but it achieves that by creating other types of harm. It is available only to persons who give up all their decision-making powers, which is a huge price to pay. Others, not willing to forfeit their autonomy, remain entirely unprotected. If they fall victim to exploitation, guardianship applied *ex-post facto* will be of little help to them. The effectiveness of guardianship's protective mechanism should therefore be evaluated in light of the narrow group of persons it is able to help.

Supported decision-making achieves a better balance of protection and autonomy, which makes protection available to a larger group of persons. In any case, the types of remedies in supported decision-making are flexible, offering various combinations of support and respect for the supported person's autonomy. Jurisdictions can apply a solution fit for their circumstances and change it when experience suggests otherwise if developments make certain abuses more or less likely.

6.2.4.2. *Abuse by Self*

Another type of abuse prevented by guardianship is harm caused by the person's own decisions. This relates to situations where no one in particular takes advantage of the person, she is unable to protect her own interests by making inappropriate decisions. Guardianship solves this problem by replacing all her decisions for which she is found to lack capacity with the decisions of her guardian.

Supported decision-making values the person's own decisions. Its aim is not simply to allow the disabled person any arbitrary decisions but to help her make decisions that are in her interest.[75] Some might object that a person with diminished capacity could not make complicated decisions. For example, she might have a preference for staying at home, but she cannot appreciate the financial consequences of her choice. Giving her the option of simply choosing between staying at home or moving to an institution can easily lead to an arbitrary answer. However, that is not how meaningful support should work. The supporters have to appreciate the consequences of certain decisions and come up with realistic options to choose from.[76] They have to explain the alternatives to the person so that she can select among those: does she want to stay at home

[75] Minkowitz, 'Abolishing Mental Health Laws' 157.
[76] Flynn and Arstein-Kerslake, 'Legislating personhood' 99.

for five more years and lose her money and then move to the institution, or does she want to move now and keep her money? Perhaps other options are possible, such as using only half of her home and accommodating a tenant in the rest or moving to a smaller apartment. Support plays its role if it allows the disabled person to choose from meaningful options, allowing her to appreciate what she is choosing from.

Supported decision-making achieves decisions of better quality also because of its pedagogic effect.[77] Everybody needs experience and practice to make good decisions. Guardianship deprives disabled persons of the opportunity to learn by making their own decisions.[78] It is thus wholly anti-pedagogic: persons subject to substitute decision-making lose even those skills they used to have before incapacitation, and their condition deteriorates.[79] When receiving support, however, they develop their skills. Simply by making more and more decisions over time and experiencing their consequences, they become gradually less dependent on their supporters.[80] Making mistakes and taking responsibility for them is an integral part of this learning process. For example, while initially they might need assistance with all their shopping, over time, they can learn how to budget their weekly or monthly income alone. It is a basic axiom of special education that everybody can learn.[81] While not everybody is able to reach the same level, supported decision-making is much better suited for achieving a person's full potential than guardianship.

Despite these positive features of supported decision-making, it cannot be denied that some supported persons will engage in behaviour that can be considered by others as harmful or otherwise not in their interest. For example, they might waste their money on useless items, leaving their basic needs unmet. This problem can be approached in a number of ways.

First, some transactions of this nature can be declared void using the safeguards described in the previous part. This would typically involve contracts with long-term obligations, such as telephone-, club membership- and other subscriptions. These are not necessarily the result of abuse by the company offering them. Nevertheless, they can be considered to have been signed by mistake, or there are other grounds available for declaring transactions void. The German experience with Betreung suggests that these are the most typical types of self-harming transactions that Germans with diminished capacity enter into, and they are easily declared void by the German courts.[82]

[77] Mental Disability Advocacy Centre (MDAC), 'A kizáró gondnokság kérdése az új Ptk.-ban' (31 March 2008) 1.

[78] Salzman, 'Guardianship for persons with mental illness' 291.

[79] I Huszár and E Kuncz, *Igazságügyi pszichiátria* (Medicina, 1978) 274.

[80] Kohn, Blumenthal, and Campbell, 'Supported Decision-Making' 1139.

[81] Oktatáskutató és Fejlesztő Intézet, 'A tantárgygondozó szaktanácsadói támogatáshoz kapcsolódó pedagógiai szintleírások – Gyógypedagógus munkakör' (2014) 16.

[82] Email from Ulrich Hellman, Legal Director of Lebenshilfe, the German Association of Persons with Intellectual Disability (27 February 2008).

Second, one has to realise that self-harm is difficult to curtail, even under guardianship. The protection provided by guardianship is often only formal, it provides the false appearance of protection instead of genuinely safeguarding the person's interests.[83] If the person has a habit of irresponsibly wasting money without the approval of her guardian, her transactions are legally invalid. Nevertheless, if she has access to cash or a credit card, her purchases are difficult to annul, especially if she has already consumed the goods she bought. Contracts with long-term obligations mentioned above are easy to declare void if the person lacks the legal capacity to sign them, but unreasonable spending of cash is much more challenging to remedy. It either requires the continuous supervision of the represented person by the guardian or limiting her access to cash by releasing pocket money to her in small instalments. Supported decision-making does not seem to be less efficient with regard to the latter option and can easily outperform guardianship with regard to the first one.

Third, it is hard to measure the prevalence of this problem because harm, in this case, is difficult to define to start with. Small purchases of an everyday nature, especially with regard to entertainment, are highly subjective. Reviewing spending of this type on the grounds of rational justification is very intrusive. This is not an issue of capacity: many, if not most, non-disabled persons would have difficulty justifying some of their expenses on rational grounds. Some suffering from alcoholism or other types of addiction, whether diagnosed as having a substance abuse problem or not, are clearly endangering their well-being. However, only disabled people's 'irresponsible wasting of money' results in legal intervention by guardianship laws. Of course, some types of spending, without a doubt, would be considered irrational by the vast majority of society.[84] However, there are no bright rules separating the vast majority of unacceptable irrational spending from the tolerable ones. Any intervention on this very shaky basis has the potential to be over-inclusive. Indeed, guardianship in practice is characterised by an invasive control over the represented person's spending, subjecting all her expenses to scrutiny by the guardian.[85] Since this intervention affects only persons with disabilities, it is possible, and even desirable, not to impose control over irresponsible spending at all. This is a better option than intervening with disabled persons' choices on the basis that their entertainment patterns derail from the expectations of their community or the rational opinion of a court.

[83] Field and Sanchez, *Equal Treatment for People with Mental Retardation*, 165.

[84] The author of this book at the age of 13 spent his very first salary, earned after two weeks of hard construction labour, on a full six-book edition of Winston Churchill's Second World War. While he still does not regret this decision, he had a very hard time justifying it to his parents, and even harder to his friends at the time.

[85] J Dallos, 'A gyámügyi előadó szemével' in Hungarian Civil Liberties Union (TASZ), *Ki a kompetens?* (TASZ, 2001) 18; excessive control over the disabled person's spending is not unique to guardians. As mentioned in chapter 5.1.2 above, the Swedish God Men (mentors) were also criticized on similar grounds.

In the absence of empirical evidence, it is hard to evaluate how reckless spending behaviour would manifest in the case of persons with diminished capacity if they could not be placed under guardianship. Instead of intervening by supervising their individual transactions, a better approach would be to ensure that whatever spending decisions they make do not endanger their well-being. Setting up automatic payments for all the person's regular expenses and releasing only the rest of the supported person's income to her as pocket money already puts a prodigal disabled person in a better position than her non-disabled peers are. This option is perfectly compatible with supported decision-making. The rest depends on how the supported person manages her money. Educating her about budgeting seems to be a preferable solution to making expense decisions on her behalf; therapy and training are a more sensible interventions than legal control. Supported decision-making is more suited for this task than guardianship due to its pedagogic qualities, especially if the supporter has closer and more frequent contact with the supported person than a professional guardian would have.

An example of a disability-neutral approach concerns the protection of persons from abuse and severe deterioration of their condition due to neglect. If the carers of a person with a disability die, authorities often proceed with placement under guardianship to ensure that they can intervene with social and healthcare services.[86] Their concern for well-being is commendable and, indeed, depending on the jurisdiction, a legal or constitutional obligation. People with disabilities are, however, not unique in having these kinds of needs; the growing elderly population is as much a recipient of similar services. The fact that these kinds of interventions can be performed without unnecessarily restricting the person's legal capacity is shown by the adult protection legislation adopted in several Canadian provinces.[87] Following the example of child protection legislation, they unify the process of providing assistance to adults in need resulting from various social crises. This approach can ensure that the needs of adult and elderly persons can be met without restricting their rights, regardless of whether they have a disability or not.

Various safeguards can also be developed in specific areas. Banks can establish a good practice of providing extra counselling to supported persons when applying for loans. Hospitals can develop procedures for the effective involvement of supporters in medical decision-making. Social protection agencies can extend their cooperation to supporters, providing them with advice relevant to the decisions of the supported person. These specific safeguards would not limit the autonomy of the disabled person, they would merely ensure that she and her supporters receive the appropriate type and amount of information to avoid particularly harmful outcomes.

[86] C Bigby, *Ageing with a lifelong disability* (Jessica Kingsley, 2004) 161.
[87] Bach and Kerzner, 'A New Paradigm' 135.

6.2.4.3. *Abuse by the Supporter*

The third type of harm threatening the well-being of a person with a disability is abuse by the person entrusted with safeguarding her interests. Guardianship poorly protects represented persons from mistreatment by the guardians.[88] Their relationship is based on the notion that the guardian makes decisions in the person's interests because the latter is incompetent to make them. Due to this presumption, it is very difficult for a person under guardianship to challenge the decisions of her guardian.[89] In some jurisdictions, it is technically impossible, because to file a complaint against the guardian, or even to learn the details of his decisions (e.g., inquire about how he manages the represented person's property), the represented person needs the guardian's consent. Even where this is not the case, the prospects of filing a complaint against the person who is the one entitled by law to make decisions on their behalf are slim.[90] Guardianship makes abuse possible by giving the guardian complete control over a vulnerable person's decisions, either entirely or in a given area, with little outside oversight into how he manages his duties.[91]

Compared to guardians, supporters have less power over the persons they are aiding. Nevertheless, the supporting relationship also has the potential to turn into an abusive one.[92] The supporter can mislead the supported person about a transaction in order to benefit from it. For example, he might convince her to sell a property below its market value to the supporter's accomplice, or to donate it to the supporter.

As a best practice rule, with transactions of significant value, more supporters should be involved. If the supporter has any interest in the transaction, he should not act as a facilitator in the process. These are not hard rules, and it is difficult to turn them to a legal requirement. Nevertheless, their breach can indicate the need for a review of the decision.

Proposals about supported decision-making usually mention that the supporter should not exert undue influence on the supported person.[93] This concept relates to some form of coercion, but is currently not very well defined psychologically, therefore it is of little help in guiding courts.[94] This lack of clarity can be overcome through developing its substance as a legal standard in the

[88] Mental Disability Advocacy Centre (MDAC), *Legal Capacity in Europe* (Hungary, 2013) 7.

[89] Callus, 'Removing obstacles' 163.

[90] Bantekas, 'Mental and Intellectual Capacity and Contractual Freedom' 586.

[91] RM Powell and MA Stein, 'People with Disabilities and Sexual and Reproductive Rights: an International Comparative Analysis' (2016) 11 *Frontiers of Law in China* 53, 77.

[92] Gordon, 'The Emergence of Assisted (Supported) Decision-Making in the Canadian Law' 75.

[93] W Martin, S Michalowski, and C Caughey, 'Safeguards against Undue Influence and Conflicts of Interest' Essex Autonomy Project, Essex University (2015); Dhanda, 'Legal Capacity in the Disability Rights Convention' 445.

[94] DC Marson, J Huthwaite, and K Hebert, 'Testamentary capacity and undue influence in the elderly: A jurisprudent therapy perspective' (2004) 28 *Law & Psychology Review* 71.

future.[95] Nevertheless, the substantive standard is insufficient to prevent abuses if it is not paired with meaningful procedural rules.

A possible reaction to abuse in guardianship is the guardian's dismissal by the body nominating him.[96] A similar procedure can be imagined for supported decision-making as well, whereby the certifying body would dismiss (de-certify) a supporter who has exerted undue influence over the supported person. Since the supported person can end the supporting relationship at any time, this procedure would help persons who are not aware of being abused or who wish to retain the supporter despite the abuse. It would overrule the choice of the person concerning who her supporter should be. Given that the standard for such overruling would be a proven case of abuse, this seems to be an acceptable intervention into personal autonomy.

Dismissing the supporter protects only from future abuse, not from the harmful consequences of abuse that has already taken place. To effectively take care of the latter, transactions concluded due to abuse have to be declared void. The same procedure used to challenge abuse by the other party, described above, can also serve to review abuse by the supporter. The substantive bases for nullity can be expanded by 'undue influence' and 'unfair advantage', but perhaps it is not even necessary – the existing grounds described above should be able to capture situations in which the supporter benefits from the abuse in some way.

A difficult question in the case of this type of abuse relates to procedural rules: who will help the person with a disability to apply to the court? A supported person is, by definition, in need of some assistance. Without the abusive supporter's help, she might not be able to initiate a court review proceeding alone. If she has other supporters, they might be able to help her, or they can have a right to initiate the review proceeding on their own. If there are no other supporters, or they are complicit in the wrongdoing, they are of no help. If the supported person cannot count on her supporters, her options are very limited. Some may be able to consult persons outside of her regular support circle and act with their help if they suspect they have been abused. This is not easy, as taking action against one's closest supporter never is. Also, these types of external advisers or services may not be available for everybody. Nevertheless, even in these circumstances, the supported person is in a better situation than if she were under guardianship: she does not need her supporter's consent to take action, the supporter cannot block her activities the way a guardian could.

If the person is unable to act alone without the help of her supporter, this safeguard will be of little use to her. However, even in this case, she is better protected than if she was under guardianship. A guardian would simply make a

[95] P Gooding, 'Navigating the 'Flashing Amber Lights' of the Right to Legal Capacity in the United Nations Convention on the Rights of Persons with Disabilities: Responding to Major Concerns' (2015) 15 *Human Rights Law Review* 45, 56.

[96] See, for example, the Hungarian Civil Code, Act no. IV of 1959 on the Civil Code of the Hungarian Republic, § 19/C.

harmful decision on her behalf, while a supporter would need to convince her to make it. Persons who are unable to take action against the supporter alone but who are nevertheless able to withdraw consent from a transaction which they do not like are, therefore, better off in supported decision-making.

Those who need to rely on their supporters entirely and are unable to detect any possible wrongdoing on their part are unprotected in this framework. This seems to be a problematic proposition, but, in fact, it is just a realistic one. Disabled persons completely unable to protect their own interests will be unable to defend themselves against their supporters, and the law is powerless to change that. A supervisory body for supporters, similar to one for guardians, can be established, which could regularly review the transactions made with the help of supporters. However, despite the formalism and increased costs this would bring to the system, its effectiveness is highly questionable in light of the experience with similar supervisory mechanisms of guardians.[97] A better oversight approach is one that concentrates on the overall well-being of the person with a disability, as described in the previous part, not on the benefit of individual transactions she concluded.

Persons in the last category are at least not worse off than they would be under guardianship. Indeed, they are, in fact, better off due to one reason: if the law cannot help persons who are entirely unable to protect their own interests, the aim of the legal capacity framework should be to ensure that there are as few such persons as possible. Supported decision-making's pedagogical qualities serve this aim better than guardianship. The more autonomous and confident the disabled person becomes, the more she understands the decisions she makes and her interests she needs to secure, the less likely it is that she will be abused. Guardianship, which deteriorates her skills, makes her more vulnerable to abuse.

Outside supervisory mechanisms should also take the importance of the pedagogical factor into account. Instead of investing in expensive oversight bodies and structures, they should develop services that would enable the disabled person to access information, advice and legal aid alone. This would unburden supporters and help the disabled person to become more independent, which are important goals in themselves. In addition, they would make abuse less likely.

6.3. COMPARING GUARDIANSHIP AND SUPPORTED DECISION-MAKING

The ideal model of supported decision-making is a superior solution to the exercise of legal capacity of persons with decision-making difficulties. Law, however, cannot enact the ideal model; it can only create institutions aspiring to achieve

[97] Mental Disability Advocacy Centre (MDAC), *Guardianship and Human Rights in Hungary* (Hungary, 2007) 70.

it. I showed above what conflicting principles the design of supported decision-making must take into account, and how the conflicts can be resolved. It remains to be seen how the results hold up to comparison with guardianship.

6.3.1. Restrictiveness

Guardianship and support differ fundamentally in their approach to the wishes of persons with disabilities. While guardians are legally entitled to substitute their decisions for those of the person they are representing, supporters cannot. In practice, it is possible for a good guardian to act indistinguishably from a good supporter. However, an ordinary guardian, not to mention bad ones, will be very different from an ordinary or bad supporter.

The cornerstone of supported decision-making law is the right of the supported person to legally express her decisions, to enter into legal transactions in her own name by her own actions. Notwithstanding how the decision was achieved and whose opinion it reflects, the supported person will remain the ultimate judge of whether she wants to be bound by the decision or not.[98] As a result, guardianship, regardless of its specific form, is always a more restrictive intervention than supported decision-making.

6.3.2. Flexibility

A major advantage of supported decision-making compared with guardianship is its flexibility. With guardianship, a court or other body has to decide in advance and in the abstract what decisions the person will be unable to make. The scope of the order can change, but this always requires a new decision with the necessary procedural safeguards. The decision is important because it allocates crucial powers between the guardian and the represented person: it decides in which areas the latter will be considered capable and in which ones the guardian will act on her behalf.[99] This leads to divergences between the represented person's actual abilities and her legal capacity, as the latter can never be specific enough to capture all the possible decisions a person will be required to make, especially if the person's skills develop or change for any other reason. In practice, a significant difference between ability and legal capacity can lead to unjustified interferences with autonomy and undermine the guardianship order's legitimacy.

With supported decision-making, there is no need for such accuracy. Since the respective powers of the actors are not tied to specific areas, and the supporter's

[98] Gooding 'Supported Decision-Making' 434.

[99] Keene, Kane, Kim, Owen, 'Mental capacity – Why look for a paradigm shift?' 346.

powers are limited in any case, there is no need to determine in advance which decisions of the supported person should be made independently and which require support. A supported person could always make the decision alone if she wants and can seek assistance only if she is unable to make the decision. The scope of decisions in which she is acting alone depends on her and on her agreement with her supporters. Nobody can support her against her objections. This is a very flexible tool for exploring how much a disabled person is able to do herself. As she is becoming more comfortable with certain tasks, such as daily shopping or dealing with the post office or public administration, she can become more independent from her supporter. Rearranging the tasks of supporters and support does not require a bureaucratic intervention and approval based on a problematic abstract prediction of abilities in imagined scenarios. It can be made by the persons that are the most knowledgeable about how far the supported person's abilities have developed: by her and her support circle.

6.3.3. The Pedagogic Effect

Guardianship leads to the deterioration of the represented person's skills.[100] Even if she is consulted in the process, it is the guardian who makes the decisions, expresses them, and bears responsibility for them. A supported person, on the other hand, even if she was heavily supported and influenced by her supporters, has to grasp the content of the decision, express it and take responsibility for it. This legal difference itself contributes to developing her skills, not to mention the potentially vastly different outcomes of the two legal interventions in this regard.

6.3.4. The Expressive Function

Law serves other functions in society besides directly regulating behaviour. The theory about the law's expressive function states that the law can create compliance also by changing the social meaning of a particular behaviour.[101] By signalling an appropriate form of action, it induces individuals to change their attitude, to internalise the particular normative obligation expressed in the rule, and it also creates a fear of bearing social sanctions for transgressing socially approved norms.[102]

[100] Salzman, 'Guardianship for persons with mental illness' 291.

[101] A Geisinger and M Stein, 'A Theory of Expressive International Law' (2007) 60 *Vanderbilt Law Review* 77.

[102] T Carney, 'Searching for workable alternatives to guardianship for vulnerable populations?' (2015) 1 *Ethics, Medicine and Public Health* 113, 115.

Notwithstanding its actual legal effects, supported decision-making serves an important expressive function by portraying the person with diminished capacity as legally capable.[103] By expressing this image in law, it signals social approval of the perception of disabled persons as autonomous individuals. In contrast, guardianship certifies that the person is incapable, which carries a powerful message affecting the negative perception of the represented person.[104]

Apart from the above symbolism, specific legal rules also have an expressive effect. Supported decision-making requires other parties to transact with the disabled person. They have to accept her as their equal before the law, they have to negotiate the contract and conclude it with her. In the case of guardianship, the contracting parties do not need to communicate with the represented person at all. The contract is negotiated and signed by the guardian on the disabled person's behalf, who does not even have to be present. This undermines the image of disabled persons as equals, leading to them becoming invisible to the broader society, turning from subjects of law to objects of care. Simply by fostering more encounters and legal transactions with persons with disability themselves, supported decision-making is an important tool for changing opinions about the skills and autonomy of persons with disability.

6.3.5. Ease of Transacting

Supported decision-making can be challenging to use in particular situations. Complicated decisions might be hard to grasp for a person with high support needs and therefore take more time and effort than for a non-disabled person. In this situation, transacting with a guardian is easier and faster from the perspective of contracting parties.

Guardianship's advantage, however, does not apply to all types of decisions. With regard to many ordinary transactions, which the disabled person is able to make alone, guardianship is more cumbersome because it requires the parties to produce the guardian to express the represented person's decision legally. Parties transacting with a supported person are in a more advantageous position because they can deal directly with her. Overall, it seems that with more complicated decisions, which are less frequent, guardianship facilitates easier deal-making for contracting parties. Supported decision-making is more advantageous with regard to less complex decisions.

[103] Barclay, 'Paternalism' 140.

[104] J Fiala-Butora, MA Stein and JE Lord, 'The democratic life of the Union: towards equal voting participation for Europeans with Disabilities' (2014) 55 *Harvard International Law Journal* 71, 101.

6.3.6. Protection from Harmful Decisions

The previous comparisons apply to all forms of supported decision-making. However, there are different ways to protect the disabled person from abuse. Support can be equipped with various safeguards with different abilities to avoid specific types of harmful decisions. Some interventions strengthen the protective features of supported decision-making without interfering with disabled persons' autonomy, as discussed above. Nevertheless, specific safeguards, which protect persons from more types of harm, limit other essential principles of supported decision-making, namely respecting the person's wishes and fostering legal certainty. The choice of safeguards, therefore, depends on resolving these trade-offs to secure the adequate level of all mentioned functions.

This conflict cannot be resolved in the abstract because perfect solutions do not exist. If a person's decision has the potential to harm her, the law can only react by respecting her wish and allowing the harm to occur, or by overruling the wish in some way. Any abstract rule chosen will have a negative effect on some persons with regard to at least one of these factors. It is an empirical question as to which harms are dangerous and widespread enough that protecting from them is necessary, even at the expense of other important goals. The answer is not static: as supported decision-making develops, its effectiveness in preventing certain harms will change. States might also develop alternative means of responding to these harms, such as the mentioned adult protection legislation. In-depth empirical research about the consequences of various stages of development is needed to fine-tune the protective features of supported decision-making in order to cause the least interference overall with its other goals.

Guardianship in practice is also not universal in its approach to harmful decisions. Nevertheless, with regard to the above principles, it can be classified as an extreme intervention in favour of prevention of harm at the expense of respecting the disabled person's wishes. However, protection from all possible and impossible harm can hardly be the most appropriate policy goal of legal capacity law. In addition, the methods of achieving even this aim in isolation from all others are highly dubious. By making the guardian the sole gatekeeper of what transactions the person with a disability enters, the latter becomes completely dependent on him, both in a legal and a factual-psychological sense. This makes abuse by guardians more likely and severe and also breeds mistreatment by others. By losing her decision-making skills, the represented person requires permanent protection from the guardian, which many guardians are unable to offer. This limits represented persons' ability to contract, and leads to complications when they are acting alone. Even though their transactions are invalid, once they consumed the goods or services purchased, it is hard to annul them against bona fide parties who did not know that the person is acting ultra vires. A person with diminished capacity with cash in hand is unlikely to be best protected by guardianship, which is not aimed at developing her skills on how to spend money. Guardianship is thus both a highly overprotective and an underprotective intervention. To paraphrase Thomas Jefferson's quote about liberty and security, a law that sacrifices the autonomy of persons with disabilities for their protection achieves neither.

As there is no one type of supported decision-making law with regard to the prevention of abuse, it is hard to compare it with guardianship in the abstract. The promise of support is that it can increase the decision-making skills of disabled persons to a level where they would be much less likely to be abused. A range of interventions can help achieve this goal, which makes support potentially superior to guardianship, even with regard to protection from abuse. Nevertheless, some procedure of overruling supported persons' decisions seems to be necessary, at least until the said potential materialises.

The above analysis indicates a possible solution that can secure all relevant principles to a high level. The point of balance is for supporters to be unable to overrule the supported person's decisions themselves, but to have a right to challenge before courts those transactions that they suspect are the result of abuse. Courts could declare the transactions void not on the basis of incapacity, but under a disability-neutral standard of abusing the person's situation.

By strengthening the protective features at the expense of respecting the disabled person's decision, supported decision-making's above-analysed advantages vis-à-vis guardianship shrink. Nevertheless, any solution carefully selecting the level on which each conflicting principle will be served is likely better than the one-sided approach guardianship law has chosen.

6.4. CONCLUSION

The above analysis showed how law can effectively pursue conflicting aims of securing the autonomy of persons with disability. By distributing power between the supporter, the supported person and other parties, legal rules can create a regime of supported decision-making that adequately respects the wishes of persons with disabilities, protects them from abuse and secures the legal certainty of transactions. This does not mean that their decisions will always be respected because that is a standard which applies to nobody. Some overturning of decisions is inevitable if society wants to protect persons from mistakes, fraud, duress, and other evils that lead to severely harmful decisions. Legal capacity law can only ensure that these considerations apply in a disability-neutral way and do not disadvantage persons with disabilities because of their perceived lack of mental capacity. By basing overturning on substantive standards related to harm but unrelated to capacity, and by making it more difficult but not impossible to initiate a review of decisions, it can eliminate discriminatory practices typical of guardianship systems. The level of intervention can be increased by small changes in the design of the system, depending on empirical outcomes. This is what the law can do. It cannot create the ideal version of supported decision-making by enacting it; it can only enact a less-perfect system with the goal of achieving the ideal system in practice. It remains to be seen how this conception of supported decision-making can be made available for persons with high support needs.

7

The Case of Persons with High Support Needs

THE PREVIOUS CHAPTER showed that the legal design of supported decision-making varies with regard to several factors, such as respecting the person's autonomy, strengthening legal certainty, and protecting the person from abuse. Yet another vital factor influences this design: the circle of persons it is available to. The solutions discussed until now presumed a person with a diminished capacity, who is nevertheless able to express a wish and make decisions with support. Now, I turn to the question of persons with high support needs who are unable to make certain decisions even with support.

Whether persons with the most severe disability can be incorporated into a support framework is one of the most challenging questions of legal capacity law.[1] It has several implications for the legal regulation of supported decision-making.[2] If these persons can be incorporated into a support model, then support is a truly universal framework capable of completely replacing guardianship.[3] If they cannot be incorporated, the retention of some form of substituted decision-making is necessary.

7.1. EXISTING SOLUTIONS AND THEIR SHORTCOMINGS

Various academic positions have been put forward to address the issue of legal capacity of persons with high support needs. I will divide them into two basic approaches, depending on whether they accept or deny that all persons with severe disabilities can make decisions with support: the Support Only[4] position

[1] JE Lord and MA Stein, 'Contingent participation and coercive care: feminist and communitarian theories of disability and legal capacity' in B McSherry and I Freckelton (eds), *Coercive care: rights, law and policy* (Routledge, 2013) 45.

[2] M Donnelly, R Harding, and E Taşcıoğlu, 'Situating the Right to Enjoy Legal Capacity' in M Donnelly, R Harding, and E Taşcıoğlu (eds), *Supporting Legal Capacity in Socio-Legal Context* (Hart, 2022) 5.

[3] MA Stein, F Mahomed, V Patel, and C Sunkel (eds), *Mental Health, Legal Capacity, and Human Rights* (Cambridge University Press, 2021) 7.

[4] For example T Minkowitz, 'The United Nations Convention on the Rights of Persons with Disabilities and the Right to Be Free from Nonconsensual Psychiatric Interventions' (2007) 34 *Syracuse Journal of International Law and Commerce* 405; A Dhanda, 'Legal Capacity in the Disability Rights Convention: Stranglehold of the Past or Lodestar for the Future?' (2007) 34

and the Some Guardianship[5] position. Both have important weaknesses, which affect differently various sub-groups of persons with disabilities. To some extent they overlap with the positions on the interpretation of the CRPD, but are not identical with them.

7.1.1. The Support Only Framework – The Complete Abolition of Guardianship

Advocates of the Support Only position argue that all persons with disabilities can make decisions with support.[6] That is, no person needs substituted

Syracuse Journal of International Law and Commerce 429; S Cifuentes and 30 other legal scholars, 'Legal Opinion on Article 12 of the CRPD' (21 June 2008); Office of the United Nations High Commissioner for Human Rights (OHCHR), 'On enhancing awareness and understanding of the Convention on the Rights of Persons with Disabilities', A/HRC/10/48 (26 January 2009); Council of Europe Commissioner for Human Rights, 'Who gets to decide? Right to legal capacity for persons with intellectual and psychosocial disabilities', CommDH/IssuePaper (Strasbourg, 20 February 2012); E Flynn and A Arstein-Kerslake, 'Legislating personhood: realising the right to support in exercising legal capacity' (2014) 10(1) *International Journal of Law in Context* 81; A Arstein-Kerslake, *Restoring Voice to People with Cognitive Disabilities* (Cambridge University Press, 2017); M Bach and L Kerzner, 'A New Paradigm for Protecting Autonomy and the Right to Legal Capacity', Paper prepared for the Law Commission of Ontario (2010); A-M Callus, 'Removing obstacles to equal recognition for persons with intellectual disability: Taking exception to the way things are' (2018) 12 *ALTER European Journal of Disability Research* 153.

[5] T Carney, 'Guardianship, Citizenship, & Theorizing Substitute-decisionmaking Law' (7 April 2012) *Sydney Law School Research Paper* No. 12/25; A Lawson, 'The United Nations Convention on the Rights of Persons with Disabilities: New Era or False Dawn?' (2007) 34 *Syracuse Journal of International Law and Commerce* 563; M Keys, 'Legal Capacity Law Reform in Europe: An Urgent Challenge' in G Quinn and L Waddington (eds), *European Yearbook of Disability Law* (Intersentia, 2009); P Weller, 'Supported Decision-Making and the Achievement of Non-Discrimination: The Promise and Paradox of the Disabilities Convention' (2008) 26(2) *Law in Context* 85; ML Perlin, 'Striking for the Guardians and Protectors of the Mind: The Convention on the Rights of Persons with Mental Disabilities and the Future of Guardianship Law' (2013) 117 *Penn State Law Review* 1159; O Lewis, 'Advancing Legal Capacity Jurisprudence' (2011) 6 *European Human Rights Law Review* 700; NA Kohn, JA Blumenthal, and AT Campbell, 'Supported Decision-Making: A Viable Alternative to Guardianship?' (2013) 117 *Penn State Law Review* 1111; P Skowron, 'Giving substance to "the best interpretation of will and preferences"' (2019) 62 *International Journal of Law and Psychiatry* 125; PS Appelbaum, 'There Are All Kinds of Rights' (2016) 46(2) *Hastings Center Report* Inside back cover; M Scholten and J Gather, 'Adverse consequences of article 12 of the UN Convention on the Rights of Persons with Disabilities for persons with mental disabilities and an alternative way forward' (2018) 44 *Journal of Medical Ethics* 226; G Szmukler, 'The UN Convention on the Rights of Persons with Disabilities: "Rights, will and preferences" in relation to mental health disabilities' (2017) 54 *International Journal of Law and Psychiatry* 90; AR Keene, NB Kane, SYH Kim, and GS Owen, 'Mental capacity – Why look for a paradigm shift?' (2023) 31(3) *Medical Law Review* 340; D Bilchitz, 'Dignity, fundamental rights and legal capacity: Moving beyond the paradigm set by the general comment on article 12 of the convention on the rights of persons with disabilities' (2016) 32(3) *South African Journal on Human Rights* 410; L Barclay, 'Paternalism, Supported Decision-Making and Expressive Respect' (2024) 27(1) *Journal of Ethics and Social Philosophy* 121; MC Freeman, K Kolappa JMC de Almeida, A Kleinman, N Makhashvili, S Phakathi, B Saraceno, G Thornicroft, 'Reversing Hard Won Victories in the Name of Human Rights: A Critique of the General Comment on Article 12 of the UN Convention on the Rights of Persons with Disabilities' (2015) 2(9) *Lancet Psychiatry* 844.

[6] Minkowitz, 'The United Nations Convention on the Rights of Persons with Disabilities' 408–09.

decision-making.[7] In this model, persons with high support needs differ from other persons with disabilities only in the degree of support they require.[8] Those with the most severe conditions should receive the highest level of support, which is sometimes described as 100 per cent support,[9] or 'total support',[10] or 'almost complete outside support'.[11]

This position relies on a reading of the CRPD according to which Article 12 forbids all substituted decision-making.[12] The state's duty, therefore, is to provide as much support as a person needs to make legally valid decisions.[13] The position is popular among NGOs[14] but is also adhered to in academia and by international organisations.[15] Importantly, the CRPD Committee's General Comment on Legal Capacity endorses the Support Only position.[16]

The Support Only position rests on a factual assumption that all persons with high support needs can make decisions with support. This may seem counterintuitive, therefore, it is important to consider it more closely. It is hard to imagine how certain persons in a persistent vegetative state, or in the final stages of dementia, or persons with severe multiple disabilities are able to make decisions.[17] State-of-the-art capacity assessment tools are all built on the presumption that mental incapacity exists; that is, at least some persons with severe disabilities are unable to make at least certain decisions.[18] That presump-

[7] Flynn and Arstein-Kerslake, 'Legislating personhood' 91.

[8] Dhanda, 'Legal Capacity in the Disability Rights Convention' 445.

[9] L Series and A Nilsson, 'Article 12 CRPD Equal Recognition before the Law' in I Bantekas, MA Stein, and D Anastasiou (eds), *The UN Convention on the Rights of Persons with Disabilities: A Commentary* (Oxford University Press, 2018) 343.

[10] P Gooding, 'Supported Decision-Making: A Rights-Based Disability Concept and its Implications for Mental Health Law' (2013) 20(3) *Psychiatry, Psychology and Law* 431, 432.

[11] E Flynn and A Arstein-Kerslake, 'The Support Model of Legal Capacity: Fact, Fiction, or Fantasy?' (2014) 31(1) *Berkeley Journal of International Law* 124, 131.

[12] OHCHR, 'On enhancing awareness' §§ 43–45.

[13] UN Committee on the Rights of Persons with Disabilities, General comment No. 1 (2014) – Article 12: Equal recognition before the law, Committee on the Rights of Persons with Disabilities, CRPD/C/GC/1 (19 May 2014), §29 a); Dhanda, 'Legal Capacity in the Disability Rights Convention' 445.

[14] International Disability Alliance (IDA) CRPD Forum, 'Principles for Implementation of CRPD Article 12, Submitted for the Day of General Discussion on "Article 12 of the CRPD – The right to equal recognition before the law" at the UN' (21 October 2009); Inclusion Europe, 'Key Elements of a System of Supported Decision-Making: Position Paper of Inclusion Europe' (Brussels, Inclusion Europe, 2008); S Trömel, 'A Personal Perspective on the Drafting History of the United Nations Convention on the Rights of Persons with Disabilities' in OM Arnadóttir and G Quinn (eds), *The United Nations Convention on the Rights of Persons with Disabilities: European and Scandinavian Perspectives* (Martinus Nijhoff, 2009) 128.

[15] Minkowitz, 'The United Nations Convention on the Rights of Persons with Disabilities', 408–411; Dhanda, 'Legal Capacity in the Disability Rights Convention'; Cifuentes, 'Legal Opinion on Article 12 of the CRPD' 4–5; OHCHR, 'On enhancing awareness' §§ 43–45; Council of Europe Commissioner for Human Rights, 'Who Gets to Decide?' 14.

[16] General comment No. 1, §8.

[17] NL Cantor, *Making Medical Decisions for the Profoundly Mentally Disabled* (MIT Press, 2005) 36.

[18] See in general T Grisso, *Evaluating Competencies: Forensic Assessments and Instruments*, Perspectives in Law and Psychology 16 (Kluwer Academic Plenum Publishers, 2nd Edition, 2003) 12.

tion is shared, or at least not disputed, by newer psychological approaches, which take support into account.[19] The Support Only position's factual claim is thus not supported by the science of psychology.

Advocates of the Support Only position provide some solutions to get around this problem. One of them is to highlight the often underestimated communication abilities of persons with high support needs.[20] One of the basic principles of communication theory for persons with severe disabilities states 'you cannot not communicate' – in other words, all persons with a disability are able to communicate in some way,[21] if only, for example, by changing the rhythm of their breathing.[22] The capacity of these persons is often denied because of their environment's inability to understand their signals.[23] The solution, therefore, is to improve communication to better understand these persons' wishes. Technology has evolved rapidly in recent years in the area of communication tools and methods for persons with disabilities; it is therefore likely that many of those who now have difficulty getting themselves understood will be able to communicate more easily in the future.[24]

This argument, however, conflates communication with the ability to decide. Denial of legal capacity on the basis of communication difficulties is indeed a problem that undermines the legitimacy of guardianship.[25] New communication technologies should be used and taken into account to overcome such exclusions.[26] Nevertheless, communication is only one of the aspects of legal capacity.[27] The fact that a person communicates a wish[28] does not automatically imply the capacity to understand alternatives and their implications and choose from them. Perhaps all persons can communicate, but that does not mean that

[19] MB Kapp, 'Assessing Assessments of Decision-Making Capacity: A Few Legal Queries and Commentary on "Assessment of Decision-Making Capacity in Older Adults"' (2007), 62B(1) *Journal of Gerontology: Psychological Sciences* P12.

[20] Bach and Kerzner, 'A New Paradigm for Protecting Autonomy' 62.

[21] S Carnaby, 'People with profound and multiple learning disabilities: A review of research about their lives', A report commissioned by MENCAP (December 2004) 9.

[22] Flynn and Arstein-Kerslake, 'The Support Model of Legal Capacity' 131.

[23] Inclusion Europe, 'Key Elements of a System of Supported Decision-Making' § 6.

[24] Inclusion Europe emphasises the importance of augmentative and alternative communication (AAC), which can compensate for impairments and severe disorders of speech-language production and/or comprehension – see Inclusion Europe, 'Key Elements of a System of Supported Decision-Making' 5, fn. 5.

[25] I Hoffman and G Könczei, 'Legal Regulations Relating to the Passive and Active Legal Capacity of Persons with Intellectual and Psychosocial Disabilities in Light of the Convention on the Rights Persons with Disabilities and the Impending Reform of the Hungarian Civil Code' (2010) 1 *Loyola Los Angeles International and Comparative Law Review* 143, 150.

[26] RD Dinerstein, 'Implementing Legal Capacity Under Article 12 of the UN Convention on the Rights of Persons with Disabilities: The Difficult Road From Guardianship to Supported Decision-Making' (2012) 19(2) *Human Rights Brief* 5.

[27] Keene, Kane, Kim, Owen, 'Mental capacity' 352.

[28] A Arstein-Kerslake and E Flynn, 'The right to legal agency: domination, disability and the protections of Article 12 of the Convention on the Rights of Persons with Disabilities' (2017) 13(1) *International Journal of Law in Context* 22, 25.

all can communicate a valid decision with regard to all the questions necessary for securing their lives and well-being.

Another solution, named facilitated decision-making, is provided by Michael Bach and Lara Kerzner, which recognises the inability of some persons to make some types of decisions.[29] According to Bach and Kerzner, the supporter's duty is to establish the person's wish from her personal values, preferences, and the environment they were raised in, in other words, from their 'life story'.[30] This approach is based on Paul Riceour's theory of narrative ethics, according to which our identity is defined by how others perceive us.[31] It is the supporter's obligation to communicate a coherent identity of the supported person based on the best knowledge of their personal history.[32]

Bach and Kerzner's solution goes a long way towards incorporating persons with high support needs into a support framework. Indeed, it goes too far. If the supporters are responsible for establishing the supported persons' decisions, their role is not materially different from substitute decision-makers, that is, guardians.[33] It is true that guardians are typically following a best interest standard, which is based on determining what would, in the guardian's opinion, serve the person's interests the most.[34] Bach and Kerzner's proposal is different in that the supporter has to determine what the person would want for herself.[35] Nevertheless, the decision is not made by the supported person. If the standard is the only difference between the two approaches, Bach and Kerzner's solution can be easily incorporated into a guardianship framework by changing the legal basis of the guardian's decisions from best interests to substituted judgment. To call a decision supported, it has to be made by the person with disability herself.[36]

Others have offered alternative solutions but have not explicitly stated how the wishes of persons with the highest support needs should be established.[37] Strong proponents of supported decision-making, such as Ann Arstein-Kerlsake[38] and

[29] Bach and Kerzner, 'A New Paradigm for Protecting Autonomy' 24.

[30] ibid, 65.

[31] P Ricoeur, *Oneself as Another*, Translated by Kathleen Blamey (University of Chicago Press, 1992).

[32] Bach and Kerzner, 'A New Paradigm for Protecting Autonomy' 24.

[33] T Minkowitz, 'Legal Capacity: Alternatives to Functional Capacity' in C O'Mahoney and G Quinn (eds), *Disability Law and Policy: An Analysis of the UN Convention* (Clarus Press, 2017) 101.

[34] N Devi, 'Supported Decision-Making and Personal Autonomy for Persons with Intellectual Disabilities: Article 12 of the UN Convention on the Rights of Persons with Disabilities' (2013) 41(4) *Journal of Law Medicine and Ethics* 792, 803.

[35] Bach and Kerzner, 'A New Paradigm for Protecting Autonomy' 65.

[36] Gooding, 'Supported Decision-Making' 434.

[37] T Minkowitz, 'Abolishing Mental Health Laws to Comply with the Convention on the Rights of Persons with Disabilities' in B McSherry and P Weller (eds), *Rethinking Rights Based Mental Health Laws* (Hart, 2010) 151.

[38] Arstein-Kerslake, *Restoring Voice to People with Cognitive Disabilities*, 201.

Eilionóir Flynn,[39] permit the possibility of making decisions on behalf of the supported person in exceptional situations without specifying the legal criteria for such interventions. The idea of providing 100 per cent support has become popular,[40] but it is unclear what precisely such support entails in practice and how it is different from a substituted decision.[41]

It seems that there is no basis to support the factual claim stated above. There is no evidence currently that all persons could be supported to make all kinds of decisions. It therefore has to be accepted that some persons are unable to make at least some types of decisions in a supported way. This is true even if the CRPD was interpreted to oblige states to provide support to everybody[42] or a law was adopted[43] to require all decisions to be made with support. A normative requirement does not overcome the factual impossibility.

It follows that unless technology radically develops or other significant changes in medicine take place in the future, some persons will be unable to make at least some types of decisions, even with support – at least if support is understood in a way described in the previous chapter, as something different from substitution. This undermines the Support Only position, but not entirely. Even though it is based on a factually incorrect assumption, there might be other reasons why its approach might be preferred over the alternatives. For that, however, we have to analyse the counter-position's disadvantages first.

7.1.2. The Some Guardianship Framework – The Need to Make Substituted Decisions

Some scholars, although welcoming the idea of supported decision-making,[44] are uneasy about its application to persons with high support needs.[45] They reject the claim that all persons with disabilities are able to make decisions with support[46] and that a supporter's claim to truly know the person's wishes can be

[39] Flynn and Arstein-Kerslake, 'Legislating personhood' 98; E Flynn and A Arstein-Kerslake, 'State intervention in the lives of people with disabilities: the case for a disability-neutral framework' (2017) 13(1) *International Journal of Law in Context* 39, 40.

[40] N Devi, J Bickenbach, and G Stucki, 'Moving towards substituted or supported decision-making? Article 12 of the Convention on the Rights of Persons with Disabilities' (2011) 5 *ALTER European Journal of Disability Research* 259, 261.

[41] Series and Nilsson, 'Article 12 CRPD' 345.

[42] General comment No. 1, §29 a).

[43] Minkowitz, 'Legal Capacity: Alternatives to Functional Capacity' 103.

[44] Carney, 'Guardianship, Citizenship, & Theorizing Substitute-decisionmaking Law' 7.

[45] J Dawson, 'A realistic approach to assessing mental health laws' compliance with the UNCRPD' (2015) 40 *International Journal of Law and Psychiatry* 70; Freeman et al, 'Reversing hard won victories' 844.

[46] Carney, 'Guardianship, Citizenship, & Theorizing Substitute-decisionmaking Law' 7.

trusted[47] or would be a good basis for authorising decisions.[48] As Paul Skowron points out, a person's narrative identity is not specific enough to decide what their future should be, and a supporter basing its decision on these factors is essentially making a decision on behalf of the supported person, even if we pretend otherwise.[49] These arguments lead to the conclusion that at least some decisions of at least some persons have to be made in a substituted way, and therefore, supported decision-making should not be available to all.[50] These scholars argue that guardianship needs to be preserved and used alongside supported decision-making, at least in exceptional situations.[51] Guardianship laws should be improved, even renamed, but nevertheless retained[52] as an exceptional measure for individuals for whom support has failed to ensure the exercise of their legal capacity.[53]

The argument is straightforward, but the position has a significant weakness: it is very difficult to ensure that guardianship would only be used exceptionally. No convincing solution to this problem has been put forward so far. There is no exact definition of the category of persons who would be unable to benefit from support – and, as shown in the previous chapters, nor do capacity assessment tools for this purpose exist.[54] Even if such tools were created, which seems possible, it is highly questionable whether the actual practice of applying them in guardianship proceedings would be able to produce the results required by theory.

Defining exceptional cases is not simply a matter of fine-tuning that could be achieved through individual litigation. Producing inflated numbers of persons unduly restricted in their legal capacity is an inherent feature of guardianship laws.[55] The available statistics show that in countries where plenary guardianship is an option, it is used at alarming rates: according to one study, of all placements under guardianship, plenary guardianships constituted 57 per cent in Hungary, 59 per cent in Moldova, 82 per cent in the Czech Republic and 89 per cent in Bulgaria and Croatia.[56] Commentators note a similar tendency of

[47] A Ward, 'Abolition of Guardianship? "Best Interests" versus "Best Interpretation"' (2015) 32 *Scots Law Times* 150, 150.

[48] L Series, 'Relationships, Autonomy and Legal Capacity: Mental Capacity and Support Paradigms' (2015) 40 *International Journal of Psychiatry* 80, 88.

[49] Skowron, 'Giving substance' 133.

[50] ibid.

[51] Carney, 'Guardianship, Citizenship, & Theorizing Substitute-decisionmaking Law' 7.

[52] See the discussion of 'facilitated decision-making' in: Mental Disability Advocacy Centre (MDAC), *Legal Capacity in Europe* (MDAC, 2013) 28.

[53] J Chesterman, 'Modernising Adult Protection in an Age of Choice' (2014) 73 *Australian Journal of Public Administration* 520.

[54] Kapp, 'Assessing Assessments of Decision-Making Capacity' at 12.

[55] M Hamilton, 'Supported Decision-making as an Alternative to Guardianship' (2023) *Trends in State Courts* 87, 88.

[56] Mental Disability Advocacy Centre (MDAC), *Legal Capacity in Europe*, 24.

the overuse of plenary guardianship in the US as well.[57] Indeed, the history of guardianship reforms offers abundant examples of systemic failures of courts to implement basic legislative changes, such as replacing plenary guardianship with partial guardianship.[58] As one commentator noted: 'New legislative wine often sours in old (judicial) bottles.'[59]

Guardianship has become a major human rights issue because the legal capacity of a large number of persons has been unduly restricted. The causes of this problem are manifold, including a prejudiced view of the ability of persons with some disabilities to make decisions on their own behalf.[60] This was reflected in mainstream international law, which was unable to protect persons with disabilities from encroachments on their legal capacity.[61] The CRPD aims to overcome existing prejudices about the incapacity of persons with disabilities, which was one of the main motives for its adoption.[62]

There is another, more technical problem with ensuring that exceptional solutions apply only to exceptional cases: the law's ability to define the exception is quite limited in the area of legal capacity and perhaps disability law in general.[63] This is known as the group to individual problem, in which a phenomenon such as persons unable to make decisions with support exist on a group or population level, but courts are unable to determine whether a particular case is an instance of the phenomenon.[64] Guardianship essentially requires the prediction of a person's decision-making ability in a future situation. It is an individualised exercise because the abilities of individuals vary depending on many factors, such as education, experience, access to and the nature of support, and others.[65] This makes comparing cases and setting up objective standards difficult. It is no surprise that decision-making often turns to the only hard data available, the nature and severity of the disability.[66] This overvalues

[57] L Salzman, 'Guardianship for persons with mental illness – a legal and appropriate alternative?' (2011) 4 *Saint Louis University Journal of Health Law and Policy* 279, 286; Grisso, *Evaluating Competencies*, 317.

[58] NA Kohn, 'Legislating Supported Decision-Making' (2021) 58 *Harvard Journal on Legislation* 313, 325.

[59] T Carney, 'Globalisation and Guardianship – Harmonisation or Postmodern Diversity?' (2001) 24 *International Journal of Law and Psychiatry* 95, 104.

[60] AJ Jackson, 'Between us: Facilitated decision-making in the relational experience of profound intellectual disability' (2023) 51(4) *Ethos* 370, 374.

[61] MA Stein, 'Disability Human Rights' (2007) 95 *California Law Review* 82, 82.

[62] P Bartlett, 'The UN Convention on the Rights of Persons with Disabilities: great opportunities and dangerous interpretations' (2019) 18(1) *World Psychiatry* 47, 49.

[63] K Kanev, 'Remarks at the New York Law School Symposium: International Human Rights Law and the Institutional Treatment of Persons with Mental Disabilities' (2002) 21 *New York Law School Journal of International and Comparative Law* 356, 358.

[64] DL Faigman and K Geiser, 'Using burdens of proof to allocate the risk of error when assessing developmental maturity of youthful offenders' (2022) 63 *William & Mary Law Review* 1289, 1290.

[65] Mental Disability Advocacy Centre (MDAC), 'A kizáró gondnokság kérdése az új Ptk.-ban' (31 March 2008) 1.

[66] Grisso, *Evaluating Competencies*, 12.

psychiatric and psychological expertise and leads to a semi-automatic placement under guardianship of persons with more severe disabilities.[67]

It should be pointed out that assessment tools can never predict capacity with absolute accuracy, even in theory. Psychiatric experts agree that evaluations are not exclusively based on objective criteria but also rely on policy and social prejudice.[68] They are more reliable in identifying clearly incapable and clearly capable individuals, but there are always persons in the middle who cannot convincingly be put in either category.[69] As Sally Hurme and Paul Appelbaum argue, there is no objective scientific cut-off point between capable and incapable.[70] How persons in the grey zone will be categorised depends on many subjective factors.[71] Classifications based on advance assessments are thus always bound to produce a certain number of errors. The proportion of persons wrongly considered capable compared with persons wrongly considered incapable can be changed by changing the assessment criteria, but neither can be eliminated entirely.[72] This means that if guardianship is available, the legal capacity of some persons who are able to make decisions with support will be limited. This takes place in theory even if the system operates according to the highest professional requirements. Faulty application in practice, which is not a possibility but a reality in most jurisdictions of the world, only severely exacerbates the problem.

The Some Guardianship position relies on the assumption that it is possible to restrict the use of substituted decision-making to exceptional situations. However, no wording of such a rule has been proposed so far. In the absence of a workable solution, the fear remains that the exception becomes the rule. This is precisely the situation currently,[73] which the introduction of supported decision-making aims to overcome, not preserve.[74]

7.1.3. Common Ground and Divergence between the Two Positions

The two positions outlined above share an assumption regarding the relationship between supported decision-making and guardianship: they both consider the former preferable for some categories of individuals. For the Support

[67] Mental Disability Advocacy Centre (MDAC), *Legal Capacity in Europe*, 24.

[68] See PS Appelbaum, '"I Vote, I Count": Mental Disability and the Right to Vote' (2000) 51 *Psychiatric Services* 849, 850.

[69] R Raad, J Karlawish, and PS Appelbaum, 'The Capacity to Vote of Persons with Serious Mental Illness' (2009) 60 *Psychiatric Services* 624.

[70] SB Hurme and PS Appelbaum, 'Defining and Assessing Capacity to Vote: The Effect of Mental Impairment on the Rights of Voters' (2007) 38 *McGeorge Law Review* 931, 962.

[71] NA Kohn, 'Preserving Voting Rights in Long-Term Care Institutions: Facilitating Resident Voting While Maintaining Election Integrity' (2007) 38 *McGeorge Law Review* 1065, 1083.

[72] Hurme and Appelbaum, 'Defining and Assessing Capacity to Vote' 962.

[73] Kohn, Blumenthal, Campbell, 'Supported Decision-Making: A Viable Alternative' 1117.

[74] Bartlett, 'The UN Convention on the Rights of Persons with Disabilities' 49.

Only position, this category comprises all persons with disabilities; for Some Guardianship, the category is narrower.

What the two positions also share is both the necessity and the inability to address the situation of persons with high support needs. The Support Only position requires that persons with severe disabilities utilise a support framework, but its proponents have so far been unable to explain how this would work in practice.

Basing the position on a factually wrong assumption does not automatically disqualify it as a normative matter. If the abilities of persons with disabilities are constantly undervalued, acting on the normative assumption that their abilities should always be treated as higher than perceived might lead to good results. Perhaps, in most cases, the outcome will be more appropriate in relation to their actual abilities and, in any case, more favourable for them than basing the normative requirements on their perceived abilities.

Indeed, there is a lot to be said for this approach. Current legal capacity laws heavily undermine the autonomous status of persons with disabilities by constantly undervaluing their abilities.[75] Given this starting point, requiring states to act on the basis of these persons being more capable than courts think they are can be a sensible advocacy approach,[76] and it might produce good outcomes. Pointing out the factual incorrectness of the assumption is not enough to disqualify this approach.

However, with regard to a small minority of persons for whom the factual assumption is wrong, the normative approach does not, in fact, have to be beneficial. The Support Only position potentially harms persons with high support needs: if substituted decisions are prohibited, some of their decisions will not be made because these persons will not be accommodated in a support framework. If important decisions are not made, this could lead to serious harm or even death. If there is a framework which could prevent these harms and, at the same time, not be worse with regard to persons with lower support needs, it should therefore be preferred over the Support Only model.

The Some Guardianship position has a solution for persons with severe disabilities: guardianship. However, it cannot ensure that substituted decisions are utilised only in their case, that they are applied only in exceptional situations of genuine inability to reach a supported decision. As a result of guardianship's inherent tendency to be overinclusive, its retention has the potential of harming a large number of persons with disabilities who are able to utilise support and who will be denied it because they will be subjected to substituted decision-making.

Both positions have advantages for different groups of persons with disabilities, and both harm others in different ways. It is impossible to balance the harms in the abstract and evaluate which position would work better for a specific

[75] Jackson, 'Between us' 374.

[76] T Steinert, 'The UN Committee's interpretation of "will and preferences" can violate human rights' (2019) 18(1) *World Psychiatry* 45, 45.

jurisdiction. My aim is different: to find another solution for the case of persons with high support needs, which would work better than the existing two.

7.2. THE MODIFIED SUPPORT FRAMEWORK – A PROPOSAL FOR A THIRD OPTION

The proposal put forward by this book, named the Modified Support Framework, is not based on the factual assumption of the Support Only position. It nevertheless incorporates persons with high support needs in a support framework. It creates space for decisions to be made on their behalf within this framework, with the accompanying safeguards. If these decisions were not made, their life and well-being could be put in grave danger. However, substituted decisions do not automatically require a guardianship framework; they can be made in other ways as well. Many negative features of guardianship do not relate to substituted decisions as such.[77] Instead, they are connected to the ex-ante categorisation of persons based on capacity assessments.[78] To justify the transfer of decision-making power from the disabled person to the guardian, courts need to establish who lacks the capacity to make those decisions. This leads to many shortcomings of the system, as explained earlier.[79]

The categorisation can be avoided if the power to make substituted decisions is based on a different source, not on court decisions and capacity assessments. I argue that disabled persons' inability to make their wishes known to an outside observer is a more useful cut-off point to determine when a substituted decision should be permitted. In the Modified Support Framework, the disabled person can make her own decisions with support if she can communicate these in a form which a third person can understand. If the disabled person cannot communicate her decisions, the supporter is entitled to make supported decisions on her behalf. The supporter should make all efforts to establish the person's wishes and achieve a supported decision if possible, but if all else fails, he can make the decision on behalf of the disabled person.

These are the proposal's main features, which themselves raise additional questions. The ex-ante categorisation of guardianship serves as an important safeguard. I therefore have to explain how the Modified Support Framework ensures that substituted decisions are not abused. It needs to be tested how it resolves specific decision-making scenarios for different categories of persons. If I can show that the Modified Support Framework is better with regard to some categories of persons with disabilities than the existing two approaches

[77] Series and Nilsson, 'Article 12 CRPD' 341.
[78] Flynn and Arstein-Kerslake, 'Legislating personhood' 95.
[79] AE Buchanan and DW Brock *Deciding for Others: The Ethics of Surrogate Decision Making* (Cambridge University Press, 1989) 19.

and not worse with regard to others, it should be accepted as superior to them.[80] If I cannot show this, I should make clear in what respect one of the existing approaches is better.

We should not expect that this proposal is perfect in the sense that it successfully protects all persons with disabilities from all possible types of harm. As I argued in the previous chapter, this is not possible. Every kind of intervention emphasises different values to the detriment of others and is, therefore, better suited for avoiding certain types of harm. Because the law can only create one specific framework, the result will likely be imperfect at least for some categories affected, for whom a different framework might be preferred. More sub-categories might be created within a framework, but this has its own disadvantages, which should be evaluated together with the other features of that particular solution. The key is therefore to be clear about what type of problems each approach solves and creates. The different approaches' overall effectiveness might depend a lot on how they are implemented in practice. Choosing between them is an exercise in evaluating and comparing the type and frequency of harm. Nevertheless, it should be clear what values each of the solutions are promoting vis-à-vis the other approaches.

7.2.1. Who are 'Persons with High Support Needs' from a Legal Perspective?

The first question to consider is who exactly belongs to the group of persons unable to make decisions even with support. As shown above, this is a contentious point because some authors deny that such a category even exists.[81] It is even more difficult to establish its contours. Defining the group is not simply an exercise in deciding on a threshold based on the severity of disability. Persons with the same degree of disability from a medical perspective, expressed in the form of IQ points or other measures, can have very different abilities due to various factors, such as training and education, experience, familiarity with the environment in which the task is carried out, and so on.[82] More sophisticated psychological tools to assess the person's ability to utilise support, similar to those developed for capacity assessments, have not yet been developed.[83] Once supported decision-making will be an established legal institution, and assessments will concentrate on the question of utilising support, such tools will hopefully be available. That, however, does not help with the current analysis.

The solution lies in specifying the categorisation's purpose. The Some Guardianship position is based on a separate legal category for persons who

[80] M Nussbaum, 'The Capabilities of People with Cognitive Disabilities' (2009) 40 *Metaphilosophy* 331.
[81] Dhanda, 'Legal Capacity in the Disability Rights Convention' 445.
[82] Mental Disability Advocacy Centre (MDAC), 'A kizáró gondnokság' 1.
[83] Kapp, 'Assessing Assessments of Decision-Making Capacity' 12.

cannot utilise support – they are the ones who need to be placed under guardianship. In the Modified Support Framework, however, formally, the same intervention – supported decision-making – applies to all types of persons. There is thus no need to authoritatively decide who belongs to which category for the purposes of this legal intervention.

The question becomes relevant in a different way. Persons with high support needs are incorporated into the Support Only proposal by proactive actions of their supporters – they receive 100 per cent support,[84] or the supporters make the decision based on their personal history using a narrative ethics approach.[85] That is support only from an idealised normative perspective – this is how supporters should behave in those circumstances. From a legal standpoint, however, there is no difference between this type of support and substitution. The decision-making process is a matter only between the supporter and the supported person.[86] An outsider cannot establish whether the ideal criteria were met because they learn about the process only from the supporter.[87] The supporter, however, is also the only one who could breach the ideal criteria, for example, by substituting his own wishes for those of the supported person. Therefore, the difference between the supporter acting in a supported or in a substituted way is legally unenforceable – an outside party, such as a judge, cannot observe the difference.

It follows that for the purposes of legal regulation, the relevant question is whether the supported person can make her wishes known to an outsider. If she can, the outsider can be sure that the decision is her own, at least in the sense that she does not reject it. She might have been misled or abused by the supporter in various ways, and thus, the decision might not reflect her true wishes.[88] For situations like this, the safeguards described in the previous chapter apply.[89] Nevertheless, by expressing the decision, the supported person herself believes the decision to be her own.

If the supported person cannot express her decision in a way that is comprehensible to an outsider, she has to rely in this respect on her supporter. From a legal perspective, it is irrelevant whether the decision expressed by the supporter was reached with support or by substitution, because only the supporter knows the answer. A third person or an outside supervisory body could review the supporter's claim only if they knew the person's personal circumstances better than the supporter, which is very unlikely. The supervisory body could review

[84] Dhanda, 'Legal Capacity in the Disability Rights Convention' 445.

[85] Bach and Kerzner, 'A New Paradigm for Protecting Autonomy' 60.

[86] CB McGeehan and L Berninger, 'Autonomous by Extension: Balancing Patient Autonomy and Vulnerability in Surrogate Decision-making' (2024) 35(3) *AACN Advanced Critical Care* 228, 236.

[87] Barclay, 'Paternalism, Supported Decision-Making and Expressive Respect' 147.

[88] Skowron, 'Giving substance' 128.

[89] See chapter 6 above.

the claim using a best interest standard, but that would be incompatible with supported decision-making.[90] The decision should therefore be respected.

The framework thus creates a cut-off point and separates disabled persons for the purposes of legal regulation into exactly two categories: those who can communicate their decisions on their own will have a right to make decisions with support, and their supporters must not make substituted decisions on their behalf; for those who can be understood only by their supporters, law cannot ensure that their decisions are indeed supported ones.

The latter category of persons, those who are unable to communicate their decision to an outsider, is wider than 'persons with high support needs' as usually understood. It includes those who truly cannot utilise support, those whose wishes cannot be understood even by their supporters, and also those who can make supported decisions but can communicate them only in a manner that their supporters can understand. As a practical matter, it is irrelevant for the Modified Support Framework to which of these categories the person belongs because all these sub-groups share the same legal fate.

Persons unable to express their decisions enter legal transactions through their supporters. It does not matter whether they are unable to communicate the specific decision they made, or whether they are unable to make the decision, or merely choose not to make it. Once they fail to communicate a decision, the supporter is entitled to communicate it on their behalf. What matters for third parties and external observers is that some decisions of persons who did not communicate a choice need to be expressed by the supporter. Only the supporter knows which of the person's decisions were or can be made with support and which need to be made by substitution. Because outsiders cannot judge how the decision was made, they have to trust the supporter that he made the greatest possible effort in establishing the person's true wishes.

The supporter is prohibited from communicating or making a decision on behalf of the supported person only if the latter communicates it herself. In this case, the supported person's will takes precedence over the supporter's. If the supported person is unable or unwilling to communicate a decision, if she does not express dissatisfaction with the decision made by the supporter, the decision will be binding on her as her own. It cannot be overturned on the ground that the disabled person's wishes were not respected since those wishes could not be established. However, that does not preclude overturning them on different grounds, as explained below.

Defining the legal cut-off point at the level of the inability to communicate one's decision sets the Modified Support Framework proposal apart from the other two models. Contrary to the Support Only position, it expressly recognises that some persons need some decisions to be made on their behalf in a substituted way. On the other hand, contrary to the Some Guardianship position, it

[90] General comment No. 1, § 29 b).

does not single out these persons and decisions for special legal intervention, such as guardianship, and does not create a separate legal status for them. Those substituted decisions can be made by their supporters, who are appointed and are acting in a supported decision-making framework.

7.2.2. The Modified Support Framework in Practice

At this point some examples might be helpful to make clear how, in fact, this book's proposal plays out for different categories of persons. This part will examine how a simple decision, such as withdrawing money from one's bank account to buy a new bed, will be executed by different individuals under the different proposals. Three individuals will be considered: A, who is able to make this decision with support and communicate it in a way that bank clerks understand; B, who is able to make it with support, but the bank clerk cannot understand her; and C, who is unable to make the decision with support.

A's situation is seemingly similar under all three proposals, at least in the normative sense: she should be treated the same way regardless of which framework is adopted. She should have a supporter who would explain the options available: how a new bed might help her sleep better and which types are available for what price. Depending on her needs, the supporter could help her understand the benefits of a more expensive bed, the value of the price difference and what it equals to so that she can choose whether she prefers the increased comfort over the equivalent of, for example, 15 music CDs. Once A has made her decision about what type of bed she needs, she can instruct the bank clerk to withdraw the money from her account. The bank clerk has, therefore, no doubts that this is what she wants.

How A ended up in this situation, however, varies across the three models. In the Support Only model and the Modified Support Framework, her case would be simple – only supporters are available, therefore she could only have a supporter. As she is able to express a decision, the supporter is not allowed to articulate a decision on her behalf, and if he does, the bank clerk is bound to follow A's decision. If the supporter was concerned that A's expressed decision was harming her interests, he should be able to turn to a court to declare it null and void, as with any supported decision.[91]

In the Some Guardianship framework, however, where guardianship is possible, a court certifying A's supporter must have established prior to the scenario that A is indeed capable of making this type of decision with support, that she does not need a guardian for it. That judgment must have been passed some time previously, with unknown precision – it is unlikely that buying a bed was precisely the question the court was considering when deciding on A's legal

[91] See chapter 6.2.4 above.

capacity. It is possible that if A was found to lack the capacity to make some types of financial decisions, she is under guardianship also with regard to buying a bed or withdrawing money from her account. Therefore, possibly she would not act with a supporter, but a guardian would act on her behalf. This is an interference with her autonomy, which is not justified by her actual skills with regard to the precise task at the given moment. This is the harm A has to suffer under this framework.

B is able to make the decision, but she is unable to communicate it to the bank clerk. In the Modified Support Framework, she would make the decision with her supporter, similarly to A above. Her supporter would then communicate it to the bank clerk in B's presence. Unless the bank clerk can establish that B wants something else, he has to accept the supporter's interpretation of what B's decision is. If B is dissatisfied with the decision as expressed by her supporter, she can turn to a court to declare it null and void, for example with the help of another supporter.[92]

In the Support Only framework, B's situation is problematic. She could make the decision with the help of her supporter, but she could not communicate it to the bank clerk. The bank clerk could not accept the supporter's interpretation of what B's decision is, because the clerk has no way of knowing whether it reflects B's will or that of the supporter. The latter, substituting the supporter's will for B's, is not allowed in this framework, and outsiders are required not to honour substituted decisions. More support would have to be provided to B until she is able to make her wish known. If that is not possible, she could not withdraw money from her account.

Under the Some Guardianship model, B would have to act through a guardian since she is unable to communicate the decision herself. This implies all the difficulties of placing B in the appropriate category with a court judgment, as explained above with regard to A. If B's status is established correctly, her position is arguably still worse than it would be in a Modified Support Framework. There, the decision is still supposed to take place in a supported way, while in the Some Guardianship model, the guardian makes a substituted decision. That difference cannot be enforced in practice. Only B and her supporter know how the decision was made; outsiders have no way of interfering with the decision-making process. One would expect supporters to make more effort in establishing B's wishes than guardians, but nobody can know whether that has indeed been the case, and certainly cannot know this with regard to a specific decision. Only if B is able to object to a supported decision would the situation be different. In the Some Guardianship framework, her objection would be irrelevant – the guardian's decision would prevail. In the Modified Support Framework, however, the bank clerk would have to accept her objections – they take precedence over the

[92] See chapter 6 above.

decision communicated by the supporter. The supporter is able to communicate a decision on behalf of B only if she is unable to do so.

C is unable to make a decision even with support, and therefore, she would have a problem in the Support Only framework. Her supporter cannot make a decision on her behalf, consequently no decision will be made. She would have to receive more support, enough for her to make her decision known to the bank clerk. If that cannot be achieved, she cannot withdraw money from her account and cannot buy a bed.

In the Some Guardianship model, C's guardian would make and communicate the decision on her behalf. A problem could arise again with the prior judicial establishment of C's lack of capacity. If she was incorrectly incapacitated with regard to this decision, she would be denied the opportunity to make her decision in a supported way. On the contrary if she was unable to make this decision but was incorrectly assumed by the court to be able to make it, she would have no guardian for this purpose and would not be able to withdraw money from her account. She would have to go through a new guardianship procedure, and her guardian's powers would have to be extended, or a new guardian would have to be appointed to cover this area.

The Modified Support Framework would work for C similarly to the Some Guardianship model. Her supporter would have to make and communicate the decision on her behalf. In this case, no court needs to establish in advance whether C is unable to make the decision with support or not. It is her supporter's duty to make all effort in establishing C's wishes. However, this cannot be supervised by the bank clerk or an outside body, except if C is able to communicate an objection to her supporter's decision – in that case, the clerk honours her objection.

The above examples highlight that the main weakness of the Some Guardianship proposal lies in its reliance on prior categorisation of persons according to their capacity with regard to various decisions. This is problematic for several reasons. First, it has a great potential for mistakes. As shown above, the practice of guardianship in many jurisdictions is characterised by heavy overuse.[93] Second, mistakes are not equally distributed. The system leads to over-caution: failure to appoint a guardian for an area is more serious because it would lead to decisions not being made.[94] Conversely, the appointment of a guardian in an area where he is not needed would only mean that the decision will be unnecessarily made in a substituted way. Third, capacity assessments are by their nature imprecise: the court has to list a reasonable number of areas in which a person has or lacks capacity, with some degree of generality. It is impossible to assess the person's capacity for all possible tasks within these categories. It is very likely that she would, in fact, be able to make some decisions

[93] RM Powell and MA Stein, 'People with Disabilities and Sexual and Reproductive Rights: an International Comparative Analysis' (2016) 11 *Frontiers of Law in China* 53, 77.

[94] Hurme and Appelbaum, 'Defining and Assessing Capacity to Vote' 962.

in the general category, but her legal capacity with regard to them would be restricted.[95] Fourth, the prior judicial establishment of her capacity status is very static. A person's ability with regard to certain tasks can change over time; it can improve or deteriorate, sometimes very quickly.[96] The person's mood in the given moment might determine whether she is able and willing to make the specific decision which is required of her. No prior assessment can capture this fluctuation, which can unnecessarily restrict the person's right to make some decisions with support, which she would be able to make in practice.

The Support Only framework's shortcomings are pretty obvious. If a person's all decisions have to be made in a supported way, at least some decisions of at least some persons will not be made, even in theory. In practice, the situation can be much worse, depending on what kind of support is available. Nevertheless, there might be reasons to prefer this framework. Perhaps its proponents believe that the number of people thus harmed is miniscule, and the interests of others in not accepting any form of substitution either in form or substance outweigh them. Perhaps if support was the only option available, society would be forced to find new ways of providing it, and also persons who are currently thought to be unable to benefit from support could be included in the framework. These are empirical claims that have to be spelt out explicitly and evaluated on their own terms. If one has to choose between different types of harm, it is essential to know how exactly everybody will be affected.

Some might object that this analysis excludes from the Support Only model decisions that can only be understood by the supporter and not the outside world. If those were accepted as legitimate supported decisions, perhaps in the way Bach and Kerzner suggest, the model would work for more people.[97] That is undoubtedly true, but as explained above, the outside world could never be confident about the nature of those decisions. Maybe they were made in a supported way by the disabled person, perhaps they are the supporter's own decisions.[98] Since the Support Only model objects to substituted decisions, the legal system's duty is to prevent them from taking place. Hence, decisions whose validity could not be ascertained should not be accepted.

7.2.3. Comparing the Three Models

The Modified Support Framework openly admits that some decisions made by supporters will be substituted ones. Since substitution is allowed, it is possible

[95] L Turner-Stokes, K Benaichouche-Motam, W Goodison, A Altaie, A Howard, P McKnight, and J Alfonso, 'Improving the systematic screening and documentation of mental capacity for patients with severe brain injury: The Mental Capacity Screening assessment tool (MCScreen)' (2024) 24(5) *Clinical Medicine, Journal of the Royal College of Physicians of London* 1.

[96] A Peterson, J Karlawish, and E Largent, 'Supported Decision Making With People at the Margins of Autonomy' (2021) 21(11) *American Journal of Bioethics* 4, 7.

[97] Bach and Kerzner, 'A New Paradigm for Protecting Autonomy' 60.

[98] Barclay, 'Paternalism, Supported Decision-Making and Expressive Respect' 147.

that some decisions that could be taken in a supported way will be made in a substituted way. Only those persons who are themselves able to raise an objection against a substituted decision will be protected from this kind of abuse. For them, the model is no worse than the Support Only model and significantly better than the Some Guardianship model: there is no prior capacity assessment, therefore anybody capable of making a particular decision at a particular moment will be allowed to utilise support, and object if the supporter abuses his position.

For persons who are unable to communicate a decision to others, the Modified Support Framework is significantly better than the Support Only model because it allows for their decisions to be, in fact, made. It is also no worse than the Some Guardianship framework because the decisions are made in the same way in both approaches. In fact, even in this situation, the Modified Support Framework has an advantage because it does not rely on prior capacity assessments and, therefore, avoids wrongful categorisations.

The Support Only model requires support to be also provided for persons unable to communicate their decisions. This normative requirement does not lead to more support because it cannot be enforced. If a third person is unable to establish whether the decision was made in a supported or substituted way, the requirement to support cannot be supervised, its violations cannot be sanctioned.[99] The supporter's exclusive knowledge makes him the best decision-maker in the question of whether support is possible or not in a given situation. This decision should be allocated to him, not to an outside reviewer.

If this assumption is correct, requiring support all the time as a normative matter does not lead to good results. The law is unable to enforce in practice the prohibition of substituted decisions against supporters who breach their obligations. Also, if the supporter willingly wishes to fulfil his obligation in situations in which it is impossible, it will hurt the supported person because a decision will not be made. It, therefore, leads to better results and, in any case, is more in line with reality if the supporter has the power to decide whether a substituted decision is required or not.

Basing this decision with the supporter is the strength of the Modified Support Framework compared with the Some Guardianship approach. In the latter approach, the type of decision, supported or substituted, always has to be determined in advance with some level of generality by outsiders. That is highly problematic, as I described earlier.

The Modified Support Framework connects the enforceability of support to the ability to communicate decisions by the supported person. In the case of the Some Guardianship approach, the standard is much higher: demonstrating legal capacity in the abstract in a court procedure removed from the decision itself.

[99] M Donnelly, 'Support Relationships in Law: Framing, Fictions and the Responsive State' in M Donnelly, R Harding, and E Taşcıoğlu (eds), *Supporting Legal Capacity in Socio-Legal Context* (Hart, 2022) 29.

The Modified Support Framework is more beneficial to persons with disabilities in general. It does not eliminate capacity assessments entirely. They can indeed be invaluable to establish what the person's skills and abilities are, and what type of support could be more suitable for her. However, these assessments cannot serve as a basis for incapacitation, they do not justify limiting rights.

One might point out that capacity assessments in guardianship also serve a crucial safeguarding function: they ensure that the guardian takes over decision-making only in areas where the person is certified not to have capacity.[100] Because this is lacking in the Modified Support Framework, the supporter could usurp powers even in areas where this is not warranted. However, this view is mistaken. The supporter has the power to make substituted decisions only where the person is uncommunicative. In these areas, substituted decisions are a certainty if guardianship is allowed. In other areas, the supporter has no right to make substituted decisions as a legal matter since third parties are bound to follow the decisions expressed by the supported person. The supporter's actions are also subject to the safeguards described in the previous chapter.

The Modified Support Framework requires the supported person's active objection to prevent the supporter from making an unjustified substituted decision. If the supported person is misled, threatened or otherwise manipulated by the supporter not to state an objection, the latter can make substituted decisions in areas where he would not have such rights even as a guardian. This situation is not different from the forms of abuse described and dealt with in the previous chapter, and the same type of safeguards would apply. This type of abuse is possible because no system is able to eliminate it completely. Supporters who have such extensive influence over the supported person are able to manipulate them in other ways as well. The Modified Support Framework will be unable to protect the person, who, although able, is not objecting and has no other supporters to help her. Outside control mechanisms to investigate abuse under a social protection or even criminal framework might be a solution, as in the case of non-disabled individuals who find themselves in a similar situation. The Modified Support Framework at least gives such represented persons the right to object to the abuse on the spot when a decision is expressed by the supporter – were they under guardianship, their situation would be even worse, as the guardian could act without them being present, and in any case their objections would have no legal relevance.

Guardianship is more convenient than the Modified Support Framework from one perspective. The latter's in-built safeguard is that the supported person must be present when a decision on her behalf is made. If she was not present, the other party could not be certain that she, in fact, is unable to communicate a decision. Always requiring the presence of a person with severe multiple

[100] T Henking and M Scholten, 'Respect for the Will and Preferences of People with Mental Disorders in German Law' in C Kong, J Coggon, P Cooper, M Dunn, and AR Keene (eds), *Capacity, Participation and Values in Comparative Legal Perspective* (Bristol University Press, 2023) 212.

disabilities can be burdensome for some carers, who would prefer to handle some matters on their own. This problem is mitigated by certain factors. Persons with high support needs are unlikely to have many legal transactions – even in a guardianship system, their contacts with their guardians are often limited to a monthly visit or even less.[101] Nevertheless, it could indeed present a severe burden in particular cases, for example, when the disabled person buys a home using a loan – one decision is made, but several signatures in different places will be required.

Simple powers of attorney could solve this problem in the Modified Support Framework. These could be issued in the represented person's home, where witnesses could certify that she did not express any objection to authorising her representative. If the state considered that more safeguards are necessary, a state body, such as the local social security office could certify these authorisations. The supporter is practically authorising himself because he is expressing the supported person's wish; therefore, the only issue to be certified is that the latter is indeed uncommunicative on the matter. The overuse of this practice of powers of attorney can lead to abuse. Supporters interested in their own convenience could be denying the opportunity for the disabled person to try to make her own supported decision. In that case, such powers of attorneys could be restricted, abolished or countered in other ways, depending on how much harm they actually cause and prevent. This is certainly not a necessary element of the model, but it should be mentioned as a possibility.

7.3. SAFEGUARDS ENSURING THAT SUPPORT DOES NOT BECOME SUBSTITUTION

There is a specific risk inherent in the Modified Support Framework: the unjust use of substituted decisions. I do not believe that a review mechanism that attempted to make sure that the supporter resorted to support to the maximum extent possible could be effective. It would be intrusive for an outside body to interfere with the relationship between the supporter and the supported person, with little basis to establish what the true nature of the decision was. Indeed, guardians are also not required to justify each of their individual decisions in a review procedure, although their powers are more extensive and the potential for abuse is higher. Any overview by administrative bodies or courts should be concerned with the supported person's well-being, as described in chapter six, not with the nature of the decisions expressed by the supporter.

The fact that there are no supervision mechanisms, however, does not mean that supporters will be no different than guardians. The system's design, first of

[101] Mental Disability Advocacy Centre (MDAC), *Guardianship and Human Rights in Hungary* (MDAC, 2007) 73.

all, ensures that to the extent supported persons are able to voice their own will, they will be able to do so, and their preferences will be legally relevant. In this regard, this model already has a significant advantage compared to guardianship. Indeed, it is likely to benefit most persons who are relatively more able to make their wishes known to others.

However, for persons unable to communicate, the status of supporters still matters. Currently, guardians in most countries are acting in a system based on substituted decisions made in the person's best interest. Non-respect for the decision-making ability of persons with disabilities is part of their institutional culture. Repressive guardianship laws, which treat the will of persons under guardianship as irrelevant, contribute to this institutional culture.

Supporters are expected by law to act differently; they are required to make all efforts to take the disabled person's wishes into account. This obligation can be enforced with regard to persons who are able to communicate their wishes. Even if the obligation cannot be enforced with regard to persons who cannot communicate with outsiders, it is reasonable to expect that this system will evolve in a different institutional culture of supporters. It should be more likely for them to act by supporting a person and not substituting her wishes simply because this is what the law requires of them, and this is what members of their profession do.

Obviously, the institutional culture of supporters is shaped by many factors other than law. Their selection, training, support provided by public bodies, workload, and public awareness about and appreciation for supported decision-making are all important considerations.[102] How the practice of supporters in a given jurisdiction develops, whether it will be better in this regard than the practice of guardians, is a question for future empirical analysis. Nevertheless, it can be stated that as a conceptual matter, the legal framework of supported decision-making, as an important factor in developing institutional culture and communicating social expectations towards all stakeholders, is promoting more supported decisions even for persons unable to communicate. That is also true of the Modified Support Framework proposal. It remains to be seen how significant this factor is. Nevertheless, in the absence of viable legal safeguards against the overuse of substitution, extra-legal factors such as institutional culture will have to be taken more seriously in implementing any system of supported decision-making.

7.4. THE EQUALITY OF PERSONS WITH HIGH SUPPORT NEEDS

Compared with the current system of guardianship, the Modified Support Framework primarily benefits persons with high support needs who are able to

[102] T Carney and D Tait, 'Adult Guardianship: Narrative Readings in the "Shadow" of the Law?' (1998) 21(2) *International Journal of Law and Psychiatry* 147, 149.

communicate a supported decision. They will be able to enjoy genuine support, with all the educational benefits for developing their skills, and take an active part in exercising their autonomy.

Those who are unable to be understood by others also benefit. They are present when their transactions are made. They have an opportunity to make supported decisions, or at least to try. Some of their decisions will be substituted, and because this cannot be supervised by outsiders, perhaps more decisions than are necessary. Nevertheless, they are not automatically excluded from the possibility of utilising support. It is their default option. More of them will be able to make use of it than if they were under guardianship.

In addition, the model also has an important expressive function. Incapacitation is stigmatising. It emphasises inability and signals to the outside world that the person is in some crucial way less capable than her fellow non-disabled citizens. It is also a marker of lack of potential for development, besides being the reason for deteriorating skills. Support, however, has a different message. Its ideology emphasises that the person is making decisions similarly to everybody else and is no different from others regarding her status. Needless to say, support in itself does not decrease the stigma already attached to disability, but at least it does not add to it, unlike guardianship.[103]

Persons who are unable to make decisions even with support benefit seemingly little from the model described here. However, they have a better opportunity than under guardianship to make use of any decision-making skills they have or new skills they happen to develop. In addition, they are better off with regard to the model's expressive function. Even if they were unable to make any decisions in practice, their human dignity is not curtailed by an unnecessary stigma of incapacity. That has an important implication for all persons with disabilities, who, in this way, are able to be incorporated into the category of legally capable individuals, at least formally, and thus achieve equality with regard to this fundamental marker of being a fully accepted member of society.

The Modified Support Framework fails to achieve the full equality of persons with high support needs the way envisaged by the Support Only model: some of them will not be able to make decisions with support and substituted decisions will have to be made on their behalf. There does not seem to be a better option. Law is an imperfect tool to overcome all inequalities in all senses of the word. Mandating supported decisions in all cases cannot be enforceable in practice for the reasons explained above, and it might even hurt rather than help persons with high support needs.

Nevertheless, even persons who need substitute decisions do not have to rely on a guardianship model characterised by ex-ante categorisations based on capacity assessments. The Modified Support Framework provides even for them

[103] J Fiala-Butora, MA Stein and JE Lord, 'The democratic life of the Union: towards equal voting participation for Europeans with Disabilities' (2014) 55 *Harvard International Law Journal* 71, 101.

a more advantageous alternative for developing their skills and benefiting from support as much as they can, without giving up on the idea of protecting them from abuse. Some will perhaps never be fully equal in their real opportunities to make supported decisions. Nevertheless, the proposal developed here provides them with a meaningful conception of equality within the support framework, closer to being fully equal than in any other proposal so far.

The Modified Support Framework provides less protection from harm than guardianship. That is a conscious choice because it emphasises the autonomy of persons with disabilities over protection. Nevertheless, it can be equipped with specific procedural safeguards to protect, for example, the disabled person's property or to facilitate decision-making in healthcare matters. The safeguards can provide various levels of oversight and protection from abuse at the expense of decreased levels of autonomy. What particular solution should be chosen in a given jurisdiction is a matter of empirical analysis of the types and severity of abuses and a value judgment about which of these should be necessarily countered. There is no one optimal set of safeguards; various levels of protection are possible within the model.

The last issue I have to consider is how the Modified Support Framework proposal, which extends supported decision-making to persons with high support needs, affects persons with disabilities with regular support needs. There is not much to say here. The Modified Support Framework opens up the possibility of substituted decisions if the supported persons do not express a decision. That could potentially lead to some additional forms of abuse compared to those described in the previous chapter. These are, however, not categorically different from those discussed previously, and do not require a different form of response. The supported person will always have the possibility to express an opinion, which will take precedence over the supporter's will. In case the supported person fails to raise an objection and becomes a victim of abuse, the regular safeguard of declaring the transaction void is available to her and any other of her supporters.

The key feature of the proposal developed here is strengthening the position of the disabled person in decisions concerning her life. The proposal reinforces her ability to take part in these decisions effectively and is also dependent on it for the best outcomes. It is the most advantageous for any person with typically milder disabilities who is seriously disadvantaged by guardianship and who could fully utilise a support option. For others, the difference will not be so obvious, but the framework developed here has either clear advantages over guardianship, or in the case of those who could make very little or no actual use of support, such as persons in a coma, it is at least not worse, and arguably better for its symbolic and expressive effect. Consequently, it offers an interpretation of Article 12 of the CRPD that provides the overall highest level of autonomy for persons with disabilities.

8

Conclusion

PERSONS WITH DISABILITIES have suffered denial of their legal capacity, and thus of legal personhood, for more than two millennia.[1] Their personal autonomy has been restricted, their human rights violated through placement under guardianship, and theories of justice have failed to include them in concepts of equal citizenship and justify their equal moral personhood.[2] This book has argued how these problems can be overcome and how persons with disabilities can be integrated into a framework of equal legal capacity.

The Convention on the Rights of Persons with Disabilities requires that all persons with disabilities enjoy legal capacity on an equal basis with others. This has provided an important impetus for the debate, but it has not resolved it,[3] mainly because the CRPD Committee's interpretation is considered unreasonable by many states:[4] while it requires the incorporation of persons with severe disabilities in a support framework, it did not explain how this could be achieved.[5] Two central positions have emerged in the academic literature on how to understand equality in this domain. One argues that all persons with disabilities are able to exercise their legal capacity with support.[6] To emancipate persons with disabilities, they therefore need to be provided support for making their decisions.[7] Incapacitation in all its forms should be abolished, and persons with disabilities should be integrated into the framework of full legal capacity.[8] The move from guardianship to supported decision-making is often described as a paradigm shift: the old paradigm, based on incapacitation, is replaced by

[1] K Blankman, 'Guardianship Models in the Netherlands and Western Europe' (1997) 20 *International Journal of Law and Psychiatry* 47.

[2] A Arstein-Kerslake, *Restoring Voice to People with Cognitive Disabilities* (Cambridge University Press, 2017) 14.

[3] AR Keene, NB Kane, KYH Kim, and GS Owen, 'Mental capacity – Why look for a paradigm shift?' (2023) 31(3) *Medical Law Review* 340, 344.

[4] R Uerpmann-Wittzack, 'The Law-Making Function of the UN Committee on the Rights of Persons with Disabilities' (2018) 8(2) *Wroclaw Review of Law, Administration & Economics* 36, 44.

[5] MA Stein, F Mahomed, V Patel, and C Sunkel (eds), *Mental Health, Legal Capacity, and Human Rights* (Cambridge University Press, 2021) 5.

[6] E Flynn and A Arstein-Kerslake, 'Legislating personhood: realising the right to support in exercising legal capacity' (2014) 10(1) *International Journal of Law in Context* 81, 91.

[7] T Minkowitz, 'CRPD and transformative equality' (2017) 13(1) *International Journal of Law in Context* 77.

[8] A Dhanda, 'Legal Capacity in the Disability Rights Convention: Stranglehold of the Past or Lodestar for the Future?' (2007) *34 Syracuse Journal of International Law & Commerce* 429.

a new paradigm based on support, in which incapacitation has no place.[9] They are two realms that have no connection with each other. In the paradigm of fully respecting the dignity of persons with disabilities, there is no guardianship.

The other position argues that supporting all persons is not possible because some will be unable to make decisions, even with the highest degree of support.[10] If certain decisions cannot be made on their behalf and they cannot make them with support, they will suffer serious detriment or might even die.[11] Guardianship in some limited form therefore needs to be maintained. It follows that persons with disability cannot be integrated into a framework of full legal capacity. It is impossible in practice. For most persons with disabilities, it remains, at best a utopian aspiration and at worst a source of serious problems.

This book offers a third approach, the Modified Support Framework, which allows for some decisions to be made on behalf of the person but rejects formal categories of incapacitation. It promotes the autonomy of persons with disabilities by leading to better results regarding each sub-category of affected persons than existing approaches. Persons without need for support, persons able to make decisions with support, and persons with severe disabilities unable to make some decisions even with support are all either better off in the proposed framework or, in some cases, at least not worse off than they would be under alternative approaches. By abolishing ex ante categorisation, the proposal avoids many of the pitfalls of current guardianship regimes and of some proposed supported decision-making models,[12] which require the prediction of a person's capacity in advance and lock people in imprecise categories that result in their autonomy being denied. Basing the threshold of substitution on the supported person's ability to communicate a decision to persons other than her supporter avoids the involvement of courts and experts. It is a question observable by lay-people on the spot in a flexible, decision-specific way. The proposal is also not at odds with other similar proposals that describe how support should be developed beyond the suggested threshold, for persons who can only be understood by their supporters.[13] I agree with many of the arguments concerning

[9] L Salzman, 'Guardianship for persons with mental illness – a legal and appropriate alternative?' (2011) 4 *Saint Louis University Journal Health Law & Policy* 279, 285.

[10] J Dawson, 'A realistic approach to assessing mental health laws' compliance with the UNCRPD.' (2015) 40 *International Journal of Law and Psychiatry* 70.

[11] MC Freeman, K Kolappa JMC de Almeida, A Kleinman, N Makhashvili, S Phakathi, B Saraceno, G Thornicroft, 'Reversing Hard Won Victories in the Name of Human Rights: A Critique of the General Comment on Article 12 of the UN Convention on the Rights of Persons with Disabilities' (2015) 2(9) *Lancet Psychiatry* 844.

[12] M Bach and L Kerzner, 'A New Paradigm for Protecting Autonomy and the Right to Legal Capacity', Paper prepared for the Law Commission of Ontario 62 (2010).

[13] Arstein-Kerslake, *Restoring Voice*; E Flynn and A Arstein-Kerslake, 'Legislating personhood: realising the right to support in exercising legal capacity' (2014) 10(1) *International Journal of Law in Context* 81–104; A Arstein-Kerslake and E Flynn, 'The right to legal agency: domination, disability and the protections of Article 12 of the Convention on the Rights of Persons with Disabilities' (2017) 13(1) *International Journal of Law in Context* 22–38; C Kong, *Mental Capacity in Relationship* (Cambridge University Press, 2017).

how supporters should behave as a normative matter, even in these situations.[14] However, I consider the distinction between support and substitution in these areas unenforceable by law. This book provides a practical solution on what legal rules can ensure the maximum level of supported decision-making for all persons with disabilities. The success of such rules also depends on other factors, notably on implementation efforts and the building of administrative capacity by states. Hopefully, in the future, with changing societal and institutional culture recognising the skills of persons with disabilities, the limits of enforceable support can be pushed even further.

It only remains to put the proposal into the context of the main question raised by this book: how can persons with disabilities be treated on an equal basis with others with regard to exercising their legal capacity? In my opinion, some existing proposals on supported decision-making that are trying to eliminate substituted decisions completely are entrenching rather than overcoming the restrictions on the autonomy of persons with disabilities. They are doing that with the laudable goal of harnessing as much support as possible for all persons with disabilities, but the consequences are nevertheless detrimental.[15] They identify legal incapacitation, the removal of a person's decision-making powers, as the source of denial of disabled persons' autonomy. They want to accommodate disabled persons in the group of legally capable persons through support. However, in the paradigm based on support, people with disabilities are still subject to and are supposed to comply with the standard of the imagined rational person – to behave as a legally autonomous subject whose competent decisions are not questioned or overruled by the law. To be equal under this standard, persons with disabilities have to make decisions that are never overruled by others.[16] They receive support to meet this task and, therefore, can exercise their autonomy in a relational way contrary to the imagined 'rational man', but they are still expected to reach a threshold which is unrealistic for many.[17] If the rational person remains the standard, people with disabilities will be unable to achieve the status of ordinary citizens. They will never be fully equal.

This book rejects the idea that support is able to raise all persons with disabilities to the level of the idealised 'rational man' – mainly for the reason

[14] E Flynn and A Arstein-Kerslake, 'State intervention in the lives of people with disabilities: the case for a disability-neutral framework' (2017) 13(1) *International Journal of Law in Context* 39, 40; C Kong, *Mental Capacity in Relationship*.

[15] GL Neuman, 'Divergent Human Rights Approaches to Capacity and Consent' in MA Stein, F Mahomed, V Patel, and C Sunkel (eds), *Mental Health, Legal Capacity, and Human Rights* (Cambridge University Press, 2021).

[16] T Minkowitz, 'Abolishing Mental Health Laws to Comply with the Convention on the Rights of Persons with Disabilities' in OM Arnadóttir and G Quinn (eds) *The United Nations Convention on the Rights of Persons with Disabilities: European and Scandinavian Perspectives* (Martinus Nijhoff, 2009) 157.

[17] G Quinn and A Rekas-Rosalbo, 'Civil Death: Rethinking the foundations of personhood for persons with a disability' (2016) 56 *Irish Jurist* 286, 318.

that such a person does not exist. In a sense, I reject a particular conception of the paradigm shift. The paradigm in which all persons' decisions are always respected cannot be reached for persons with disabilities because it does not exist for non-disabled persons either. The law has always treated the decisions of legally capable individuals as potentially subject to being overruled by the court system in their own interest.[18] Persons with disabilities would not be equal if their decisions could never be overruled; they would indeed surpass non-disabled persons. Instead, the law should provide several tools to overrule certain decisions to protect individuals with and without disabilities alike on an objective basis from fraud, mistakes, abuse and other types of harm. Protection of one's interests, including protection from abuse and self-abuse, is a legitimate goal and should not be thrown out of the window in the name of equality.[19] The equality of persons with disabilities requires that paternalistic tools are applied to them on the same basis as they are applied to others.[20]

This book proposes a framework in which the legitimate interests of protection from harm can be taken into account and applied to persons with disabilities on the same basis as to non-disabled individuals. The rationales for overruling their decisions should not be related to formal categories of legal capacity established through capacity assessments but to goals preventing specific harms established on the basis of objective criteria, which are not based on disability. I do not wish to prescribe how much protection a particular jurisdiction should offer to any person. Instead, I have explained how values such as personal autonomy, legal certainty and protection from harm can be balanced in the framework of supported decision-making to achieve a result suitable for particular situations. A range of options is possible, from minimal interference and maximum autonomy to allowing substituted decisions for persons who are unable to communicate a decision with support. Different jurisdictions could opt for different levels of protection; therefore, the possible solutions should be imagined as a continuum rather than two opposing paradigms. They differ in allocating the burden to challenge decisions, in whether the right to overrule decisions rests with a court or administrative body or an individual, in whether certain decisions need automatic approval or if they can be contested retroactively, and in other features, each representing a specific resolution of balancing the basic values mentioned above. More or less paternalistic systems can be designed using the proposed framework, but each of them will provide persons with disability more autonomy than guardianship. Future empirical evidence

[18] I Bantekas, 'Mental and Intellectual Capacity and Contractual Freedom: Assistive Decision-Making Matters' (2023) 21(2) *Seattle Journal for Social Justice* 569, 586.

[19] RAC Caycho, 'The flag of imagination: Peru's new reform on legal capacity for persons with intellectual and psychosocial disabilities and the need for new understandings in private law' (2020) 14 *Age of Human Rights Journal* 155, 170.

[20] A Arstein-Kerslake and E Flynn, 'The General Comment on Article 12 of the Convention on the Rights of Persons with Disabilities: a roadmap for equality before the law' (2016) 20(4) *The International Journal of Human Rights* 471, 482.

about abuse can be invaluable in guiding legislators to decide on what the type and frequency of some harms are, and thus what specifically they want to protect persons with disabilities from, and what trade-offs are involved.

It is quite possible that in the described framework, decisions of some persons with disabilities will be overruled more frequently than decisions of non-disabled persons, even though not on the ground of legal capacity.[21] That, however, is not in itself a sign of a lack of equality with regard to exercising legal capacity. Those persons with disabilities who are more vulnerable than others because of their lack of education, economic dependence, social dependence (lack of friends and other social contacts), and ability to take care of themselves will more often be subject to interventions aimed at protecting their interests.[22] Legal capacity law can and should treat them equally, but it cannot overcome all obstacles undermining their autonomy to pursue their own interests. At best, it can aim at strengthening rather than weakening their decision-making abilities, but it cannot compensate for all social disadvantages.[23]

What the book rejects are current formal categories of legal capacity and incapacity. In that sense it is endorsing another conception of the paradigm shift: guardianship and other disability-specific methods of substituted decision-making based on capacity criteria are not part of the range of imagined solutions. Formal incapacitation should be discarded. However, that is not enough to achieve the exercise of legal capacity by persons with disabilities on an equal basis with others. Nor is providing support sufficient to meet this goal. A system of combining support with protection, described in this book, comes in its practical implications the closest to ensuring that persons with disabilities are indeed treated like anybody else with regard to enjoying their personal autonomy and can exercise supported decision-making as a legally protected and enforceable right to the maximum extent possible.

Some authors argue that support can easily turn into substitution in the case of persons with high support needs. I believe they are right, but they draw the wrong conclusion from this. I do not consider this a reason to acknowledge substituted decision-making formally. Treating all decisions formally as support and normatively requiring that support be utilised to the maximum extent possible is a more promising approach and leads to better results than formally distinguishing support and substitution in law. The alternative would be to accept some form of incapacitation, which would unavoidably lead to unjustly limiting the legal capacity of some persons due to the inherent features of ex-ante formal categorisation based on a prediction of mental capacity without

[21] G de Beco, *Disability in International Human Rights Law* (Oxford University Press, 2021) 104.

[22] M Donnelly, 'Judging Values in a Time of Transition: An Irish Perspective' in C Kong, J Coggon, P Cooper, M Dunn, and AR Keene (eds), *Capacity, Participation and Values in Comparative Legal Perspective* (Bristol University Press, 2023) 66.

[23] M Keys, 'Article 12' in VD Fina, R Cera, and G Palmisano (eds), *The United Nations Convention on the Rights of Persons with Disabilities. A Commentary* (Springer, 2017) 269.

offering any advantages in the form of increased protection for those considered incapable. Because of the in-built safeguards (i.e., the supporter can only express a decision if the supported person does not express any), the proposed solution can legally enforce the requirement of support to as many decisions as possible; even beyond that, in the realm of unenforceable support, persons with disabilities are better off than in a guardianship framework.

This solution is different from a very well-functioning guardianship system in one important respect. An optimal guardianship system might limit a person's ability in a specific area to authorise the guardian to make decisions, but the good guardian will take into account any relevant wishes of the person. In my framework, the good supporter will act similarly concerning wishes of the person only he can interpret (and in that area, he is legally speaking in a similar territory to a good guardian), but in the case of any relevant wishes that a third persons can understand, these are legally binding on them and cannot be ignored neither by the supporter nor by the other parties. In an optimal guardianship, it is in the guardian's discretion to take the represented person's decisions into account – here, it is the supported person's right for her expressed wishes to be taken into account and everybody else's obligation to respect them.

Article 12 of the CRPD does not determine a particular vision of equality in exercising legal capacity. Its text is ambiguous enough to allow for differing interpretations. The solution described in this book is in line with Article 12 but others can be too. However, since the overall purpose of the CRPD is to protect the dignity and rights of persons with disabilities, a framework that maximises personal autonomy without sacrificing other important values should be seen as superior to others in interpreting and applying the CRPD. My proposal is in line with the CRPD Committee's General Comment on Legal Capacity, provided that the distinction between enforceable and unenforceable support is accepted. It offers specific obligations for states on what legal rules can achieve the accommodation of persons with high support needs in a supported framework, and how problematic decisions and abuse can be addressed. It also provides space for support to be provided to persons who are unable to express their decisions in a way which could be understood by third parties. I believe the book's proposal offers the highest level of decision-making autonomy for all persons with disabilities in the framework set by the CRPD. For that reason, to fulfil the goal of the CRPD, it can become an interpretation accepted by all stakeholders and, in that sense, the preferred interpretation. At least until newer forms of enforcing support, providing an even higher level of decision-making autonomy, are discovered.

Bibliography

Appelbaum, PS, 'Assessment of Patients' Competence to consent to treatment' (2007) 357 *New England Journal of Medicine* 1834–1840

Appelbaum, PS and M Trachsel, 'The Doctrine of Informed Consent Doesn't Need Modification for Supported Decision Making' (2021) 21(11) *American Journal of Bioethics* 27–29

Appelbaum, PS, '"I Vote, I Count": Mental Disability and the Right to Vote' (2000) 51 *Psychiatric Services* 849–863

Appelbaum, PS, 'There Are All Kinds of Rights' (2016) 46(2) *Hastings Center Report* (2016) 46(2), inside back cover

Appelbaum, PS, SA Mirkin, and AL Bateman, 'Empirical assessment of competency to consent to psychiatric hospitalization' (1981) 138 *American Journal of Psychiatry* 1170–1176

Arai, M and A Homma, 'Guardianship for adults in Japan: Legal reforms and advances in practice' 24 (Supplement June 2005) *Australasian Journal on Ageing* S19–S24

Arnardóttir, OM and G Quinn (eds), *The UN Convention on the Rights of Persons with Disabilities: European and Scandinavian Perspectives* (Martinus Nijhoff Publishers, 2009)

Arstein-Kerslake, A and E Flynn, 'The General Comment on Article 12 of the Convention on the Rights of Persons with Disabilities: a roadmap for equality before the law' (2016) 20(4) *The International Journal of Human Rights* 471–490

Arstein-Kerslake, A and E Flynn, 'The right to legal agency: domination, disability and the protections of Article 12 of the Convention on the Rights of Persons with Disabilities' (2017) 13(1) *International Journal of Law in Context* 22–38

Arstein-Kerslake, A, *Legal Capacity and Gender* (Springer, 2021)

Arstein-Kerslake, A, *Restoring Voice to People with Cognitive Disabilities* (Cambridge University Press, 2017)

Arstein-Kerslake, A, *The Right to Legal Personhood of Marginalised Groups* (Oxford University Press, 2024)

Aust, A, *Modern Treaty Law and Practice* (Cambridge University Press, 2012)

Bach, M 'Securing Self-Determination: Building the Agenda in Canada', TASH Newsletter (1998)

Bach, M and L Kerzner, 'A New Paradigm for Protecting Autonomy and the Right to Legal Capacity', Paper prepared for the Law Commission of Ontario (October 2010)

Bach, M, 'Overview of the Supported Decision-Making Model and Legal Provisions in Canada', Include 1/2007, Inclusion Europe Newsletter (2007)

Bach, M, 'Supported Decision Making under Article 12 of the UN Convention on the Rights of Persons with Disabilities', Presentation to the Conference on Legal Capacity and Supported Decision Making, Athlone, Ireland (3 November 2007)

Badenhoop, L, S Baisch, S Penger, and J Haberstroh, 'The Role of Different Aspects of Communication Behavior in the Assessment of Capacity to Consent' (2023) 36(4) *GeroPsych: The Journal of Gerontopsychology and Geriatric Psychiatry* 227–235

Bantekas, I, 'Mental and Intellectual Capacity and Contractual Freedom: Assistive Decision-Making Matters.' (2023) 21 *Seattle Journal for Social Justice* 569–587

Bantekas, I, MA Stein, and D Anastasiou (eds), *The UN Convention on the Rights of Persons with Disabilities: A Commentary* (Oxford University Press, 2018)

Barclay, L, 'Paternalism, Supported Decision-Making and Expressive Respect' (2024) 27(1) *Journal of Ethics and Social Philosophy* 121–149

Bartlett, P, 'Implementing a paradigm shift: Implementing the convention on the rights of persons with disabilities in the context of mental disability law' in *Torture in healthcare settings: Reflections on the special rapporteur on Torture's 2013 thematic report* (American University Washington College of Law: Center for Human Rights & Humanitarian Law, 2014) 169–179

Bartlett, P, 'The UN Convention on the Rights of Persons with Disabilities: great opportunities and dangerous interpretations' (2019) 18(1) *World Psychiatry* 47–48

Bartlett, P, 'Thinking About the Rest of the World: Mental Health and Rights Outside the "First World"' in B McSherry and P Weller (eds), *Rethinking Rights Based Mental Health Laws* (Hart, 2010) 397–418

Basa, I, 'Gondnokság a római jogban' (2006) 43 *Állam- és Jogtudomány* 407–443

Beaudry, J-S, *The Disabled Contract: Severe Intellectual Disability, Justice and Morality* (Cambridge University Press, 2021)

Benincasa, Z and M Nowak, 'Outline of the legal situation of persons with mental disabilities (furiosi) in Roman law' in M Domański and B Lackoroński (eds), *Models of Implementation of Article 12 of the Convention on the Rights of Persons with Disabilities (CRPD); Private and Criminal Law Aspects* (Routledge, 2024) 47–60

Besson, S, 'Sources of International Human Rights Law: How General is General International Law' in S Besson and J d'Aspremont (eds), *The Oxford Handbook on the Sources of International Law* (Oxford University Press, 2017) 837–870

Bigby, C and J Douglas, *Support for Decision Making – A Practice Framework* (Living with Disability Research Centre, La Trobe University, 2015)

Bigby, C, *Ageing with a lifelong disability* (Jessica Kingsley, 2004)

Bigby, C, S Anderson, and N Cameron, 'Identifying conceptualizations and theories of change embedded in interventions to facilitate community participation for people with intellectual disability: A scoping review' (2018) 31(2) *Journal of Applied Research in Intellectual Disabilities* 165–180

Bilchitz, D, 'Dignity, fundamental rights and legal capacity: Moving beyond the paradigm set by the general comment on article 12 of the convention on the rights of persons with disabilities' (2016) 32(3) *South African Journal on Human Rights* 410–437

Blackstone, W, *Commentaries on the Laws of England: A Facsimile of First Edition of 1765–1769 with an Introduction by Stanley N. Katz* (Blackwells, 1979)

Blankman, K, 'Guardianship Models in the Netherlands and Western Europe' (1997) 20 *International Journal of Law and Psychiatry* 47–57

Boros, Zs, 'A cselekvőképesség korlátozásának hazai tendenciái a nemzetközi elvárások tükrében' (2023) 21 *Családi Jog* 19–25

Buchanan, AE and DW Brock, *Deciding For Others: The Ethics of Surrogate Decision Making* (Cambridge University Press, 1989)

Burch, M, 'Autonomy, respect, and the rights of persons with disabilities in crisis' (2017) 34(3) *Journal of Applied Philosophy* 389–402

Bushko, M, 'Toxic: A Feminist Legal Theory Approach to Guardianship' (2022) 81 Ma*ryland Law Review Online* 141–178

Callus, A-M, 'Removing obstacles to equal recognition for persons with intellectual disability: Taking exception to the way things are' (2018) 12 *ALTER European Journal of Disability Research* 153–165

Canadian Association for Community Living (CACL), Report of the Task Force on Alternatives to Guardianship (1992)

Cantor, NL, *Making Medical Decisions for the Profoundly Mentally Disabled* (MIT Press, 2005)

Carnaby, S, 'People with profound and multiple learning disabilities: A review of research about their lives', A report commissioned by MENCAP (December 2004)

Carney, T 'Guardianship, Citizenship, & Theorizing Substitute-decisionmaking Law' (2012) 12/25 *Sydney Law School Research Paper* 1–26

Carney, T and D Tait, 'Adult Guardianship: Narrative Readings in the "Shadow" of the Law?' (1998) 21/2 *International Journal of Law and Psychiatry* 147–162

Carney, T and D Tait, 'Caught Between Two Systems? – Guardianship and Young People with a Disability' (1997) 20 *International Journal of Law and Psychiatry* 141–166

Carney, T, 'Australian Guardianship Tribunals: An adequate response to CRPD disability rights recognition and protection of the vulnerable over the lifecourse?' (2017) 10 *Journal of Ethics in Mental Health* 1–16

Carney, T, 'Clarifying, Operationalising, and Evaluating Supported Decision Making Models' (2014) 1(1) *Research and Practice in Intellectual and Developmental Disabilities* 46–50

Carney, T, 'Globalisation and Guardianship – Harmonisation or Postmodern Diversity?' (2001) 24 *International Journal of Law and Psychiatry* 95–116

Carney, T, 'Prioritising Supported Decision-Making: Running on Empty or a Basis for Glacial-To-Steady Progress?' (2017) 6(4) *Laws* 18–32

Carney, T, 'Searching for workable alternatives to guardianship for vulnerable populations?' (2015) 1 *Ethics, Medicine and Public Health* 113–119

Carney, T, 'Supported Decision-Making for People with Cognitive Impairments: An Australian Perspective?' (2015) 4 *Laws* 37–59

Carney, T, SN Then, C Bigby, I Wiesel, J Douglas, and E Smith, 'Realising "will, preferences and rights": reconciling differences on best practice support for decision-making?' (2019) 28 *Griffith Law Review* 357–379

Castillo-Wyszogrodzka, S, 'Implementation of Article 12 of the UN Convention on the Rights of Persons with Disabilities in France' in M Domański and B Lackoroński (eds), *Models of Implementation of Article 12 of the Convention on the Rights of Persons with Disabilities (CRPD); Private and Criminal Law Aspects* (Routledge, 2024) 200–227

Catterall, HT, *Judicial Cases Concerning Slavery and the Negro* (Carnegie Institution of Washington, 1926)

Cavalli-Sforza, LL, *The Great Human Diasporas: the history of diversity and evolution* (Perseus Books, 1995)

Caycho, RAC and RAB Lazarte, 'A Four-Speed Reform: A Typology for Legal Capacity Reforms in Latin American Countries' (2023) 12(3) *Laws* 45–59

Caycho, RAC, 'The flag of imagination: Peru's new reform on legal capacity for persons with intellectual and psychosocial disabilities and the need for new understandings in private law' (2020) 14 *Age of Human Rights Journal* 155–180

Chayes, A and AH Chayes, *The new sovereignty: compliance with international regulatory agreements* (Harvard University Press, 1995)

Chesterman, J, 'Modernising Adult Protection in an Age of Choice' (2014) 73 *Australian Journal of Public Administration* 517–524

Christoffersen, J, 'Impact on General Principles of Treaty Interpretation', in MT Kamminga and M Scheinin (eds), *The Impact of Human Rights Law on General International Law* (Oxford University Press, 2009) 37–62

Cifuentes, S and 30 other legal scholars, 'Legal Opinion on Article 12 of the CRPD' (21 June 2008)

Comm. on Soc. Affairs, Health and Sustainable Dev., *Putting an End to Coerced Sterilisations and Castrations*, Doc. 13215 (28 May 2013) (by Liliane Maury Pasquier)

Council of Europe Commissioner for Human Rights, 'Who gets to decide? Right to legal capacity for persons with intellectual and psychosocial disabilities', CommDH/IssuePaper (Strasbourg, 20 February 2012)

Crane, SA, 'Is Guardianship Reform Enough? Next Steps in Policy Reforms to Promote Self-Determination among People with Disabilities' (2015) 8 *Journal of International Aging Law and Policy* 177–210

Csehi, Z, 'A 2009. évi CXX. törvényről, az Új Polgári Törvénykönyv meghiúsult kísérletéről, annak előkészítéséről és tartalmáról' (2010) 3 *Iustum Aequum Salutare* 71–103

Dallos, J, 'A gyámügyi előadó szemével' in Hungarian Civil Liberties Union (TASZ), *Ki a kompetens?* (TASZ, 2001) 15–20

Dawson, J and G Szmukler, 'Fusion of Mental Health and Incapacity Legislation' (2006) 188 *British Journal of Psychiatry* 504–509
Dawson, J and G Szmukler, 'The "Fusion Law" Proposals and the CRPD' in MA Stein, F Mahomed, V Patel, and C Sunkel (eds), *Mental Health, Legal Capacity, and Human Rights* (Cambridge University Press, 2021) 95–108
Dawson, J, 'A realistic approach to assessing mental health laws' compliance with the UNCRPD.' (2015) 40 *International Journal of Law and Psychiatry* 70–79
Dayan, C, *The Law Is a White Dog: How Legal Rituals Make and Unmake Persons* (Princeton University Press, 2013)
de Almeida, JMC, 'The UN Committee's interpretation of "will and preferences" can violate human rights' (2019) 18(1) *World Psychiatry* 45–46
de Beco, G, *Disability in International Human Rights Law* (Oxford University Press, 2021)
de Bhailís, C and E Flynn, 'Recognising legal capacity: commentary and analysis of Article 12 CRPD' (2017) 13(1) *International Journal of Law in Context* 6–21
Degener, T, 'Challenges and Compliance of the UN CRPD' (2013) Working Paper of the Academy of European Law
Devi, N, 'Supported Decision-Making and Personal Autonomy for Persons with Intellectual Disabilities: Article 12 of the UN Convention on the Rights of Persons with Disabilities' (2013) 41(4) *Journal of Law Medicine and Ethics* 792–806
Devi, N, J Bickenbach, and G Stucki, 'Moving towards substituted or supported decision-making? Article 12 of the Convention on the Rights of Persons with Disabilities' (2011) 5 *ALTER European Journal of Disability Research* 249–264
Dhanda, A, 'Advocacy Note on Legal Capacity', World Network of Users and Survivors of Psychiatry (2009)
Dhanda, A, 'Constructing a new Human Rights Lexicon: Convention on the Rights of persons with Disabilities' (2008) 8 *SUR International Journal on Human Rights* 43–60
Dhanda, A, 'Legal Capacity in the Disability Rights Convention: Stranglehold of the Past or Lodestar for the Future?' (2007) 34 *Syracuse Journal of International Law and Commerce* 429–462
Dinerstein, R, EG Grewa and J Martinis, 'Emerging International Trends and Practices in Guardianship Law for People with Disabilities' (2016) 22 *ILSA Journal of International and Comparative Law* 435–460
Dinerstein, RD 'Implementing Legal Capacity Under Article 12 of the UN Convention on the Rights of Persons with Disabilities: The Difficult Road from Guardianship to Supported Decision-Making' (2012) 19 *Human Rights Brief*
Disability Rights Center, 'Proposal for implementing Article 12 of the Convention on the Rights of Persons with Disabilities in Croatia' (9 February 2013)
Domański, M and B Lackoroński, 'Comparative analysis of the transposition of Article 12 of the UN Convention on the Rights of Persons with Disabilities' in M Domański and B Lackoroński (eds), *Models of Implementation of Article 12 of the Convention on the Rights of Persons with Disabilities (CRPD); Private and Criminal Law Aspects* (Routledge, 2024) 600–605
Domański, M and B Lackoroński, *Models of Implementation of Article 12 of the Convention on the Rights of Persons with Disabilities (CRPD); Private and Criminal Law Aspects* (Routledge, 2024)
Donnelly, M, 'Deciding in dementia: The possibilities and limits of supported decision-making' (2019) 66 *International Journal of Law and Psychiatry* 101466:1–7
Donnelly, M, 'Judging Values in a Time of Transition: An Irish Perspective' in: C Kong, J Coggon, P Cooper, M Dunn, and AR Keene, *Capacity, Participation and Values in Comparative Legal Perspective* (Bristol University Press, 2023) 65–84
Donnelly, M, 'Support Relationships in Law: Framing, Fictions and the Responsive State' in M Donnelly, R Harding, and E Taşcıoğlu (eds), *Supporting Legal Capacity in Socio-Legal Context* (Hart, 2022) 19–37

Donnelly, M, *Healthcare Decision-Making and the Law: Autonomy, Capacity and the Limits of Liberalism* (Cambridge University Press 2010)
Donnelly, M, R Harding, and E Taşcıoğlu, 'Situating the Right to Enjoy Legal Capacity' in M Donnelly, R Harding, and E Taşcıoğlu (eds), *Supporting Legal Capacity in Socio-Legal Context* (Hart, 2022) 1–16
Donnelly, M, R Harding, and E Taşcıoğlu, *Supporting Legal Capacity in Socio-Legal Context* (Hart, 2022)
Doron, I, 'Elder Guardianship Kaleidoscope – a Comparative Perspective' (2002) 16 *International Journal of Law, Policy and the Family* 368–398
Doron, I, 'From Lunacy to Incapacity and Beyond – Guardianship of The Elderly and Ontario's Experience in Defining "Legal Incapacity"' (1999) 19(4) *Health Law in Canada* 95–114
Earp, BD, J Demaree-Cotton, and J Savulescu, 'Against Externalism in Capacity Assessment – Why Apparently Harmful Treatment Refusals Should Not Be Decisive for Finding Patients Incompetent' (2022) 22(10) *American Journal of Bioethics* 65–70
Enck, GG, 'Healthcare Decisions Are Always Supported Decisions' (2021) 21(11) *American Journal of Bioethics* 29–32
European Union Agency for Fundamental Rights, *Legal capacity of persons with intellectual disabilities and persons with mental health problems* (February 2013)
Faigman, DL and K Geiser, 'Using burdens of proof to allocate the risk of error when assessing developmental maturity of youthful offenders' (2022) 63 *William & Mary Law Review* 1289–1316
Fattah, HM, 'Kuwait Grants Political Rights to Its Women', *New York Times,* 17 May 2005
Fiala-Butora, J and MA Stein, 'The Law as a Source of Stigma or Empowerment: Legal Capacity and Persons with Intellectual Disabilities' in K Scior and S Werner (eds), *Intellectual Disability & Stigma: Stepping out from the Margins* (Palgrave Macmillan, 2016) 195–207
Fiala-Butora, J, 'Disabling Torture: The Obligation to Investigate Ill-treatment of Persons with Disabilities' (2013) 45 *Columbia Human Rights Law Review* 214–280
Fiala-Butora, J, 'The CRPD and legal capacity reform in Hungary: Compromise of what?' in C O'Mahoney and G Quinn (eds), *Disability Law and Policy – An Analysis of the UN Convention* (Clarus Press, 2017) 127–136
Fiala-Butora, J, 'The influence of the convention on the rights of persons with disabilities on the European court of human rights in the area of mental health law: Divergence and unexplored potential' (2024) 94 *International Journal of Law and Psychiatry* 101965:1–12
Fiala-Butora, J, 'A Polgári törvénykönyv cselekvőképességi szabályainak értékelése a nemzetközi jog és a hazai tapasztalatok szemszögéből' (2019) 17(4) *Családi Jog* 8–14
Fiala-Butora, J, MA Stein and JE Lord, 'The democratic life of the Union: towards equal voting participation for Europeans with Disabilities' (2014) 55 *Harvard International Law Journal* 71–104
Field, MA and VA Sanchez, 'Equal Treatment for People with Mental Retardation' (Harvard University Press, 1999)
Fina, VD, R Cera, and G Palmisano (eds), *The United Nations Convention on the Rights of Persons with Disabilities: A Commentary* (Springer, 2017)
Fitzmaurice, M, 'Dynamic (Evolutive) Interpretation of Treaties, Part I', *Hague Yearbook of International Law XXI* (Martinus Nijhoff, 2008)
Fitzmaurice, M, 'Interpretation of Human Rights Treaties' in D Shelton (ed), *The Oxford Handbook of International Human Rights Law* (Oxford University Press, 2013) 739–771
Flynn, E and A Arstein-Kerslake, 'Legislating personhood: realising the right to support in exercising legal capacity' (2014) 10 *International Journal of Law in Context* 81–104
Flynn, E and A Arstein-Kerslake, 'State intervention in the lives of people with disabilities: the case for a disability-neutral framework' (2017) 13(1) *International Journal of Law in Context* 39–57
Flynn, E and A Arstein-Kerslake, 'The Support Model of Legal Capacity: Fact, Fiction, or Fantasy?' (2014) 31(1) *Berkeley Journal of International Law* 124–143

Flynn, E, 'The (Contested) Role of the Academy in Activist Movements for Legal Capacity Reform: A Personal Reflection' in M Donnelly, R Harding, and E Taşcıoğlu (eds), *Supporting Legal Capacity in Socio-Legal Context* (Hart, 2022) 117–134

Flynn, E, A Arstein-Kerslake, C de Bhailís, and ML Serra, *Global Perspectives on Legal Capacity Reform Our Voices, Our Stories* (Routledge, 2019)

Foner, E and J Brown, *Forever Free: A Story of Emancipation and Reconstruction* (Knopf, 2005)

Freeman, MC, K Kolappa JMC de Almeida, A Kleinman, N Makhashvili, S Phakathi, B Saraceno, G Thornicroft, 'Reversing Hard Won Victories in the Name of Human Rights: A Critique of the General Comment on Article 12 of the UN Convention on the Rights of Persons with Disabilities' (2015) 2(9) *Lancet Psychiatry* 844–50

Frintová, D, 'Implementation of Article 12 of the UN Convention on the Rights of Persons with Disabilities in the Czech Republic' in M Domański and B Lackoroński (eds), *Models of Implementation of Article 12 of the Convention on the Rights of Persons with Disabilities (CRPD); Private and Criminal Law Aspects* (Routledge, 2024) 140–166

Frolik, LA, 'Guardianship Reform: When the Best is the Enemy of the Good' (1998) 9 *Stanford Law & Policy Review* 347–353

Ganzini, L, W Nelson, and A Derse, 'Pitfalls in Assessment of Decision-Making Capacity' (2003) 44(3) *Psychosomatics* 237–243

Gardiner, R, 'The Vienna Convention on Treaty Interpretation' in DB Hollis (ed), *The Oxford Guide to Treaties* (Oxford University Press, 2012) 474–506

Gardner, H, *Frames of Mind. The Theory of Multiple Intelligences,* 10th edn (Basic Books Publisher, 1993)

Geisinger, A and M Stein, 'A Theory of Expressive International Law' (2007) 60 *Vanderbilt Law Review* 77–131

Georg Nolte, Special Rapporteur, International Law Commission, Fourth report on subsequent agreements and subsequent practice in relation to the interpretation of treaties, UN Doc A/CN.4/694 (7 March 2016)

German Statement on the Draft General Comment on Article 12 CRPD, Federal Republic of Germany (20 February 2014)

Glen, KB, 'Introducing a New Human Right: Learning from Others, Bringing Legal Capacity Home' (2018) 49 *Columbia Human Rights Law Review* 1–98

Gombos, G, I Hoffman, G Könczei, Z Nagy, and G Szabó, *A támogatott döntéshozatal elmélete és gyakorlata* (Eötvös Lóránd University Bárczi Gusztáv Faculty of Special Education, 2009)

Gooding, P, *A New Era for Mental Health Law and Policy* (Cambridge University Press, 2017)

Gooding, P, 'Legal Capacity in the UN Convention on the Rights of Persons with Disability and its Challenges to a Rawlsian Theory of Justice', Melbourne University Postgraduate Legal Theory Conference (2010)

Gooding, P, 'Navigating the 'Flashing Amber Lights' of the Right to Legal Capacity in the United Nations Convention on the Rights of Persons with Disabilities: Responding to Major Concerns' (2015) 15 *Human Rights Law Review* 45–71

Gooding, P, 'Psychiatrists' Perceptions of Supported Decision-Making: A Victorian Empirical Study' (2014) 22 *Psychiatry, Psychology and Law* 701–722

Gooding, P, 'Supported Decision-Making: A Rights-Based Disability Concept and its Implications for Mental Health Law' (2013) 20(3) *Psychiatry, Psychology and Law* 431–451

Gordon, RM, 'The Emergence of Assisted (Supported) Decision-Making in the Canadian Law of Adult Guardianship and Substitute Decision-Making' (2000) 23 *International Journal of Law and Psychiatry* 61–77

Gosney, P and P Bartlett, 'The UK Government Should Withdraw from the Convention on the Rights of Persons with Disabilities' (2020) 216(6) *British Journal of Psychiatry* 296–300

Griffin J, *On Human* Rights (Oxford University Press, 2008)

Grisso, T, *Evaluating Competencies: Forensic Assessments and Instruments,* Perspectives in Law and Psychology 16 (Kluwer Academic Plenum Publishers, 2nd Edition, 2003)

Grunewald, K, 'The Swedish System of Legal Capacity and Supported Decision Making Concerning Adults with Intellectual Disabilities', Inclusion Europe, Europe in Action, Citizen's Right for All, Warsaw (10–12 May 2007)

Guardianship reform coalition of 15 Hungarian organisations, 'A gondnoksági rendszer módosításának javasolt alapelvei' (22 June 2007)

Gulya, F and I Hoffman, 'A támogatott döntéshozatal sorsa Magyarországon' (2019) 5(2) *Fogyatékosság és Társadalom* 22–36

Gulya, F and I Hoffmann (eds), *A nagykorúak cselekvőképességének korlátozása Magyarországon* (ORAC Kiadó, 2024)

Gurbai, S, 'Unfulfilled Dream about Moving from Civil Death to Visible Citizens: Legal Capacity Law Reform in Hungary' in C O'Mahoney and G Quinn (eds), *Disability Law and Policy – An Analysis of the UN Convention* (Clarus Press, 2017) 137–147

Guzelian, CP, MA Stein, and HS Akiskal, 'Credit Scores, Lending and Psychosocial Disability' (2015) 95 *Boston University Law Review* 1807–1868

Hamilton, M, 'Supported Decision-making as an Alternative to Guardianship' (2023) *Trends in State Courts* 87–95

Harrison, W, *Representation Agreements in British Columbia: Who is Using Them and Why?* (M.A. thesis, Simon Fraser University, 2008)

Hellmann, U, 'Civil Rights for Everybody!' (2007) Include 1/2007, Inclusion Europe Newsletter, 11.

Henckes, N, 'Between tutelage and assistance: The debate over the reform of the 1838 French law on insane people from the 1870s to the 1910s' (2017) 35(2) *Sciences sociales et santé* 81–108

Henking, T and M Scholten, 'Respect for the Will and Preferences of People with Mental Disorders in German Law' in C Kong, J Coggon, P Cooper, M Dunn, and AR Keene (eds), *Capacity, Participation and Values in Comparative Legal Perspective* (Policy Press, 2023) 203–225

Herr, SS, 'Self Determination, Autonomy, and Alternatives for Guardianship' in SS Herr, LO Gostin, and HH Koh (eds), *The Human Rights of Persons with Intellectual Disabilities* (Oxford University Press, 2003) 429–450

Herring, J, *Caring and the Law* (Hart, 2013)

Hoffman, I and G Könczei, 'Legal Regulations Relating to the Passive and Active Legal Capacity of Persons with Intellectual and Psychosocial Disabilities in Light of the Convention on the Rights' (2010) 33 *Loyola of Los Angeles International and Comparative Law Review* 143–172

Hoffmann, I, F Gulya, and B Tőkey, 'A nagykorúak cselekvőképességének korlátozása – hazai jogi keretek és az azzal kapcsolatos főbb adatok' in F Gulya and I Hoffmann (eds), *A nagykorúak cselekvőképességének korlátozása Magyarországon* (ORAC Kiadó, 2024) 87–110

Hungarian Civil Liberties Union (TASZ), *Ki a kompetens?* (TASZ, 2001)

Hurme, SB and PS Appelbaum, 'Defining and Assessing Capacity to Vote: The Effect of Mental Impairment on the Rights of Voters' (2007) 38 *McGeorge Law Review* 931–1014

Huszár, I and E Kuncz, *Igazságügyi pszichiátria* (Medicina, 1978)

Hynes, Á, *Irish Capacity Law and Assisted Decision-Making* (Bloomsbury Publishing, 2018)

Inclusion Europe, 'Key Elements of a System of Supported Decision-Making: Position Paper of Inclusion Europe' (Inclusion Europe, 2008)

International Disability Alliance (IDA) CRPD Forum, 'Principles for Implementation of CRPD Article 12', Submitted for the Day of General Discussion on 'Article 12 of the CRPD – The right to equal recognition before the law' at the UN (21 October 2009)

International Law Commission, 'Subsequent practice and subsequent agreements in relation to the interpretation of treaties: Text of the draft conclusions', UN Doc A/CN.4/L.907 (11 May 2018)

Jackson, AJ, 'Between us: Facilitated decision-making in the relational experience of profound intellectual disability' (2023) 51(4) *Ethos* 370–384

Jackson, E, 'The relationship between medical law and good medical ethics' (2015) 41 *Journal of Medical Ethics* 95–98

Jameson, JM, T Riesen, S Polychronis, B Trader, S Mizner, J Martinis, and D Hoyle, 'Guardianship and the Potential of Supported Decision Making With Individuals with Disabilities' (2015) 40 *Research and Practice For Persons With Severe Disabilities* 36–51

Johns, AF, 'Guardianship Folly: The Misgovernment of Parens Patriae and the Forecast of its Crumbling Linkage to Unprotected Older Americans in the Twenty-first Century – A March of Folly? Or just a Mask of Virtual Reality?' (1997) 27 *Stetson Law Review* 28–66

Kanev, K, 'Remarks at the New York Law School Symposium: International Human Rights Law and the Institutional Treatment of Persons with Mental Disabilities' (2002) 21 *New York Law School Journal of International and Comparative Law* 356–361

Kant, I, *Lectures on Ethics* (Harper Torchbooks, 1963)

Kanter, AS, *The Development of Disability Rights under International Law: From Charity to Human Rights* (Routledge 2014)

Kapp, MB, 'Assessing Assessments of Decision-Making Capacity: A Few Legal Queries and Commentary on "Assessment of Decision-Making Capacity in Older Adults"' (2007) 62B(1) *Journal of Gerontology: Psychological Sciences* P12–P13

Katona, V and A Sándor, 'A támogatott döntéshozatal külföldi gyakorlatai egy célzott szakirodalomelemzés tükrében' in F Gulya and I Hoffmann (eds), *A nagykorúak cselekvőképességének korlátozása Magyarországon* (ORAC Kiadó, 2024) 70–86

Kayess, R and P French, 'Out of Darkness into Light? Introducing the Convention on the Rights of Persons with Disabilities' (2008) 8 *Human Rights Law Review* 1–34

KC Glass, 'Refining definitions and devising instruments: Two decades of assessing mental competence' (1997) 20 *International Journal of Law and Psychiatry* 5–33

Keene, RA, NB Kane, SYH Kim, and GS Owen, 'Mental capacity – Why look for a paradigm shift?' (2023) 31(3) *Medical Law Review* 340–357

Kelemen, G, 'A fogyatékosság jelensége a pszichiátriában' in P Zászkaliczky and T Verdes (eds), *Tágabb értelemben vett gyógypedagógia* (Budapest, ELTE Eötvös Kiadó, 2004) 123–140

Kerzner, L, 'Paving the way to Full Realization of the CRPD's Rights to Legal Capacity and Supported Decision-Making: A Canadian Perspective', Prepared for In From the Margins: New Foundations for Personhood and Legal Capacity in the 21st century (April 2011).

Keys, M, 'Article 12' in VD Fina, R Cera, and G Palmisano (eds), *The United Nations Convention on the Rights of Persons with Disabilities. A Commentary* (Springer, 2017) 263–280

Keys, M, 'Legal Capacity Law Reform in Europe: An Urgent Challenge' in G Quinn and L Waddington (eds), *European Yearbook of Disability Law* (Intersentia, 2009) 59–88

Kiss, V, A Maléth, B Tőkey, and I Hoffman, 'An empirical study of actions on custodianship in Hungary' (2021) 78 *International Journal of Law and Psychiatry* 101719:1–13

Kiss, V, A Maléth, B Tőkey, I Hoffman, K Zsille, and B Dombrovszky, 'A gondnoksági perek empirikus vizsgálata' (2021) 62(2) *Állam-És Jogtudomány* 84–114

Kiss, V, A Maléth, B Tőkey, I Hoffman, K Zsille, and B Dombrovszky, 'A gondnoksági perek empirikus vizsgálata' in F Gulya and I Hoffmann (eds), *A nagykorúak cselekvőképességének korlátozása Magyarországon* (ORAC Kiadó, 2024) 33–70

Kittay, EF, 'The Personal Is Philosophical: a Philosopher and Mother of a Cognitively Disabled Person Sends Notes From the Battlefield' (2009) 40 *Metaphilosophy* 606–627

Kohn, NA and JA Blumenthal, 'A critical assessment of supported decision-making for persons aging with intellectual disabilities' (2014) 7 *Disability and Health Journal* S40–S43

Kohn, NA, 'Legislating Supported Decision-Making' (2021) 58 *Harvard Journal on Legislation* 313–356

Kohn, NA, 'Preserving Voting Rights in Long-Term Care Institutions: Facilitating Resident Voting While Maintaining Election Integrity' (2007) 38 *McGeorge Law Review* 1065–1111

Kohn, NA, 'Realizing Supported Decision-Making: What It Does – and Does Not – Require' (2021) 21(11) *American Journal of Bioethics* 37–40

Kohn, NA, JA Blumenthal, and AT Campbell, 'Supported Decision-Making: A Viable Alternative to Guardianship?' (2013) 117 *Penn State Law Review* 1111–1157

Kong, C, J Coggon, P Cooper, M Dunn, and AR Keene, *Capacity, Participation and Values in Comparative Legal Perspective* (Policy Press, 2023)

Kong, C, *Mental Capacity in Relationship* (Cambridge University Press, 2017)

Kőrös, A, '"Jót s jól!" – helyes célok, alkalmatlan megoldások a cselekvőképesség tervezett szabályozásában' (2009) 2 *Magyar Jog* 104–112
Lawson, A, 'The United Nations Convention on the Rights of Persons with Disabilities: New Era or False Dawn?' (2007) 34 *Syracuse Journal of International Law and Commerce* 563–619
Lazarte, RAB and RAC Caycho, 'Legal Capacity in Peruvian Law. Qualitative Analysis of Court Ruling of Restitution on Legal Capacity and Designation of a Support Person under the Framework of the Legislative Decree 1384' (2023) 44 *Revista de Derecho Privado* 15–27
Letsas, G, 'Strasbourg's Interpretive Ethic: Lessons for the International Lawyer' (2010) 21(3) *The European Journal of International Law* 510–541
Lewis, O, 'Advancing Legal Capacity Jurisprudence' (2011) 6 *European Human Rights Law Review* 700–714
Lewis, O, 'Council of Europe' in L Waddington and A Lawson, *The UN Convention on the Rights of Persons with Disabilities in Practice: A Comparative Analysis of the Role of Courts* (Oxford, Oxford University Press, 2018) 89–130
Lewis, O, 'Disabling Legal Barriers' (2017) 1 *European Human Rights Law Review* 49–58
Lewis, O, 'Mental Disability Law in Central and Eastern Europe: Paper, Practice, Promise' (2014) *International Journal of Mental Health and Capacity Law* 293–303
Lewis, O, 'Protecting the Rights of People with Mental Disabilities: The European Convention on Human Rights' (2002) 9 *European Journal of Health Law* 293–320
Liga lidských práv, 'Zásady pro poskytování asistence při rozhodování osobám s duševní poruchou' (2007)
Locke, J, *An Essay Concerning Human Understanding* (Roger Woolhouse ed, Reprint edn, Penguin Classics 1998)
Lord, JE and MA Stein, 'Contingent participation and coercive care: feminist and communitarian theories of disability and legal capacity' in B McSherry and I Freckelton (eds), *Coercive care: rights, law and policy* (Routledge, 2013) 31–47
Mackay, K and P McCusker, 'Adult safeguarding legislation: Navigating the borderlands between mental capacity, mental health and social care law and practice' (2024) 94 *International Journal of Law and Psychiatry* 101964:1–9
Mackenzie, C and S Natalie, *Relational Autonomy: Feminist Perspectives on Autonomy, Agency, and the Social Self* (Oxford University Press, 2000)
Mackenzie, C, 'The Importance of Relational Autonomy and Capabilities for an Ethics of Vulnerability' in C Mackenzie, W Rogers, and S Dodds (eds), *Vulnerability: New Essays in Ethics and Feminist Philosophy* (Oxford University Press, 2014)
Maléth, A, 'Fogyatékossággal élő felnőtt személyek lehetséges útja a támogatott döntéshozatal felé és az igazságszolgáltatáshoz történő hozzáférés' in N Rékasi, A Sándor, B Bányai, and Z Kondor (eds), *Széttartó Összhang* (ELTE Eötvös Kiadó, 2021) 132–150
Maléth, A, 'Az intellektuális képességzavarral élő személyek társadalmi inklúziója – gondolatok és javaslatok a cselekvőképesség korlátozását érintő hazai szabályokról' 2018 *Családi Jog* 9–17
Marshall, P, P Vasquez, V Purin, and L Godoy, 'Are We Closing the Gap? Reforms to Legal Capacity in Latin America in Light of the Convention on the Rights of Persons with Disabilities' (2023) 56(1) *Vanderbilt Journal of Transnational Law* 119–180
Marson, DC, J Huthwaite, and K Hebert, 'Testamentary capacity and undue influence in the elderly: A jurisprudent therapy perspective' (2004) 28 *Law & Psychology Review* 71–96
Martin, W and S Michalowski, 'The Legal Status of General Comments', Essex Autonomy Project, Essex University (23 May 2014)
Martin, W, 'Respect for the Will of the Person' in M Bach and N Espejo-Yaksic (eds), *Legal capacity, disability and human rights* (Larcier Intersentia, 2023) 31–48
Martin, W, S Michalowski, and C Caughey, 'Safeguards against Undue Influence and Conflicts of Interest', Essex Autonomy Project, Essex University (2015)
Martin, W, S Michalowsky, T Jütten, and M Burch, 'Achieving CRPD Compliance, Is the Mental Capacity Act of England and Wales Compatible with the UN CRPD? If not, what next?', Essex Autonomy Project, Essex University (2014)

Martinez-Pujalte, A, 'Legal Capacity and Supported Decision-Making: Lessons from Some Recent Legal Reforms' (2019) 8(1) *Laws* 1–22
Mattsson, T, 'Autonomy, Capacity, and Vulnerability: Making Decisions on Social Services for Persons with Dementia in Sweden' in M Donnelly and R Harding, and E Taşcıoğlu (eds), *Supporting Legal Capacity in Socio-Legal Context* (Hart, 2022) 235–253
McCarthy, AM and D Howard, 'Supported Decision-Making: Non-Domination Rather than Mental Prosthesis' (2023) 14(3) *AJOB Neuroscience* 227–237
McGeehan, CB and L Berninger, 'Autonomous by Extension: Balancing Patient Autonomy and Vulnerability in Surrogate Decision-making' (2024) 35(3) *AACN Advanced Critical Care* 228–237
McMahan, J, *The Ethics of Killing: Problems at the Margins of Life* (Oxford University Press, 2003)
McSherry, B and P Weller, *Rethinking Rights Based Mental Health Laws* (Bloomsbury Publishing, 2010)
McSherry, B, 'Legal Capacity under the Convention on the Rights of Persons with Disabilities' (2012) 20 *Journal of Law and Medicine* 22–27
Mechlem, K, 'Treaty Bodies and the Interpretation of Human Rights' (2009) 42 *Vanderbilt Journal of Transnational Law* 905–947
Mental Disability Advocacy Centre (MDAC), 'A kizáró gondnokság kérdése az új Ptk.-ban' (31 March 2008)
Mental Disability Advocacy Centre (MDAC), *Cage Beds: Inhuman and Degrading Treatment in Four EU Accession Countries* (MDAC, 2003)
Mental Disability Advocacy Centre (MDAC), *Guardianship and Human Rights in Bulgaria* (MDAC, 2007)
Mental Disability Advocacy Centre (MDAC), *Guardianship and Human Rights in Georgia* (MDAC, 2007)
Mental Disability Advocacy Centre (MDAC), *Guardianship and Human Rights in Hungary* (MDAC, 2007)
Mental Disability Advocacy Centre (MDAC), *Guardianship and Human Rights in Kyrgyzstan* (MDAC, 2007)
Mental Disability Advocacy Centre (MDAC), *Guardianship and Human Rights in Lithuania* (MDAC, 2007)
Mental Disability Advocacy Centre (MDAC), *Guardianship and Human Rights in Russia* (MDAC, 2007)
Mental Disability Advocacy Centre (MDAC), *Guardianship and Human Rights in Serbia* (MDAC, 2006)
Mental Disability Advocacy Centre (MDAC), *Guardianship and Human Rights in the Czech Republic* (MDAC, 2007)
Mental Disability Advocacy Centre (MDAC), *Legal Capacity in Europe* (MDAC, 2013)
Ministerstvo práce, sociálnych vecí a rodiny Slovenskej republiky, 'Národný akčný plán prechodu z inštitucionálnej na komunitnú starostlivosť v systéme sociálnych služieb na roky 2011–2015' (December 2011)
Egészségügyi Minisztérium, *Az Egészségügyi Minisztérium szakmai protokollja: Az ECT kezelés* (Budapest, Egészségügyi Közlöny, 2005)
Minkowitz, T, 'Abolishing Mental Health Laws to Comply with the Convention on the Rights of Persons with Disabilities' in B McSherry and P Weller (eds), *Rethinking Rights Based Mental Health Laws* (Hart, 2010) 151–177
Minkowitz, T, 'CRPD and transformative equality' (2017) 13(1) *International Journal of Law in Context* 77–86
Minkowitz, T, 'Legal Capacity: Alternatives to Functional Capacity' in O'Mahoney, C and G Quinn (eds), *Disability Law and Policy: An Analysis of the UN Convention* (Clarus Press, 2017) 101–110
Minkowitz, T, 'The United Nations Convention on the Rights of Persons with Disabilities and the Right to Be Free from Nonconsensual Psychiatric Interventions' (2007) 34 *Syracuse Journal of International Law and Commerce* 405–428

Montoya, TF, 'Supported Decision-Making in Swedish Law – Is the "Good Man" a Good or Bad Guy in Light of the CRPD?', English translation of 'Unterstützte Entscheidungsfindung im schwedischen Recht – der "Gute Mann": Held oder Schurke im Licht der UN-BRK?" in M Zinkler, C Mahlke, R Marschner (eds), *Selbstbestimmung und Solidarität Unterstützte Entscheidungsfindung in der psychiatrischen Praxis* (Psychiatrie Verlag, 2019) 222–232

Morss, JR, 'But for the Barriers: Significant Extensions to Children's Capacity' (2004) 11 *Psychiatry, Psychology and Law* 319–322

Moye, J and DC Marson, 'Assessment of decision-making capacity in older adults: An emerging area of practice and research' (2007) 62(1) *Journal of Gerontology: Psychological Sciences* P3–P11

Naci, L and AM Owen, 'Making Every Word Count for Nonresponsive Patients' (2013) 70 *JAMA Neurology* 1235–1241

Neisser, U, G Boodoo, TJ Bouchard, AW Boykin, N Brody, SJ Ceci, DF Halpern, JC Loehlin, R Perloff, RJ Sternberg, and S Urbina, *Intelligence: Knowns and Unknowns,* (1996) 51 American Psychologist 77–101

Neuman, GL, 'Divergent Human Rights Approaches to Capacity and Consent' in MA Stein, F Mahomed, V Patel, and C Sunkel (eds), *Mental Health, Legal Capacity, and Human Rights* (Cambridge University Press, 2021) 56–69

Neuman, GL, 'Human Rights and Constitutional Rights: Harmony and Dissonance' (2003) 55 *Stanford Law Review* 1863–1900

Neuman, GL, 'Submission to the Committee on the Rights of Persons with Disabilities Regarding Draft General Comment on Article 5, Equality and Non-Discrimination', UN OHCHR (18 June 2017)

Nilsson, A, *Compulsory Mental Health Interventions and the CRPD: Minding Equality* (Hart, 2021)

Nolan, A, '"Aggravated Violations", Roma Housing Rights and Forced Expulsions in Italy: Recent Development under the European Social Charter Collective Complaints System' (2011) 11 *Human Rights Law Review* 343–361

Nowak, M, *U. N. Covenant on Civil and Political Rights: CCPR Commentary* (N.P. Engel, 1993)

Nussbaum, M, 'The Capabilities of People with Cognitive Disabilities' (2009) 40 *Metaphilosophy* 331–351

Nussbaum, M, *Frontiers of justice: disability, nationality, species membership* (Harvard University Press, 2006)

Nyírőné Kiss, I, 'A gondnoksági perek joggyakorlat-elemzésének tanulságai' (2023) 21(3) *Családi Jog* 1–7

O'Connor, D, J Braun, N Marriette, and K Purser, 'Assessing mental capacity in the context of abuse and neglect: A relational lens' (2024) 97 *International Journal of Law and Psychiatry* 102027:1–8

O'Keeffe, S, 'Functional Capacity Assessments by Healthcare Professionals: Problems and Mitigating Strategies' in M Donnelly, R Harding, and E Taşcıoğlu (eds), *Supporting Legal Capacity in Socio-Legal Context* (Hart, 2022) 75–95

O'Mahoney, C and G Quinn (eds), *Disability Law and Policy: An Analysis of the UN Convention* (Clarus Press, 2017)

Office of the United Nations High Commissioner for Human Rights (OHCHR), 'On enhancing awareness and understanding of the Convention on the Rights of Persons with Disabilities', A/HRC/10/48 (26 January 2009)

Office of the United Nations High Commissioner for Human Rights, Thematic Study on enhancing awareness and understanding of the Convention on the Rights of Persons with Disabilities, A/HRC/10/48 (26 January 2009)

Oktatáskutató és Fejlesztő Intézet, 'A tantárgygondozó szaktanácsadói támogatáshoz kapcsolódó pedagógiai szintleírások – Gyógypedagógus munkakör' (2014)

Parker, M, 'Getting the Balance Right: Conceptual Considerations Concerning Legal Capacity and Supported Decision-Making' (2016) 13 *Bioethical Inquiry* 381–393

Pathare, S and LS Shields, 'Supported decision-making for persons with mental illness: a review' (2012) 34(2) *Public Health Review* 1–40

Pavlich, G, 'Criminal Justice and Cape Law's Persons' (2014) 23 *Social and Legal Studies* 55–72

Perju, V, 'Constitutional Transplants, Borrowing, and Migrations' (2011) *Boston College Law School Faculty Papers* 360

Perlin, ML, 'Striking for the Guardians and Protectors of the Mind: The Convention on the Rights of Persons with Mental Disabilities and the Future of Guardianship Law' (2013) 117 *Penn State Law Review* 1159–1190

Perlin, ML, *International human rights and mental disability law: when the silenced are heard* (Oxford University Press, 2012)

Peterson, A, J Karlawish, J, and E Largent, 'Supported Decision Making With People at the Margins of Autonomy' (2021) 21(11) *American Journal of Bioethics* 4–18

Pickering, N, G Newton-Howes, and G Young, 'Harmful Choices, the Case of C, and Decision-Making Competence' (2022) 22(10) *American Journal of Bioethics* 38–50

Powell, RM and MA Stein, 'People with Disabilities and Sexual and Reproductive Rights: an International Comparative Analysis' (2016) 11 *Frontiers of Law in China* 53–85

Quinn, G and A Arstein-Kerslake, 'Restoring the 'human' in 'human rights': personhood and doctrinal innovation in the UN disability convention' in C Gearty and C Douzinas (eds), *The Cambridge Companion to Human Rights Law* (Cambridge University Press, 2012) 36–55

Quinn, G and A Rekas-Rosalbo, 'Civil Death: rethinking personhood for persons with a disability' (2019) 56 *Irish Jurist* 286–325

Quinn, G, 'An Ideas Paper', Eur. Foundation Centre, Seminar on Legal Capacity, Brussels (4 June 2009)

Quinn, G, 'Personhood and Legal Capacity – Perspectives on the Paradigm Shift of Article 12 CRPD', Harvard Law School Project on Disability Conference presentation (2010).

Raad, R, J Karlawish, and PS Appelbaum, 'The Capacity to Vote of Persons with Serious Mental Illness' (2009) 60 *Psychiatric Services* 624–628

Rees, N, 'The Fusion Proposal: A Next Step?' in B McSherry and P Weller (eds), *Rethinking Rights Based Mental Health Laws* (Hart, 2010) 73–93

Rehabilitation International, 'Legal Capacity and Guardianship of Persons with Disabilities in Mexico, Seminar on Legal Capacity and Access to Justice' (2010)

Response from the Government of Denmark with regards to Draft General Comment on Article 12 of the Convention – Equal Recognition before the Law, Ministry of Children, Gender Equality, Integration and Social Affairs (20 February 2014)

Richardson, G, 'Mental Disabilities and the Law: From Substitute to Supported Decision-Making?' (2012) 65 *Current Legal Problems* 333–354

Ricoeur, P, *Oneself as Another*, Translated by Kathleen Blamey (University of Chicago Press, 1992)

Rioux, M, J Gilmour, and N Angel, 'Negotiating capacity: legally constructed entitlement and protection' in B McSherry and I Freckelton (eds), *Coercive care: rights, law and policy* (Routledge, 2013) 51–75

Rodley, N, 'The Role and Impact of Treaty Bodies' in D Shelton (ed), *The Oxford Handbook of International Human Rights Law* (Oxford University Press, 2013) 621–648

Rothke, SE, GJ Demakis, and HM Amsbaugh, 'State statutes regarding the role of psychologists in performing capacity evaluations for guardianship determinations' (2019) 50(4) *Professional Psychology: Research and Practice* 228–239

Salzman, L, 'Guardianship for persons with mental illness – a legal and appropriate alternative?' (2011) 4 *Saint Louis University Journal of Health Law & Policy* 279–329

Schaefer, LA and TJ Farrer, *A Casebook of Mental Capacity in US Legislation. Assessment and Legal Commentary* (Routledge, 2022)

Scheinin, M, 'The Art and Science of Interpretation in Human Rights Law' in BA Andreassen, HO Sano, and S McInerney-Lankford (eds), *Research Methods in Human Rights: A Handbook* (Edward Elgar, 2017) 17–37

Schlütter, B, 'Aspect of Human Rights Treaty Interpretation by the UN Treaty Bodies' in H Keller and G Ulfstein (eds), *UN Human Rights Treaty Bodies: Law and Legitimacy* (Cambridge University Press, 2012) 261–319

Scholten, M and J Gather, 'Adverse consequences of article 12 of the UN Convention on the Rights of Persons with Disabilities for persons with mental disabilities and an alternative way forward' (2018) 44 *Journal of Medical Ethics* 226–233

Scholten, M, E Braun, J Gather, and J Vollmann, 'Combining Supported Decision-Making with Competence Assessment: A Way to Protect Persons with Impaired Decision-Making Capacity against Undue Influence' (2021) 21(11) *American Journal of Bioethics* 45–47

Scholten, M, J Gather, and J Vollmann, 'Equality in the Informed Consent Process: Competence to Consent, Substitute Decision-Making, and Discrimination of Persons with Mental Disorders' (2021) 46(1) *Journal of Medicine and Philosophy* 108–136

Series, L and A Nilsson, 'Article 12 CRPD Equal Recognition before the Law' in I Bantekas, MA Stein, and D Anastasiou (eds), *The UN Convention on the Rights of Persons with Disabilities: A Commentary* (Oxford University Press, 2018) 339–382

Series, L, 'Relationships, Autonomy and Legal Capacity: Mental Capacity and support Paradigms' (2015) 40 *International Journal of Law and Psychiatry* 80–91

Sheehan, MM, 'The Influence of Canon Law on the Property Rights of Married Women in England' (1963) 25 *Medieval Studies* 109–124

Silvers, A and LP Francis, 'Thinking About the Good: Reconfiguring Liberal Metaphysics (or not) for People with Cognitive Disabilities' (2009) 40 *Metaphilosophy* 475–498

Sinclair, C, J Bajic-Smith, M Gresham, M Blake, RS Bucks, S Field, JM Clayton, H Radoslovich, M Agar, and S Kurrle, S., 'Professionals' views and experiences in supporting decision-making involvement for people living with dementia' (2021) 20(1) *Dementia* 84–105

Singer, P, 'Speciesism and Moral Status' (2009) 40 *Metaphilosophy* 567–581

Skarsaune, SN and HM Hanisch, 'Holding and Professional Care: On Self-Determination for Persons With Profound Intellectual and Multiple Disabilities' (2023) 48(1) *Research and Practice for Persons with Severe Disabilities* 25–40

Skowron, P, 'Giving substance to 'the best interpretation of will and preferences' (2019) 62 *International Journal of Law and Psychiatry* 125–134

Smith, MS and MA Stein, 'The Disabled Contract: Severe Intellectual Disability, Justice and Morality by Jonas-Sébastien Beaudry' (2022) 44 *Human Rights Quarterly* 839–845

Stein, MA and A Silvers, 'Essentially Empirical: The Role of Biological and Legal Classification in Effectively Prohibiting Genetic Discrimination' in R Figueroa and S Harding (eds), *Science and Other Cultures: Issues in Philosophies of Science and Technology* (Routledge, 2003) 129–153

Stein, MA, 'Disability Human Rights' (2007) 95 *California Law Review* 75–121

Stein, MA, F Mahomed, V Patel, and C Sunkel (eds), *Mental Health, Legal Capacity, and Human Rights* (Cambridge University Press, 2021)

Steinert, T, 'The UN Committee's interpretation of "will and preferences" can violate human rights' (2019) 18(1) *World Psychiatry* 45–46

Sundram, CJ, 'A Discussion of Legal Capacity in the Draft Convention on Disability', National Disability Authority, Dublin, Ireland (15 June 2006)

Szegediné Sebestyén, K, 'A gondnokság alá helyezés iránti perekről' (1982) 7 *Magyar Jog* 606–615

Szerletics, A, 'Paternalism', The Essex Autonomy Project, Essex University (2011)

Szmukler, G and BD Kelly, 'We should replace conventional mental health law with capacity-based law' (2016) 209(6) *British Journal of Psychiatry* 449–453

Szmukler, G, '"Capacity", "best interests", "will and preferences" and the UN Convention on the Rights of Persons with Disabilities' (2019) 18(1) *World Psychiatry* 34–41

Szmukler, G, 'The UN Convention on the Rights of Persons with Disabilities: "Rights, will and preferences" in relation to mental health disabilities' (2017) 54 *International Journal of Law and Psychiatry* 90–97

Szmukler, G, R Daw, F Callard, 'Mental health law and the UN convention on the rights of persons with disabilities' (2014) 37(3) *International Journal Law Psychiatry* 245–252

The Montreal Declaration on Intellectual Disabilities, Pan-American Health Organization and World Health Organization, Montreal, Canada (6 October 2004).

Then, S-N, H Patrick, and N Smith, 'Reinforcing guardianship regimes through assisted decision-making: a Scottish perspective' (2014) *The Juridical Review* 263–279

Trömel, S, 'A Personal Perspective on the Drafting History of the United Nations Convention on the Rights of Persons with Disabilities' in OM Arnadóttir and G Quinn (eds), *The United Nations Convention on the Rights of Persons with Disabilities: European and Scandinavian Perspectives* (Martinus Nijhoff, 2009) 115–138

Turner-Stokes, L, K Benaichouche-Motam, W Goodison, A Altaie., A Howard., P McKnight, and J Alfonso, 'Improving the systematic screening and documentation of mental capacity for patients with severe brain injury: The Mental Capacity Screening assessment tool (MCScreen)' (2024) 24(5) *Clinical Medicine, Journal of the Royal College of Physicians of London* 100236

Uerpmann-Wittzack, R, 'The Law-Making Function of the UN Committee on the Rights of Persons with Disabilities' (2018) 8(2) *Wroclaw Review of Law, Administration & Economics* 36–46

United Nations High Commissioner for Human Rights, Mental health and human rights, Report, UN Human Rights Council, Thirty-fourth session, A/HRC/34/32 (27 February–24 March 2017)

Vékás, L, 'Szakértői Javaslat az új Polgári Törvénykönyv tervezetéhez' (CompLex, 2008)

Verdes, T and M Tóth, *A per tárgya* (Budapest, ELTE Eötvös Kiadó, 2010)

Villiger, M, *Commentary on the 1969 Vienna Convention on the Law of Treaties* (Martinus Nijhoff, 2009)

Ward, A, 'Abolition of Guardianship? "Best Interests" versus "Best Interpretation"' (2015) 32 *Scots Law Times* 150–154

Weller, P, 'Supported Decision-Making and the Achievement of Non-Discrimination: The Promise and Paradox of the Disabilities Convention' (2008) 26(2) *Law in Context* 85–110

Wildeman, S, 'Protecting Rights and Building Capacities: Challenges to Global Mental Health Policy in Light of the Convention on the Rights of Persons with Disabilities' (2013) 41 *The Journal of Law, Medicine and Ethics* 48–73

Winick, BJ, 'The Side Effects of Incompetency Labeling and the Implications for Mental Health' (1995) 1 *Psychol Public Policy and Law* 6–42

Wolfensberger, W, *The principle of normalization in human services* (National Association for Mental Retardation, 1972)

Wright, MS, 'Implementing Ethical and Legal Supported Decision Making: Some Unresolved Issues. (2021) 21(11) *American Journal of Bioethics* 40–42

Združenie na pomoc ľuďom s mentálnym postihnitím (ZPMP), 'Osnova návrhu reformy opatrovníctva v Slovenskej republike' (2011)

Index

Absolutist Position
common ground with Constricted Position, 38
failure of current approach, 47
literal reading of Article 12, 30–1
strengths and weaknesses
CRPD's text, 35–8
persons with severe disabilities, 32–3
role of mental capacity, 34–5
Abstract thinking, 81
Abuse *see* **Protection from harmful decisions and abuse**
Access to information
abuse by self, 105
abuse by supporter, 108
functional approach, 57
legal regulation of supported decision-making, 92–4
supported decision-making as a legal institution, 87
Administration
Administration and oversight
different legal approaches to guardianship, 63–5
guardianship and supported desion-making compared
ease of transacting, 111
expressive function, 110–11
flexibility, 109–10
pedagogic effect, 110
protection from harmful decisions and abuse, 112–13
restrictiveness, 109
ideal version of supported decision-making, 90–2
institutional aspect, 45–7
legal regulation of supported decision-making
guardian's right to be present and access information, 92–4
legal certainty, 96–7
protection from harmful decisions, 97–108
role of supporters, 94–6
Modified Support Framework, 141
Article 12 of the CRPD
alignment with Modified Support Framework, 144
broad scope for different interpretations, 28
conflicting views on interpretation
Absolutist Position, 30–1
common ground, 38
Constricted Position, 31
failure of current approaches, 47–8
strengths and weaknesses of alternative positions, 32–8
denial of legal personhood on the basis of disability, 28–9
detailed analysis of the text
consensual aspect, 39–43
institutional aspect, 45–7
suprapositive principles, 43–5
VCLT's requirements, 39
emergence of supported decision-making, 70–1
implications of legal capacity as a human right
procedural rights, 23–5
substantive rights, 25–6
important impetus for persons with disabilities, 139
need to resolve difficulties with current interpretation, 28
new understanding of legal capacity, 4–5
overview of chapter 3, 8
overview of chapter 8, 8–9
prohibition of discrimination based on disability, 29
replacement of guardianship, 29
significant step towards recognising the rights of persons with disabilities worldwide, 27
Support Only model, 117
Autonomy
adverse effects of substituted decision-making, 67–8
assumption of individuals as rational atomistic beings, 5–6
desirability of framework that maximises autonomy, 49

existing landscape of legal capacity, 2–3
historical denial for persons with disabilities, 139
impact of legally recognised incapacity, 1–2
Modified Support Framework, 140, 144
supported decision-making, 70, 98, 113

Capacity *see* **Legal capacity**; **Mental capacity**
Capacity assessments
disproportionately effect on persons with disabilities, 34
functional approach, 62
Modified Support Framework, 125, 131, 133–4, 137, 142
persons with high support needs, 126
psychological assumptions behind supported decision-making
based on abstract thinking, 81
legal and clinical incompetence, 84
measure of logical and linguistic intelligence, 82–3
no support, 83
overview, 78, 80–1
reliability, 53
substituted decision-making, 121
Support Only model, 117
Capacity to act
see also **Legal capacity**
Article 12 of the CRPD, 40, 42
human right, 17
legal capacity, 12
Capacity to have rights
see also **Legal capacity**
human right, 17
legal capacity, 12
Certainty *see* **Legal certainty**
Competence, see **Incompetence**
Consensual adoption of human rights norms
absence of clear consensus, 42–3
failure of current approach, 48
general rule of treaty interpretation, 39–40
instruments of ratification, 40
legal capacity, 41–2
preparatory works as supplementary means of interpretation, 40
text produced by working group, 40–1
Constricted Position
common ground with Absolutists, 38
failure of current approach, 47
narrower reading of the CRPD, 31
strengths and weaknesses
CRPD's text, 35–8
persons with severe disabilities, 32–3
role of mental capacity, 34–5
Convention on the Rights of Persons with Disabilities (2006)
Article 12 *see* **Article 12 of the CRPD**
entry into force, 27
Costs
different legal approaches to guardianship, 61
CRPD Committee
binding power of its views, 45–8
continuing ambiguity, 36–7
implementation of Article 12, 36–7
insufficient clarification of Article 12, 28
lack of international support for its views, 139
prohibition on substituted decision-making, 5
rejection of the mental capacity approach, 34
reliance on the CRPD's norms, 45
support for Absolutist Position, 30
supported decision-making, 71–2, 117

Decision-making
alternative mechanisms for limiting decision-making, 14
criteria for decision-making, 87
existing landscape of legal capacity, 2–3
impact of legally recognised incapacity, 2
Modified Support Framework
equality, 136–9
framework in practice, 129–32
legal classification of relevant persons, 126–9
main features, 125–6
safeguards against substituted decision-making, 135–6
origins on law of decision-making, 11
persons with high support needs
comparison of the three models, 132–5
Some Guardianship model, 120–3
Support Only model, 116–20
the two positions compared, 123–5
recent human rights challenges to guardianship
assumption of individuals as rational atomistic beings, 5–6
new paradigm of Article 12, 4–5

substituted decision-making *see* **Substituted decision-making**
supported decision-making *see* **Supported decision-making**
suprapositive principles, 44
underlying assumption of guardianship, 51
Differential treatment
Absolutist and Constricted Positions compared, 30
ambiguity of Article 12, 29
textual interpretation, 36–7
Dignity
Article 12 of the CRPD, 44
Modified Support Framework, 140, 144
persons with high support needs, 137
Domestic law
reservations or interpretative declarations when ratifying CRPD, 40
tailored approaches to guardianship, 60
violations concerning essence of guardianship, 22
Domestic laws
see also **International law**
revision of guardianship legislation, 76–7
supported decision-making
Canada, 72–4
Germany, 75
overview, 72
Sweden, 74–5

Equality
aims of CRPD, 40
Article 12(2), 29
assumption of individuals as rational atomistic beings, 5
consensual adoption of human rights norms, 39
expressive function, 111
historical denial for persons with disabilities, 139
impact of legally recognised incapacity, 1–2
important impetus from CRPD, 139
least restrictive form of guardianship, 68
legal regulation of supported decision-making, 100
Modified Support Framework, 136–9, 141, 144
new paradigm of Article 12, 4, 27
prohibition of discrimination based on disability, 29
recent challenges to guardianship, 4–7
recognition of international case-law on guardianship, 23
supported decision-making, 70–1
suprapositive principles, 44
European Court of Human Rights (ECtHR)
guardianship
evaluation of different approaches, 60
functional approach, 57–8
outcome approach, 55–6
substituted decision-making, 50
interpretation of CRPD Article 12
Absolutist Position, 33, 36
conflicting views on interpretation, 29
institutional aspect, 46
legal capacity as a human right
emergence as important issue, 18–19
implications for CRPD, 23–6
violations concerning essence of guardianship, 21–2
violations of procedural rights, 20
violations of substantive rights, 20–1
legitimacy of substituted decision-making, 50–1
outcome approach to guardianship, 55–6
supported decision-making, 71
Expressive function
guardianship and supported decision-making compared, 110–11
persons with high support needs, 137

Functional approach to legal capacity
costs, 59–60
ease of administration and oversight, 63–5
evaluation of different approaches, 65–6
legal approach to guardianship
legal certainty, 61–2
protection from abuse, 62–3
ranking the different approaches, 59–60

Guardianship
see also **Supported decision-making as a legal institution**
Absolutist Position
common ground with Constricted Position, 38
literal reading of Article 12, 30–1
strengths and weaknesses of alternative positions, 32–8
alternative mechanisms for limiting decision-making, 14
central feature of legal capacity, 13
concerns aimed at improving it, 67

consensual adoption of human rights norms, 40
Constricted Position
common ground with Absolutists, 38
narrower reading of the CRPD, 31
strengths and weaknesses of alternative positions, 32–8
desirability of framework that maximises autonomy, 49
different legal approaches
costs, 61
ease of administration and oversight, 63–5
evaluation of different approaches, 65–6
functional approach, 57–8
legal certainty, 61–2
outcome approach, 55–6
protection from abuse, 62–3
quasi-functional approach, 58–9
quasi-status approach, 54
ranking the different approaches, 59–60
status approach, 53–4
existing landscape of legal capacity, 3
institutional aspect, 46–7
key questions, 6–7
legal capacity as a human right, 21–2
legitimacy of substituted decision-making, 50–1
meaning and scope, 13
overview of chapters 4 and 6, 8
paradigm shift to supported decision-making, 139–40
persons with high support needs
Some Guardianship model, 120–3
Support Only model, 116–20
the two positions compared, 123–5
problematic features from a human rights perspective, 49–50
recent human rights challenges
academic literature, 6
assumption of individuals as rational atomistic beings, 5–6
new paradigm of Article 12, 4–5
replacement under Article 12, para.3, 29
supported decision-making as alternative, 68
supported decision-making as an alternative, 87–9
supported decision-making compared
flexibility, 109–10
protection from harmful decisions and abuse, 112–13
restrictiveness, 109
underlying assumptions
correlation between presumption and reality, 53
legal capacity, 51–2
legal certainty, 52–3
legitimacy, 51
singling out persons with disabilities, 51

Harmful decisions *see* **Protection from harmful decisions**
High support needs *see* **Persons with high support needs**
Human rights
consensual adoption of human rights norms, 39–43
historical denial for persons with disabilities, 139
institutional aspect, 45–7
legal capacity
core problems, 17
ECtHR jurisprudence, 18–19
Europe's Committee of Ministers' Recommendation R(99)4, 19
international conventions, 17–18
violations concerning essence of guardianship, 21–2
violations of procedural rights, 20
violations of substantive rights, 20–1
persons with high support needs, 122
problematic features of guardianship, 49–50
recent challenges to guardianship
academic literature, 6
assumption of individuals as rational atomistic beings, 5–6
new paradigm of Article 12, 4–5
suprapositive principles, 43–5
undermining role of guardianship, 3

Incompetence
outcome approach, 55–6
psychological assumptions behind supported decision-making, 84
severe communication difficulties, 88
Information *see* **Access to information**
Institutional perspectives
effectiveness of oversight of compliance with human rights norms by human rights bodies, 45–7
supported decision-making as a legal institution
ideal version of supported decision-making, 90–2

legal regulation of supported decision-making, 92–108
Intelligence
basis of supported decision-making, 82–3
persons with high support needs, 126
Interdependent decision-making
analysis of assumptions underlying supported decision-making, 37
analysis of assumptions underlying supported decision-making, 78–80
dichotomy of competence, 83
International law
see also **Article 12 of the CRPD; Domestic laws**
emergence of supported decision-making
Montreal Declaration on Intellectual Disabilities 2004, 71
negotiations of CRPD, 70–1
obligations under CRPD, 71–2
interpretation of treaties, 39
legal capacity as a human right, 17–18
tailored approaches to guardianship, 60
textual interpretation, 35–6

Legal agency, 12
see also **Legal capacity**
Legal capacity
see also **Mental capacity**
central feature, 13
conflicting views on interpretation of Article 12
Absolutist Position, 30–1
common ground, 38
Constricted Position, 31
strengths and weaknesses of alternative positions, 32–8
criteria for decision-making, 87
defined, 12
different legal approaches to guardianship
costs, 61
ease of administration and oversight, 63–5
evaluation of different approaches, 65–6
functional approach, 57–8
legal certainty, 61–2
outcome approach, 55–6
protection from abuse, 62–3
quasi-functional approach, 58–9
quasi-status approach, 54
ranking the different approaches, 59–60
status approach, 53–4
existing landscape
autonomy to make decisions, 2–3
comparisons with other groups, 3–4
undermining role of guardianship, 3
historical overview
changes over time, 14–16
origins in Roman law, 14
as a human right
core problems, 17
ECtHR jurisprudence, 18–19
Europe's Committee of Ministers' Recommendation R(99)4, 19
implications for CRPD, 23–6
international conventions, 17–18
violations concerning essence of guardianship, 21–2
violations of procedural rights, 20
violations of substantive rights, 20–1
impact of legally recognised incapacity, 1–2
implications for CRPD, 21–2
new paradigm of Article 12, 4–5
origins on law of decision-making, 11
overview of chapter 2, 7–8
overview of chapter 8, 8–9
prohibition of discrimination based on disability, 29
recent challenges to guardianship
academic literature, 6
assumption of individuals as rational atomistic beings, 5–6
rejection of current formal categories of legal capacity, 143
restrictions on a wide circle of persons, 12–13
supported decision-making, 69, 78
textual analysis
consensual adoption of human rights norms, 41–2
suprapositive principles, 44
underlying assumption of guardianship, 51–2
Legal certainty
different legal approaches to guardianship, 61–2
legal regulation of supported decision-making, 96–7
underlying assumption of guardianship, 52–3
Legal standing, 12
see also **Legal capacity**
Linguistic intelligence, 82–3

Mental capacity
see also **Legal capacity**
Absolutist and Constricted Positions compared, 34–5
academic literature, 6
conflicting aims in pursuit of autonomy, 113
ex-ante formal categorisation based on a prediction of mental capacity, 143
functional approach, 57
inter-dependant decision-making, 78
supported decision-making, 86
Modified Support Framework
alignment with Article 12 of the CRPD, 144
alterative proposal, 140–1
comparison of the three models, 132–5
equal treatment of persons with disabilities, 141
equality, 136–9
framework in practice, 129–32
legal classification of relevant persons, 126–9
main features, 125–6
protection from harmful decisions and abuse, 142–3
rejection of current formal categories of legal capacity, 143
rejection of idealised 'rational man' approach, 141–2
safeguards against substituted decision-making, 135–6, 143–4
wishes of persons with disabilities, 144

Outcome approach to legal capacity
costs, 59–60
ease of administration and oversight, 63–5
evaluation of different approaches, 65–6
legal approach to guardianship, 55–6
legal certainty, 61–2
protection from abuse, 62–3
ranking the different approaches, 59–60
Oversight *see* **Administration and oversight**

Partial guardianship
ease of administration and oversight, 64
evaluation of different approaches, 59–60, 65
legal certainty, 62
meaning and scope, 13
protection from abuse, 63
quasi-functional approach, 58–9
replacement of plenary guardianship, 67, 122
Pedagogic effect
guardianship and supported decision-making compared, 110
supported decision-making, 103, 108
Personhood
denial to various marginalised groups, 12–13
historical denial for persons with disabilities, 139
impact of legally recognised incapacity, 1–2
new paradigm of Article 12, 4–5, 28–9
Persons with disabilities
see also **Persons with high support needs; Persons with severe disabilities**
Absolutist and Constricted Positions compared, 32–3
continuing restrictions on legal capacity, 15–16
desirability of framework that maximises autonomy, 49
existing landscape of legal capacity
autonomy to make decisions, 2–3
comparisons with other groups, 3–4
undermining role of guardianship, 3
impact of legally recognised incapacity, 1–2
important impetus from CRPD, 139
legal capacity, see **Legal capacity**
persons with high support needs *see* **Persons with high support needs**
recent human rights challenges to guardianship
assumption of individuals as rational atomistic beings, 5–6
new paradigm of Article 12, 4–5
significance of CPRD, 27
substituted decision-making *see* **Substituted decision-making**
supported decision-making *see* **Supported decision-making**
terminology, 9–10
underlying assumption of guardianship, 51
Persons with high support needs
see also **Persons with severe disabilities**
comparison of the three models, 132–5
existing solutions and their shortcomings
overview, 115–16
Some Guardianship model, 120–3
Support Only model, 116–20
the two positions compared, 123–5
Modified Support Framework
comparison with other models, 132–5
equality, 136–9

framework in practice, 129–32
legal classification of relevant persons, 126–9
main features, 125–6
safeguards against substituted decision-making, 135–6, 143–4
overview of chapter 7, 8–9
Persons with severe disabilities
see also **Persons with high support needs**
Article 12 of the CRPD, 32–3, 48, 139
communication theories, 88
incorporation into a support framework, 5
Modified Support Framework, 140
omission from theories of justice, 1
personhood, 2
Some Guardianship model, 124
Support Only model, 117–18, 124
Plenary guardianship
ease of administration and oversight, 64–5
evaluation of different approaches, 65–6
inflated numbers of persons unduly restricted, 121–2
legal certainty, 62
meaning and scope, 13
most effective in preventing abuse, 102
phasing out since 1960s, 15
protection from abuse, 63
quasi-status approach to guardianship, 54
ranking of different approaches, 59–60
replacement with partial guardianship, 132
untenable from an international law perspective, 67
violation of right to private life, 19
Powers of attorney, 67, 135
Procedural rights
implications for CRPD, 23–5
legal capacity as a human right, 19–20
Protection from harmful decisions and abuse
conflicting aims of securing autonomy, 113
different legal approaches to guardianship, 62–3
guardianship and supported decision-making compared, 112–13
legal regulation of supported decision-making
abuse by others, 99–102
abuse by self, 102–5
abuse by supporter, 102–8
overview, 97–9
Modified Support Framework, 142–3
underlying assumption of guardianship, 51–2
Psychological perspectives
age-old attitudes towards persons with disabilities, 16
basis of supported decision-making
abstract thinking and context, 81
capacity assessment as a distinct field of research, 80–1
legal and clinical incompetence, 84
logical/linguistic intelligence, 82
no support, 83
different legal approaches to guardianship
costs of assessments, 61
functional approach to legal capacity, 57
quasi-functional approach to legal capacity, 58
existing landscape of legal capacity, 4
interdependent decision-making, 78
persons with high support needs, 123, 126
protection from harmful decisions, 112
Support Only model, 118
undue influence, 106

Quasi-functional approach to legal capacity
costs, 59–60
ease of administration and oversight, 63–5
evaluation of different approaches, 65–6
legal approach to guardianship, 58–9
legal certainty, 61–2
protection from abuse, 62–3
ranking the different approaches, 59–60
Quasi-status approach to legal capacity
costs, 59–60
ease of administration and oversight, 63–5
evaluation of different approaches, 65–6
legal approach to guardianship, 54
legal certainty, 61–2
protection from abuse, 62–3
ranking the different approaches, 59–60

Right to be present, 92–4, 134

Severe disabilities *see* **Persons with severe disabilities**
Some Guardianship model
comparison of the three models, 132–5
emergence as one of two central positions, 140
Modified Support Framework in practice, 129–32
persons with high support needs, 120–3
Support Only model compared, 123–5

Status approach to legal capacity
costs, 59–60
ease of administration and oversight, 63–5
evaluation of different approaches, 65–6
legal approach to guardianship, 53–4
legal certainty, 61–2
protection from abuse, 62–3
ranking the different approaches, 59–60
Stigmatisation, 1–2, 137
Substantive rights
implications for CRPD, 23, 25–6
legal capacity as a human right, 20–1
Substituted decision-making
see also **Supported decision-making as a legal institution**
Absolutist Position
common ground with Constricted Position, 38
literal reading of Article 12, 30–1
strengths and weaknesses of alternative positions, 32–8
concerns aimed at improving guardianship, 67
consensual adoption of human rights norms, 40
Constricted Position
common ground with Absolutists, 38
narrower reading of the CRPD, 31
strengths and weaknesses of alternative positions, 32–8
institutional aspect, 46–7
safeguards against in Modified Support Framework, 135–6, 143–4
shift to supported decision-making under CRPD, 71–2
unjust restrictions of autonomy, 67–8
valid concerns over legitimacy, 50–1
Support Only model
Article 12 of the CRPD, 117
comparison of the three models, 132–5
emergence as one of two central positions, 139–40
equality, 137
Modified Support Framework
framework in practice, 129–32
legal classification of relevant persons, 127
overcoming problems
absence of supporting evidence, 120
exceptional situations, 119–20
focus on communication abilities of persons with high support needs, 118–19
identifying wishes from personal values, preferences and upbringing, 119
persons with high support needs, 116–17
Some Guardianship model compared, 123–5
underlying assumption, 117–18
Supported decision-making
alternative to guardianship, 68
analysis of assumptions underlying theoretical model
interdependent decision-making, 78–80
psychological basis of supported decision-making, 80–4
assumption of individuals as rational atomistic beings, 5–6
chapter overview, 68–9
distribution of power, 113–14
in domestic laws
Canada, 72–4
Germany, 75
overview, 72
Sweden, 74–5
emergence in international law
Montreal Declaration on Intellectual Disabilities 2004, 71
negotiations of CRPD, 70–1
obligations under CRPD, 71–2
forms of support
as an alternative to guardianship, 87–9
as the natural way to make decisions, 85
overview, 85
as a principle, 86–7
guardianship compared
ease of transacting, 111
expressive function, 110–11
flexibility, 109–10
pedagogic effect, 110
protection from harmful decisions and abuse, 112–13
restrictiveness, 109
ideal and existing models
co-decision-making procedures, 75–6
essential features, 77
revision of guardianship legislation, 76–7
institutional aspect, 45–6
key questions, 6–7
as a legal institution
ideal version of supported decision-making, 90–2
legal regulation of supported decision-making, 92–108

legal regulation
guardian's right to be present and access information, 92–4
legal certainty, 96–7
protection from harmful decisions, 97–108
role of supporters, 94–6
meaning and scope, 69–70
new paradigm of Article 12, 4–5
overview of chapters 5 and 6, 8
paradigm shift from guardianship, 139–40
recognition of autonomy, 70
Supporters
Suprapositive principles
failure of current approach, 48
importance of decision-making and legal capacity, 44
non-legal principles superior to their embodiment in positive law, 43
text as a useful starting point, 43–4
valuable source of inspiration, 44–5

Terminology, 9–10
Textual analysis
Absolutist and Constricted Positions compared, 35–8
detailed analysis of Article 12
consensual aspect, 39–43
institutional aspect, 45–7
suprapositive principles, 43–5
VCLT's requirements, 39

UN Committee on the Rights of Persons with Disabilities *see* **CRPD Committee**

Wishes of persons with disabilities
comparing alternative models, 133
guardianship and supported decision-making compared
protection from harmful decisions, 112
restrictiveness, 109
Modified Support Framework, 125, 127–31, 144
persons with high support needs, 118–19
safeguards against substituted decision-making, 136
Some Guardianship model, 120
supported decision-making
abuse by others, 99, 101
as an alternative to guardianship, 88
distribution of power, 113
in domestic laws, 74
ideal version of supported decision-making, 92
as a principle, 86
protection from harmful decisions, 98
role of supporters, 95–6
underlying concept, 70

www.ingramcontent.com/pod-product-compliance
Ingram Content Group UK Ltd.
Pitfield, Milton Keynes, MK11 3LW, UK
UKHW021907150926
475560UK00003B/222

9 781509 980321